Fantasies
of the Feminine

Fantasies
of the Feminine

The Short Stories
of Silvina Ocampo

Patricia Nisbet Klingenberg

Lewisburg
Bucknell University Press
London: Associated University Presses

Associated University Presses
440 Forsgate Drive
Cranbury, NJ 08512

Associated University Presses
16 Barter Street
London WC1A 2AH, England

Associated University Presses
P.O. Box 338, Port Credit
Mississauga, Ontario
Canada L5G 4L8

The paper used in this publication meets the requirements
of the American National Standard for Permanence of Paper
for Printed Library Materials Z39.48-1984.

Library of Congress Cataloging-in-Publication Data

Klingenberg, Patricia Nisbet, 1950–
    Fantasies of the feminine : the short stories of Silvina Ocampo /
Patricia Nisbet Klingenberg.
        p.   cm.
    Includes bibliographical references (p.   ) and index.
    ISBN 0-8387-5389-2 (alk. paper)
    1. Ocampo, Silvina—Criticism and interpretation.   2. Women in
literature.   I. Title.
PQ7797.O293Z67   1999
863—dc21   98-20795
                                                          CIP

PRINTED IN THE UNITED STATES OF AMERICA

To Charles, of course

Oh desmedido territorio nuestro
violentísimo y párvulo. Te
muestro en un infiel espejo.
                    —Silvina Ocampo

Contents

Preface and Acknowledgments

SILVINA OCAMPO HAS BEEN LONG RECOGNIZED AS ONE OF ARGENTINA'S important contributors to a whole school of fiction which challenges normal perceptions of reality and the conventions of reading itself. The present study expands this view of her work to see it also as a prolonged assault on every aspect of literary representation of the feminine. This feminist analysis of Silvina Ocampo's short stories is addressed primarily to scholars interested in Latin American authors. Every effort has been made, however, to facilitate a reading by the nonspecialist. Translations of all quotations are provided in the text, critical terms are explained as thoroughly as possible, and footnotes provide additional clarification.

Several people deserve my thanks for their help and support in the long writing process. Thomas C. Meehan introduced me to Silvina Ocampo in the first place. His is the model I take with me into my own classes and whose continued friendship through the years is deeply appreciated. I am forever grateful to the generosity and graciousness shown to me during my 1980 trip to Buenos Aires by Enrique Pezzoni, Adolfo Bioy Casares and Silvina Ocampo. As I was completing the final draft of this book, I learned of Silvina Ocampo's death. Although she did not approve of the academic and journalistic "interpreters" of literature and claimed no alliance to feminism, I like to think that she would be pleased anyway with this tribute to her wonderful stories. In the frontispiece of the copy of the newly reprinted version of *Las invitadas* that she presented to me at the end of our month together, she wrote "No me olvides" [Don't forget me]. No chance of that.

Shari Benstock, the editor of the *Tulsa Studies in Women's Literature* during the time in which I was a new faculty member in my first job, taught a graduate course on feminist theory which I audited and which had a profound effect on my development as a scholar. "The Little Red House" on the University of Tulsa campus, which she directed, provided a library of feminist theoretical texts, a visiting speaker's program, and a group of talented graduate students and faculty always eager to debate. It was, as I look back on it, a remarkable beginning. Other colleagues have offered moral support, but I mention one, Kathleen O'Gorman, with special feeling. An early, anonymous, reader offered practical suggestions that greatly improved the manuscript and whose intelligent, insightful analysis sustained me during many subsequent disappointments. My daughter, Alix, has grown up during the writing of this book; she is present in its every line. As a stepfather, husband, colleague, and friend, Charles Ganelin works to redefine the scope and meaning of all these roles. He was first reader and kind editor of the manuscript, which quite simply could not have been written without him.

Abbreviations of Story Collections, in Chronological Order

Vo	*Viaje olvidado.* Buenos Aires: Sur, 1937.
AI	*Autobiografía de Irene.* Buenos Aires: Sur, 1948.
F	*La furia y otros cuentos.* Buenos Aires: Sur, 1959.
I	*Las invitadas.* Buenos Aires: Losada, 1961.
Ldn	*Los días de la noche.* Buenos Aires: Sudamericana, 1970.
Y así	*Y así sucesivamente.* Barcelona: Tusquets, 1987.
Cornelia	*Cornelia frente al espejo.* Barcelona: Tusquets, 1988.

Introduction

BIOGRAPHICAL NOTE

SILVINA OCAMPO (1903–93) LIVED AND WROTE WITHIN ONE OF THE most exciting and productive literary circles of the twentieth century, the one which came into being in Buenos Aires in the 1930s and 1940s, yet her name has not become a household word even among scholars of Latin American literature. The figures who surrounded her personal and professional life, her sister Victoria, her husband, Adolfo Bioy Casares, her friend Jorge Luis Borges, among others loosely associated with the literary magazine, *Sur*, dominate any history of twentieth-century Argentine literature. Silvina Ocampo was a prominent member of this group from the beginning, yet her status has remained unclarified and her works relatively unexamined. It is clear that part of this obscurity was a deliberate strategy on her part. Matilde Sánchez, editor of a recent anthology of Ocampo's stories, confirms my experience in attempting to establish biographical data, "toda biografía de Ocampo habrá de encontrarla no como una ayuda sino como un obstáculo" [any biography of Ocampo will find her a hinderance rather than a help].[1] Ocampo preferred to hide herself and to a certain extent her work, avoiding whenever possible the journalistic interviews, speeches, and public appearances, which Sánchez aptly describes as the "career" of the literary figure. In the few interviews that Ocampo conceded over the years, she refused to name names or to specify dates; rather, she maintained flatly that her life had nothing to do with what she wrote.[2] This study in part confirms that assessment—that her life in some important ways has little to do with her work—and the distance she strove to place between herself and her fictional creations is surprisingly easy to respect.

One consequence of her reluctance to speak about herself, or to pay attention to what others said, is a series of inaccuracies involving several basic facts. The date of her birth, 21 July 1903, is listed as other with frequency and several sources list her

husband's daughter, Marta, as her own.[3] Fortunate for anyone
wishing to know something about Ocampo's life, the people
around her have been less reticent, and glimpses can be had of
her through accounts of their lives.[4] Silvina Ocampo was born
into one of Argentina's old, distinguished families, the youngest
of six daughters. As a child, she seemed destined to become a
painter, and in her twenties she studied briefly in Paris with
both Giorgio de Chirico and Fernand Léger. An account of one
exhibit in which her art was presented is available in the pages
of *Sur*.[5] From the era slightly before her marriage to Bioy Casares in 1940 to her death on 14 December 1993, however, her
life was dedicated to creative writing, almost equally divided
between poetry and the short story.

    Her elder sister, Victoria, fifteen years her senior, was one of
the best-known figures of the first half of the century. Victoria
published Silvina's early works, and served as first reviewer, but
the two sisters are a study in contrasts. Victoria maintained a
high profile both literarily, as director of *Sur*, and as an active
participant in national politics: A committed feminist, opponent
of the Perón regime, she deliberately sought fame and famous
people. Silvina avoided all these. A prolific writer, Victoria is
renowned for her efforts at self-representation in multiple volumes of both her *Testimonios* and her *Autobiografía*. Silvina
published no nonfictional account of either her life or her approach to literature. Victoria was married and divorced very
young, and spent the rest of her life as a single woman, engaged
in a public career at a time when none of this was common or
acceptable. Silvina married late and well. She was thirty-seven
years old when she married a handsome young writer, ten years
her junior, who soon became known as one of Argentina's best-
known authors. One element that the sisters have in common
is their rejection of the education they received as young ladies
of the upper class. Both in their distinctive ways viewed this
upbringing as a barrier rather than a privilege. Victoria's stance
can be viewed as an ambivalent one with pride and repudiation
an uneasy combination.[6] Silvina's fictional accounts, on the
other hand, present a scathing denunciation of life in the great
houses of the oligarchy. In my talks with her, and throughout
the interview with Ulla, it is clear that Silvina as a child, like
her many fictional characters, lived a lonely existence, relieved
primarily by the companionship of various household workers.
She spoke to me with particular affection for the sewing room
in the upper part of the house, where she was allowed to play

with the mannequin and create clothing of her own design. This, then, is the place from which her works emerge, from memory and identification with those identified as other. When she says her life has nothing to do with her work, I think she means her adult life as an intellectual, as part of a distinguished group of celebrated artists, as a cosmopolitan, well-traveled citizen of the modern world. Her works, in contrast to the most obvious public aspect of her life, are set in a timeless, almost archaic, imaginary space.

Noemí Ulla says in her introductory remarks to the book-length interview, *Encuentros con Silvina Ocampo,* that the author refused to answer questions regarding her life with Bioy Casares. In my talks with her in March 1980 (probably since she allowed no tape recorder), she was a bit more forthcoming. She told me, for instance, that she scandalized her family by living with Bioy (whom she always referred to as "Adolfito") at his country estate, "Rincón Viejo," before they were married. She recounted, as does Oscar Hermes Villordo in his biography of Bioy Casares, the highjinks of their wedding day in 1940, in which Borges served as witness.[7] The stiff, formal portrait of the event, which she described as "cursi" [affected], is reproduced in Kovacci. The comments she made to me and to others regarding her life with Bioy are uniformly positive, tending toward the lyrical. When I asked her about the title of the novel they wrote together, *Los que aman odian* [Those who love hate] and the contradictory nature of love, she responded that love, with all its imperfections, is the best source of happiness. In a written reply to Danubio Torres Fierro on his question regarding her life with a fellow writer, she replies, "Convivir con un escritor es espléndido: es el a.b.c. de mi vida" [Living with a writer is splendid: he is the a.b.c. of my life].[8] The recurring themes of jealousy and betrayal in both her poetry and stories contradict the vision of harmony that Ocampo's public remarks portray; the existence of Marta, Bioy's child with another woman, is a subject on which she is resolutely silent.[9] My own analysis of her fiction suggests that Ocampo worked to formulate a new approach to love, freed from the conventions of courtly romance. I will avoid speculation about how well she may have succeeded in that endeavor in her own life. What is clear even from a distance is that her biography is as paradoxical as her fiction: From a position of wealth and privilege, she wrote movingly about all manner of marginalized beings; from a stated resistence to feminism, she created some of the most subversive

fictions of her time; out of what many consider the confines
of marriage, she and Bioy forged a most creatively productive
partnership.

Bioy Casares and Silvina Ocampo together formed a social and
professional nucleus for a number of creative people, including
Borges. No life of Borges can be written without including them,
as he was a regular visitor in their home for most of their adult
lives as well as collaborator on several important projects. The
photographs that Sánchez reproduces create a vivid image of the
fellowship they all shared, both professionally, in formal portraits taken for *Sur,* and privately, at the Bioys' beach house in
Mar del Plata. The elements from these photos which appear in
Ocampo's stories, however, are primarily the country scenes and
the dogs that she clearly adored. The artists and writers which
surround her in the photographs are not to be found in her
fiction, except for a handful of her approximately two hundred
stories. Bioy's work includes novels as well as short stories,
many of which present a wry view of the international jet set
with which the couple came in contact. Ocampo's works are
more like Borges's in that she concentrates on the genres of
poetry and short narrative, and like his, her works are often
difficult to situate in time and space.

The list of Ocampo's complete works supposes a discipline of
uncommon constancy. Author of seven large volumes of short
stories and as many volumes of poetry, hardly a year between
1937, the year of her first published work, and 1988, the year
of her last, went by without seeing something new appear, including a number of adaptations of stories for the theater. The
scholarly response to this work, a growing list of articles, translations, new editions, and anthologies, however, barely changes
the assessment posited by Torres Fierro in 1975. He describes
her position in the literary world as vague and imprecise; not
ignored or disregarded, but marginalized. He speculates that no
one has known how to read her works: "Es que en las paredes
huecas de los relatos de la Ocampo hay gatos encerrados. Y más:
tienen un doble fondo" [In the hollow walls of Ocampo's stories
there are hidden secrets and false bottoms].[10] Silvina Ocampo's
uncertain standing as a literary figure owes something to a deliberate strategy on her part. It owes something else to the complex
thread of difference from and similarity to the writers around
her. And it owes yet another something to the odd combination
of erudition and feminine "cursilería" (bad taste or vulgarity),
observable in her work, quite unlike that of any other writer.

CRITICAL APPRAISAL

Starting with the 1936 publication of the story, "Siesta en el cedro," Silvina Ocampo published creative works in *Sur* on an average of once a year until its closing in the 1970s. Most of these individual pieces were collected into the volumes of stories and poems as they also appeared every several years for some fifty years. The collections were reviewed in the pages of *Sur* by other, now well-known, writers of the period, including sister Victoria, Ezequiel Martínez Estrada, Rosa Chacel, and Eduardo González Lanuza.[11] These early assessments note the importance of the child's perspective and of ordinary objects. For instance, Victoria's review of *Viaje olvidado,* Silvina Ocampo's first published collection, comments that one has the impression that the characters are things and the things characters, as in childhood. The four fantastic stories in this first volume introduce themes that will become constants: "La familia Linio Milagro" is a kind of ghost story in which a family is haunted by the sound of a dead daughter playing the piano; "La cabeza pegada al vidrio" is a horror tale in which a young governess sees repeatedly the face of a man in flames; "El corredor ancho de sol" is a highly chaotic internal monolog which, however, hints that the main character, a convalescing woman in a hospital, has the power to predict the future; and "La enemistad de las cosas" suggests that an article of clothing exercises a subtle control over a man's affairs. All four stories contain elements that Ocampo will develop further: The young governess will be a favorite victim, the piano player foreshadows other Ocampo characters whose pleasant traits turn into some horror or other; the sick, hallucinating woman, perhaps on the brink of madness, nevertheless, possesses an unsuspected power, as does the otherwise insignificant garment. The twenty-eight stories collected in *Viaje olvidado* produce a recognizable Argentine setting of country estates and city houses, the dreamlike narrations situated within minutely detailed surroundings. About half center the narrative around a child character; several stories are reminiscent of fairy tales, four can be considered fantastic, but none contain the humor for which the author will later be best known. Victoria's review, the first ever published on Silvina's works, objects to her negligence of correct grammar and describes certain images as strained, "que parecen atacadas de tortícolis" [they seem to be suffering from a stiff neck], a criticism

that Silvina Ocampo discusses some forty-five years later with
Noemí Ulla.[12] Though she does not blame Victoria, Silvina notes
that she continued to write short fiction during an extended
period following without offering them for publication.

Ocampo collaborated in this early stage with Borges and Bioy
Casares on two anthologies, the *Antología de literatura fantástica* (1940) and the *Antología poética argentina* (1941).[13] The
former, reissued in revised form several times in subsequent
years, is considered a landmark in the literary development of
Argentina, Bioy Casares's prologue to the original edition a frequently cited early study of fantastic fiction. With Bioy, Ocampo
wrote a detective novel set, as they both have noted, in a resort
hotel they visited near Mar del Plata, called in the novel Bosque
del Mar.[14] The detective of *Los que aman odian* is a medical
doctor on vacation, a hedonistic follower of a strange science
that recommends the ingesting of small doses of poisons as a
healthful measure. He is consequently a suspect as well as narrator. Rosa Chacel's 1946 review of the novel, to my knowledge
the only critical evaluation of the work which has appeared,
notes the novel's attention to atmosphere and elaborate poetic
language, its pretensions, in short, to status as "art," not just
popular fiction. She also notes its debt to English detective style,
suggesting at the same time that this is the novel's flaw. I will
add that the importance of its child character most obviously
signals Ocampo's contribution to a genre she never again
attempted.

By this time, several major volumes of poetry had also appeared: *Enumeración de la patria* (1942), which won Buenos
Aires's Municipal Prize for poetry that year, *Espacios métricos*
(1942), and *Los sonetos del jardín* (1946).[15] These early collections are noted for the erudition of their references and the
strict metrical forms which Ocampo later calls "una jaula bien
ajustada" [a very tight cage].[16] Several connections to the fiction
can be seen here: a repeated interest in the Eumenides, or Furies, which will title a later volume of short stories; and several
other story titles that appear first in the poetry, such as "Del
diario de Porfiria" and "Autobiografía de Irene."

The five stories collected in *Autobiografía de Irene* (1948)
differ in many important ways from the rest of Ocampo's fiction.
Their exotic ambience, structural complications, and length set
them apart. "El impostor," at eighty pages, is Ocampo's longest
fictional work. Structural experimentation in the collection includes "El impostor's" two narrators, the second of whom de-

nounces the first as false. "Epitaflo romano" concludes with three optional endings, one reasonably realistic, one supernatural, and one that tends toward crime fiction. The title story contains a character who "remembers" her future; cut off from her past she is doomed to repeat it within an autobiography of her own creation. "Fragmentos del libro invisible" is a parody of religious and philosophical discourse centered on a character who believes himself to be a prophet. "La red" presents an exotic setting and interest in Eastern philosophy that contrast markedly with the remainder of Ocampo's fiction, known for its attention to the ordinary and everyday. Most critics have noted the similarity of these works to those of Borges, however, John King views the rich production of this period as a group effort:

> The theory and practice of "fantastic" literature were to be evolved throughout these years and were to reach their culmination in the creative outburst of Borges in the early 1940s. Borges is the best-known writer of this period, but it will be argued that the development of these theories was very much a group practice, and that the contribution of Adolfo Bioy Casares, Silvina Ocampo and to a lesser extent José Bianco should not be underrated.[17]

Lamentably, any serious comparison between the works of Ocampo and those of the other writers of the period is beyond the scope of this study. It is the case, however, that Ocampo evolved rapidly in and out of this period, and that her later works differ in both theme and structure from these elaborate conceits.

Two collections of poetry, *Poemas de amor desesperado* (1949) and *Los nombres* (1953) which won second prize in the Argentine national literary competition that year, and *Los traidores* (1956), a drama-in-verse written in collaboration with Juan Rudolfo Wilcock, establish Silvina Ocampo as a major poet. *Lo amargo por dulce* (1962) won the first prize for poetry, making her poetry far more officially awarded than her stories. Very few serious studies of these works have appeared, a serious gap in scholarship which Noemí Ulla's *Invenciones a dos voces* (1993) only begins to rectify.[18]

With the publication of *La furia y otros cuentos* (1959) and *Las invitadas* (1961), Silvina Ocampo had reached the height of her powers. *La furia* was reviewed twice in back-to-back sections of *Sur*.[19] Eugenio Guasta recognizes several characteristic elements of the stories: their brevity; their simple narrative structure, which usually culminates in a surprise ending; the frequent enumeration of apparently trivial objects; and a narrative tone reminiscent of fairy tales in their calm narration of the most gory horrors. While many of the characters seem to him to be derived from paintings by Goya and Bosch, he ends his review on a note repeated many times in commentary about Ocampo, a recognition of a spiritual undertone:

> *La furia* es un todo poético. . . . La poesía es un modo de acercarse al misterio. No olvidemos, además que si la poesía tiene en su origen una función lúdica, también tiene otra, que es sacra. Quien se entrega a ese alto ejercicio, puede hasta profetizar, a veces, y sin quererlo. (ibid., 64)

> [The Fury is a poetic whole. . . . Poetry is a mode of approaching life's mystery. Let us not forget, that if poetry has as its origen a playful function it also has another, which is sacred. Whoever devotes herself to that high calling may even prophesy, at times, without intending it.]

In his part of this double review, Mario A. Lancelotti also notes the poetic tone; in addition he describes Ocampo's vision of Buenos Aires marked by the supernatural and a wry humor. Two years later Lancelotti wrote the review of *Las invitadas* for *Sur*.[20] Here the word *cruel* appears with emphasis, a word that continues to be associated with Ocampo's works. What none of the commentators noted at the time is the humor combined with the cruelty. Guasta's mention of Goya and Bosch suggests the mixture of humor and horror, which begins in the stories of *La furia* and becomes fully developed in those of *Las invitadas,* a black humor I have associated as he does more indirectly with the grotesque.

Soon after the publication of these major works, José Bianco prepared an anthology of her stories selected from the four published volumes to date. His introduction to *El pecado mortal* (1966) and that of Edgardo Cozarinsky to his anthology, *Informe del cielo y del infierno* (1970), were among the first commentaries to consider Ocampo's fiction in its entirety as of that time.[21] Bianco's study stresses the use of fantastic themes: play with time and space, animation of inanimate objects such as portraits and fountain pens. He also notes an emphasis on the everyday and an approach to sexual themes. Cozarinsky speaks of a triviality redeemed and the sacred invested in humble beings. The minutely described atmosphere, approaching realism, is constantly subverted by fantastic elements and by a dispassionate banality. Cozarinsky sees traces of Kafka, James Purdy, and Katherine Mansfield; and later, Isak Dinesen, James, and Joyce. A tone that he describes as *faux naïf,* self-consciously childlike, serves to depict a fundamental brutality combinined with unabashed bad taste ("la cursilería vigorosa"). Of the story that titles his collection, "El pecado mortal," he says insightfully that its horror is not derived from the disturbing games between a girl and a servant but from the idea of sin imposed by religion on the silence kept during confession. The contradictory quality of Ocampo's style, which is at once childlike and highly literary, innocent and crude, defines the paradoxical nature of these stories.

In 1970 Ocampo published another large collection of original narratives, *Los días de la noche.* Longer in general than those of either *La furia* or *Las invitadas,* they also are noted for the interest they show in characterization. Whereas the titles of the previous two collections, as noted by Sylvia Molloy, tend to denote objects, these are predominantly names of characters: "Ana Valerga," "Livio Roca," and "Celestino Abril," for example.[22] There is a notable expansion of the use of colloquial speech, already visible in the previous two volumes; the added length of the stories can be attributed to characterization by way of dialog. While animals have frequently formed part of the stories, they are main characters in stories such as "Nueve perros," "Carl Herst," "Keif," and "La soga."

Three short stories for children appeared in separate books in the early 1970s: *El caballo alado, El cofre volante,* and *El tobogán.* In 1977 Ocampo published a sizable collection intended for children, *La naranja maravillosa: Cuentos para chicos grandes y grandes chicos.*[23] Several of her previously published stories were adapted for this collection. In all cases the grotesque humor of the originals is softened: For instance, the original ending of "La soga," in which the child character is "bitten" and dies as a result of the rope's metamorphosis into a snake, is changed to allow the child character to take his rope *cum* snake to the zoo. The nine original stories produced for the volume follow more traditional lines of classic fairy tales. In 1972 another major volume of poetry, *Amarillo celeste,* appeared. Several distinguished critics offer studies of Ocampo's works, starting in the late 1960s, including Alejandra Pizarnik, Sylvia Molloy, Rosario Castellanos and Blas Matamoro.[24] The latter's chapter on Ocampo has remained the longest and most complete study of her short fiction almost to the present. A new anthology of Ocampo's stories appeared in French translation with introductory remarks provided by Borges and Calvino.[25] A long article by Giulia Poggi on one of Ocampo's stories from *Los días de la noche,* "Las vestiduras peligrosas," enunciates the unusual blend of narrating conventions employed by Ocampo, which in this case combines a realistic mode with traditional components of ancient fables.[26] The dangerous dresses of the story's title are related in Poggi's analysis to those in Perrault's "Cinderella." The ending to Ocampo's story veers from the fairy-tale structure in a move that Poggi defines as feminist: The contradictions in the narrative levels announce the impossiblity of the female character's desire for autonomy. Though her analysis differs in method from my own of chapter 3, our conclusions are entirely compatible.

In the 1980s Dan Balderston's English translation of a selection of Ocampo's stories included Borges's prologue to the Gallimard edition. To my knowlege these are still the only available in English translation.[27] Tusquets brought out two new volumes of unpublished works, *Y así sucesivamente* (1987) and *Cornelia frente al espejo* (1988), Ocampo's last published works. Many of the stories probably date from earlier periods in the author's career for they continue the same vein. Indeed, two stories originally published in *Sur* are collected here for the first time.[28] The themes of metamorphosis and doubling are repeated with some irony and perhaps a touch of self-parody. The structural ruptures noted all along become more marked in both volumes. Ocampo always showed an interest in dreamlike narratives with minimal plot, absurd dialog in which people speak without listening, listen without hearing, and behave in inexplicable ways. All these tendencies are exaggerated in the final volumes. *Cornelia* as a collection calls attention to the connections between individual stories such that one must read "La máscara" and "Con pasión" together and "El para otra" with the poem "La alfombra voladora" for real comprehension. In interviews with me and with Noemí Ulla Silvina Ocampo mentioned the many manuscripts that she had yet to publish, among them several novels, essays, adaptations for theater, and poetry. There may yet be more forthcoming from this prolific writer as posthumous publications.

Around the 1980s articles in the United States began to appear on Ocampo's stories. Thomas C. Meehan noted the odd and magical children which populate Ocampo's stories; Dan Balderston proposed a kind of aesthetic of cruelty to define works by

Ocampo and poet Juan Rudolfo Wilcock (with whom she had coauthored the verse drama, *Los traidores*).[29] Barbara Aponte and Helena Araújo both compare Ocampo's "El pecado mortal" to contemporary narratives by Arguedas, Roa Bastos and Alba Lucía Angel.[30] Susan Bassnett mentions Ocampo as one of the female literary voices to which more attention was finally being directed: "The family of male writers has started to realize it has sisters, daughters and mothers who are emerging from their attic rooms and speaking in voices loud enough to be heard by all."[31] Later Bassnett marks the relationship between the explicit violence of Alejandra Pizarnik's "La condesa sangrienta" and the more implicit or concealed violence of Clarice Lispector and Silvina Ocampo. My own articles of that time discuss the fantastic and grotesque aspects of her work, study female violence as part of her preoccupation with the double, and examine issues of aethetics and subjectivity.[32] Recently detailed studies have appeared on individual stories. Cristina Ferreira-Pinto notes the deliberate ambiguity of authorial voice in "La continuación" and its conscious confusion of the various fictive levels.[33] Marjorie Agosín compares Ocampo's "La casa de azúcar" with the use of domestic space by María Luisa Bombal, noting that both writers transform the "safe" female enclosure into something more menacing.[34] Cynthia Duncan, in an analysis of the same story, notes that the fantastic element of "La casa de azúcar" can be read as either a supernatural metamorphosis or as a tale told by a psychologically twisted narrator.[35] Alejandra Rosarossa's study of "La red" discusses its narrative focalization as a source of ambiguity.[36] The cultural complexity of the narrative voices, the dreamlike quality of its spacial orientation, and the story's structural ambiguity contribute to its problematization of perception and identity.

In 1991 the Mexican Fondo de Cultura Económica, published the hard-back anthology, compiled by Matilde Sánchez that was cited earlier. The stories are organized into four large divisions which group Ocampo's works thematically into works of cruelty, metamorphosis, fiction (by which she seems to mean play with time and memory), and miniatures. It also contains a section devoted to poetry translated by Ocampo from foreign authors: John Donne, Andrew Marvell, Alexander Pope, Charles Baudelaire, Paul Verlaine, Pierre de Ronsard, and Emily Dickinson. As mentioned earlier, in relation to Ocampo's biography, it contains the best set of photographs of the author and her millieu to date. A collection of Noemí Ulla's essays on Ocampo's work appeared in 1992 in Argentina with the title *Invenciones a dos voces*. Despite the promising title, the essays seem to be reproduced with no adaptation for their publication as a group, and are quite repetitive, offering no overall sense of how Ocampo's works have been selected for discussion. She describes only a tiny fraction of Ocampo's total production, concentrating in terms of the fiction—inexplicably in my view—on her earliest works. Ulla's studies do draw associations between the poetry and prose and situate Ocampo with the writers most closely connected to her chronologically and personally, Borges, Bioy Casares, Cortázar, and in poetry, Neruda and Paz. She notes the frequent use of documents—letters, diaries, and so forth—as framing devices for the short stories.[37] She mentions briefly the rhetorical strategies which Ocampo's prose and poetry have in common: oxymoron, visible in such titles as *Los días de la noche* [The Days of the Night] and *Lo amargo por dulce* [Bitter Because Sweet]; images which make imaginative use of colors and sounds; and the use of metonymy, ellipsis, and enumeration. The latter starts, like Neruda, with elements of nature, but eventually the enumerated series are filled with familiar objects which replace natural ones. This enumeration of objects produces in Ocampo's works an air of *kitsch*, a term which I also associate with Ocampo in chapter 3 of the present study. Ulla's insightful analysis of the sonnet "Amor" (*Amarillo celeste*) and the short story "Amada en el amado" coincides with my conclusions below regarding Ocampo's break with what Ulla calls a whole culture of courtly love. Ulla's analysis of "La continuación," like my own of chapter 3, views the story as an "ars poetica."

As the present volume was being prepared for publication the first systematic book-length study of Ocampo's short stories appeared in Argentina. Graciela Tomassini's *El espejo de Cornelia* uses a structuralist and reader response methodology to analyze the entire opus of Ocampo's short fiction (excepting, as I do here, the works specifically written for children).[38] Tomassini focuses her comments around a central idea, that Ocampo's fictional world is characterized, both structurally and linguistically, by paradox, "donde lo trivial suele expresar lo sobrenatural, la banalidad puede servir a un planteo metafísico y la belleza abre cauces en lo abyecto, lo cruel, lo insignifante o lo estereotipado" [where the trivial expresses the supernatural, the banal can pose a metaphysical issue and beauty opens channels to the abject, the cruel, the insignificant or the cliched].[39] Starting from that premise, Tomassini offers thorough discussions of structural elements, such as point of view, and of such linguistic patterns as irony, exaggeration, enumeration, and use of colloquialisms, popular sayings and other "debased" language codes in combination often with the most lyrical of prose poetry. Divided into four chapters, she discusses the stories in chronological order. This is perhaps the book's weakness, for she deals in separate chapters with narratives judged to be early efforts (*Viaje olvidado*), stylistic detours (*Autobiografía de Irene*), and later repetitions (*Y así sucesivaemente* and *Cornelia frente al espejo*), leaving only one chapter to discuss the three volumes that contain the majority of Ocampo's best work. Since I have done exactly the opposite, concentrated on the three volumes of her mature work (i.e., *La furia, Las invitadas,* and *Los días de la noche*) and given others less comprehensive attention, Tomassini's study provides a nice complement to the current one. Though her bibliography of Ocampo's works includes several book reviews and interviews to which I have not had access, it is puzzlingly incomplete in other ways, omitting important studies by Rosario Castellanos, Blas Matamoro, and Silvia Molloy, as well as nearly everything published in the United States.

In 1995, Cynthia Duncan edited a special issue of *Inti* which contains three articles dealing in whole or in part with Ocampo. The article by Duncan, "An Eye for an 'I,'" reads three of Ocampo's fantastic stories from *La furia* with stories by Elena Garro and Elvira Orphee. The three authors have in common a play with point of view which subverts "normal" modes of organizing and articulating experience by giving both vision and voice to otherwise marginalized beings. María B. Clark fills a gap in the current study, for she analyzes a story not mentioned here, "Hombres animales enredaderas," from Ocampo's *Los días de la noche.* Clark's psychoanalytic approach reinforces arguments made below regarding the structuring properties of the gaze, the blurring of gender and species boundaries, and the playful indeterminacy of the enunciating voice visible in Ocampo's texts. My article in the collection presents an early version of the argument elaborated in chapter 4 below regarding identity construction depicted in Ocampo's works, paying special attention to the crisis of feminine identity portrayed throughout her last published work, *Cornelia frente al espejo.*[40]

The present study will be the first critical book in English on Silvina Ocampo's short stories. Its feminist approach is long overdue as statements like Alberto Manguel's attest. Referring to women writers left out by the "boom" of interest within the

United States in Latin American literature, he says: "among the authors translated, there were hardly any women. A few . . . crept onto the publishers' lists. But where were the others? Where was Silvina Ocampo, surely one of the ten best writers writing in Spanish today?"[41] John King comments in an aside (in "Victoria Ocampo") that Silvina Ocampo is "perhaps the most underrated of all Argentinian writers."[42] One of the questions which palpitates behind the writing of this book is why, given Silvina Ocampo's undeniably central position in the intellectual ferment and creative "boom" in Latin America, the steady if unspectacular interest shown in her work, have feminist scholars been relatively uninterested in this writer? The answer, ironically, seems to be inherent in the question: because she is so central, because she has so little claim to the margins from which resistance can be expected. To discard this remarkable writer as an elitist, oligarchical figure of little interest to Anglo-American feminist politics of revolution and change is to impoverish our understanding of where resistance to the status quo can arise. The present study reevaluates Ocampo's works from a feminist perspective and seeks to demonstrate their importance for scholars interested in the renovation of language which may permit the emergence of a feminine voice and a locus for change.

THEORETICAL APPROACH

Silvina Ocampo's works represent a most complex and fascinating account of the feminine, recognized early on in Eduardo González Lanuza's review of *Autobiografía de Irene,* which he describes as having "ese no sé qué inasible pero tan irreductiblemente feminino" [an indescribable but irreducibly feminine something].[43] Although Ocampo declines the label "feminist" for herself, as do many other Latin American writers, the attention she has paid to the female in representation makes her work of vital interest to an account of the constitution of the feminine in fiction. Amy Kaminsky and Debra Castillo both discuss at some length the limits, the dangers, and the promise of applying international feminist perspectives to the specifics of Latin American women writers.[44] The "nagging" questions regarding the dangers of imperialist appropriation (Castillo), the difficulties of "translating" cultures and languages of analysis (Kaminsky) have haunted my own thinking. Finally, however, one must simply begin.

Thanks in particular to Castillo's apology for utilizing "a pinch of this, and a smidgen of that," I no longer feel the need to explain at length the eclectic use I have made of contemporary literary theories. My readings of Ocampo's short stories utilize primarily the terminology of psychoanalysis in order to articulate the ways in which gender is inscripted in the language of her fictions. The critics most influential in this process are those born of North America's academic feminist tradition which by now has produced a substantial body of works attentive both to the deconstructive power of the French school and to an activist political agenda of "real women" both as writers and readers, unwilling to restrict themselves to woman as discursive category. It has been profoundly reassuring to note that Debra Castillo lists many of the strategies that organize my book: an interest in "bad taste" as a political position, in surface details particularly of the female body as aesthetic category, in silence as a specific mode of communication, in the role of the maternal in the creative process.[45] According to Castillo, Latin American women writers' "cultivation of superficiality" allows the surface reading, traditionally associated with poor reading, even decadent, morally deficient reading, to be reclaimed to express an "amoral forgotten truth." The image Castillo invokes to exemplify her point, in reference to Rosario Castellanos's works, is a feminine image infrequent in North American fiction, but perfectly describes what I have called *la madre terrible* and anticipates many issues under discussion in what follows:

> She [Castellanos] rejects the meek, tidy housewife and evokes instead the unmistakable image of the bored upper-class woman, filing her nails (sharpening her claws?), slipping menacingly out of her Eve-snake skin, creating herself affirmatively in the appropriation of the polished, superficial, adjectival existence allotted her. . . . Is excessive ornamentation belittled as the sign of an overly emotional femininity? Fine: she adopts wanton elegance as her rhetorical style and flaunts its seductiveness. The mirror is her talisman, is, like those flashing mirrors worn by the famous Knight of the Mirrors in *Don Quijote,* a weapon for dispelling, as it creates, illusion: aesthetics and politics brought home, as it were, from their travels, made homey, personal, private, quotidian.[46]

The word not used here, but certainly implied, is *decadent.* Castillo's argument regarding superficial, or bad, reading corresponds well with Naomi Schor's recent study of the (overly) ornamental surface of bad writing, or more broadly, bad art. Naomi Schor argues that "the association of details, femininity, and decadence" is one of our most persistent legacies.[47]

The final chapter of Jane Gallop's collected essays entitled *Thinking Through the Body* gives a clear idea of the method's limits. Gallop quotes from Freud's article, "The Moses of Michelangelo," in which she through Freud acknowledges that psychoanalytic criticism of art attends more to its subject matter than to what the artist values most, the "formal and technical qualities."[48] Though both Freud and Gallop may be evidencing undue modesty in this respect, I also find that I have paid more attention to the subject matter, and have dwelt on issues of structure or recurring figures of speech, for instance, less comprehensively than these deserve. My expectation, of course, is that my readings will inspire others to fill the inevitable gaps. What I hope becomes clear here is the richness of Ocampo's works, their abundant scope for feminist inquiry, and the ways in which the women writers active today have benefited from her groundbreaking success in reconfiguring the feminine in Latin American fiction.

Sylvia Molloy has stated that she is ready to identify and recognize the female tradition on which she as creative writer stands, and names Silvina Ocampo as part of this tradition.[49] Silvina Ocampo's voice has much to tell us about how a woman proceeds when attempting the unexpected, writing. Josefina Delgado puts to rest the issues of money and class in speaking about Victoria Ocampo, and anticipates the strategies of her sister Silvina:

> Sin duda a Victoria Ocampo no le resultó más sencillo que a Alfonsina llevar adelante su proyecto de ser ella, a pesar de las facilidades que indudablemente da el dinero. . . . Nada más apasionante para una mujer que leer las memorias de Victoria Ocampo. Haciéndolo se derriban las barreras de las diferencias sociales, porque allí está, para quien necesite corroborarlo, el mismo fervor, el mismo miedo, la misma inseguridad que cualquier mujer siente cuando decide hacer lo que no se espera de ella. Y escribir es algo que puede hacerse de muchas maneras: como Scherezada para que no le corten la cabeza, o para mirarse en un espejo despiadado pero verdadero.[50]

> [Without doubt it was no easier for Victoria Ocampo than for Alfonsina Storni to carry out the project of being herself, in spite of the advantages which money undeniably provides. . . . Nothing more moving for a woman than to read the memoires of Victoria Ocampo. In doing so the barriers of social class are toppled, because there it

is, for whomever needs proof, the same ferver, the same fear, the same insecurity that any woman feels when she decides to do what no one expects from her. And writing is something that can be done in many ways: like Scherezade in order to save your neck, or in order to look in a pitiless, but truthful mirror.

Silvina Ocampo's works concern themselves with issues of class and power. My analyses try to demonstrate the complex ways in which Ocampo weaves the threads of ideology and gender. Silvina holds up a mirror to herself and her society, but she describes it, not as "verdadero" [truthful] but in the terms of the postmodern, which she certainly anticipates, as "infiel" [unfaithful]. Her preoccupations with the fantastic and the grotesque are reflected in an early poem, which Enrique Pezzoni used to characterize her fiction and which serves as epigraph to this book. As Pezzoni says, "Infiel espejo será la fórmula que mejor definirá la obra futura de Silvina Ocampo" [The unreliable mirror will be the formula which best defines the future work of Silvina Ocampo].[51] The words "violentísimo" [violent] and "párvulo" [childlike, candid] define her world view as well, in which destructive forces are found within life's minimal, quotidian details, described with an innocence that forms an essential component of her narratives' humor and horror.

The fifty-six speakers who gathered in Buenos Aires in 1989 to discuss women and writing almost all needed to take a moment to define the word "femenina" which when combined with "literatura" means in Spanish both women's writing and feminine writing.[52] With the French theorists many seemed to agree that male writers could write "feminine" works, and Proust and Flaubert were frequently mentioned as examples. My concern is wholly with the first option, with writing done by women, by the half of the human species who takes up the culturally constituted position as woman however constructed we may ultimately believe that position to be. Martha Mercader says to this effect:

> Creo que las mujeres y los hombres somos distintos en nuestro ser y en nuestro hacer. Hombres y mujeres utilizamos el mismo código labrado por los balbuceos y los discursos, los gritos y susurros de la inclasificable humanidad. El mismo código, las mismas reglas lingüísticas, pero a partir de lugares distintos.[53]

> [I think that women and men are different in our being and our actions. Men and women utilize the same code forged from babbling and from argument, the cries and whispers of unclassifiable human-

ity. The same code, the same linguistic rules, but starting from different places.]

Mercader thus locates the point of departure for this book, an
examination of that different place of women's writing.

Naomi Schor writes that for the moment we are stuck in binary oppositions of male and female and must uncover the "dark
continent" of female desire in order to avoid becoming subsumed to the masculine.[54] Schor suggests, like Jessica Benjamin
and Kaja Silverman, that instead of being less integrated into
the symbolic and having a more privileged relationship to the
real than do men (as argued by French feminists), women instead have developed a double vision: They are more aware of
the costs of the symbolic and consequently less willing to view
the imaginary as thoroughly regressive. Part 1 of this study explores Ocampo's validation of the preconscious realm of the
imaginary: Governed by the duality of mother/child, often re-
garded as violent and mute even in its nurturing intimacy of
bodies and being, it provides a powerful locus for undercutting
the sterility of the symbolic realm. The subversive function of
the imaginary entails an exploration of the experience of female-
ness, the construction of the subject as female. Part 2, therefore,
in Teresa de Lauretis's phrase, takes psychoanalytic theory at
its word, that femininity is but the underside of masculinity.[55]
Recognizing "the continued existence and the functioning of
patriarchy as a structure of subjectivity" (ibid., 165), the following chapters analyze the creative ways in which Ocampo brings
that different social and psychic positioning to fiction. De Lauretis's precise definition of the important word *experience* proves
particularly useful: "I use the term not in the individualistic,
idiosyncratic sense of something belonging to one and exclusively her own even though others might have 'similar' experiences; but rather in the general sense of a *process* by which,
for all social beings, subjectivity is constructed." That process
includes "material, economic, interpersonal" relations which
may be perceived as individual, but that "are in fact social, and
in a larger perspective, historical" (ibid., 159). The fluidity of the
process, its ongoing construction, rather than fixed achieve-
ment, are important considerations for a deeper understanding
of Ocampo's fictional feminine.

This book begins with issues long associated with Ocampo's
works to pose questions of gender not addressed by the usual
approaches to these genres. Using a psychoanalytic approach to

the fantastic and grotesque, chapter 1 identifies the subversive function of preadolescent female characters who become a particularly potent locus for both magical power and violent rebellions against the status quo. Chapter 2 then explores the ways in which the subject/object grammar of plot structures is altered to make way for a desire marked as feminine. Ocampo redirects narrative desire from the standard women's plots whose endings resituate the heroine within patriarchal positions of marriage or death to more open-ended narratives which hold up both male/subject and female/object positions to ridicule. The chapter explores Ocampo's ironic approach to the romance plot, the insistent reappearance of female doubles, the transgressive mother, the rebellious daughter, and the troubling issues of sexual perversion as particularly fertile stagings for female subjectivity. Turning to the specific strategies which make up Ocampo's revision of the feminine, chapter 3 derives a conception of Ocampo's aesthetics from metafictional commentary involving artists and writers within her fiction. The ideal artist is intimately associated with the maternal, while the authorial· presence is envisioned as androgynous. The aesthetic fantasies which associate writing with a problematized female body set the stage for a consideration of Ocampo's use of details as a kind of secret code. A view of *kitsch* or bad taste as itself a political statement uncovers the moral center of Ocampo's works. Chapter 4 explores recurring elements frequently associated (negatively) with women's writing: letters, mirrors, and silence as a mode of communication. Ocampo's epistolary fiction refuses to put the female "in her place"; the mirror becomes a mode of rejecting the absoluteness of the body's defining power; and finally, feminine recourse to silence haunts Ocampo's tales of rape, marking the limits of language's capacity to relay experience.

The confluence of fantastic, grotesque, and feminine subversions works to undermine dominant depictions of power, class, aesthetics, and gender. Resistance consistently lies with the children of Ocampo's fiction, particularly with little girls whose secret knowledge, sardonic laughter, and real victimization combine to create a force for disruption and change. Feminist literary theory and theories of the fantastic and grotesque have in common their critique of dominant values. My argument suggests that Ocampo's works operate on the contradictions inherent in our culture's apprehension of reality, specifically, that her works focus on what de Lauretis has identified as a critical endeavor, to expose the operations of normative discourse: "The most exciting work in cinema and in feminism today is not anti-narrative or anti-Oedipal; quite the opposite. It is narrative and Oedipal with a vengeance, for it seeks to stress the duplicity of that scenario and the specific contradictions of the female subject in it, the contradiction by which historical women must work with and against Oedipus" (ibid., 157). Duplicity and contradiction, these are Silvina Ocampo's favorite tools which she brings to every scenario, including the oedipal one.

Fantasies
of the Feminine

Part I
Discourses of Subversion

Bотн THE FANTASTIC AND THE GROTESQUE MODES OF FICTION HAVE been traced by their theorists to ancient times.[1] Indeed, it is easy to imagine prehistoric men and women, huddled around a fire, listening to a storyteller relate something like a precursor to modern fantastic or grotesque fictions. Freud theorized that animism, or a magical outlook, coincides with early stages of both civilization and of individuals, i.e., with primitives and children.[2] In Latin America and elsewhere in the twentieth century the genre of fantastic fiction has been the site of a comprehensive exploration of conventions of reality by writers with interests far removed from either the recognizably primitive or with childhood. Borges, Bioy Casares, and Cortázar, the best-known writers of Silvina Ocampo's generation, have been acknowledged as legitimate heirs of turn-of-the-century precursors such as Henry James and Kafka. My readings of Ocampo's fictions situate her among these writers as a modernist and postmodernist author who, nevertheless, consciously evokes the ancient origins of her art. However literate, condensed and contemporary her stories, the "voice" of the storyteller haunts their pages like another of the ghosts. This fragmented and partial remnant of archaic origins opens the possibility of establishing gender for the "I" of these texts, the possibility that a female narrating voice may have held audiences rapt around that ancient campfire as now within the pages of its modern equivalent, the short story.

My arguments suggest that Ocampo's fiction subverts notions of reality as part of her interest in the fantastic and grotesque and that an important element of that subversion encompasses inherited expectations regarding gender. Ocampo's exploration of the Imaginary implies a magical outlook, which is examined in chapter 1, and an interest in the early bond between mother and child, discussed in chapter 2. The element that remains somewhat veiled in these sections is the moral, spiritual component, which is also considered to be part of Lacan's Imaginary realm. Though this element will be considered briefly in part 2, it is worth noting here that Frederic Jameson posits modern fantastic fiction as a descendant of medieval romance, itself a degraded version of ancient myth. He, therefore, places the fantastic in the position which these other forms occupied in those other times, that is, as fictions in which everyday tribulations, "the humdrum contingencies of an ordinary finite and mortal existence" are transformed into a struggle between magical forces of higher and lower realms, between good and evil.[3] In secularized contemporary fiction the sacred is gradually replaced by absence: "the 'fantastic' seeks to convey the sacred, not as a presence, but rather as a determinate, marked absence at the heart of the secular world."[4] In a later article, he makes the connection with the Imaginary:

> It will be appropriate to designate this primordial rivalry of the mirror stage as a relationship of otherness: nowhere better can we observe the violent situational content of those judgements of good and evil which will later on cool off and sediment into the various systems of ethics. Both Nietzsche and Sartre have exhaustively explored the genealogy of ethics as the latter emerges from just such an archaic valorization of space, where what is "good" is what is associated with "my" position, and "bad" simply characterizes the affairs of my mirror rival.[5]

Ocampo's stories reevaluate the Imaginary which is intimately associated with ethics and morality, with the primitive relationship between mother and the child, and with the body and its magical connection to all things in order to overturn modern obsession with the Symbolic. Many critics have noticed that modern culture's hierarchical ranking of Symbolic over Imaginary implies the primacy of the father over the mother and, hence, men over women. Part 1 of this study explores in depth Ocampo's assault on all aspects of this preference.

Ocampo's works generally undermine readerly assumptions about the structures by which we order and define notions of reality. By placing the female at their center her narratives dismantle many cherished assumptions regarding the traditional positioning of the feminine in culture. I argue that Ocampo's disturbing antisocial fantasies pose challenges to both the culturally constituted subject and the larger social order, that the subversion of the symbolic visible in these texts privileges a female subjectivity, and further, that part of the "official culture"

under attack by Ocampo's works is not only the oligarchy, identified in general by Bakhtin and more particularly by Blas Matamoro's lengthy study of Ocampo's work, but the patriarchy in
which we all live. In particular, Ocampo's *nenas terribles,* her
wicked little girls, become her ultimate fantastic and grotesque
image and the locus of an important female subversion. The
subversive energy of these characters emerges from their systematic challenge to the conventions of female representation,
from their marginalized vantage "from below," and from their
grotesque laughter. A recognition of Silvina Ocampo's unique
appropriation of discourses of subversion as a sustained critique
of inherited structures serves to introduce the rest of the book,
which examines the problematized representations of the subject as female, and the ways in which this engendering of the
"I" makes all the difference.

1

The Fantastic and the Grotesque

DEFINITIONS

Fᴀɴᴛᴀꜱᴛɪᴄ ꜰɪᴄᴛɪᴏɴ ɪᴍᴀɢɪɴᴇꜱ ᴛʜᴇ ꜱᴜᴘᴇʀɴᴀᴛᴜʀᴀʟ. ᴛᴢᴠᴇᴛᴀɴ ᴛᴏ-dorov's structural approach defines it as a type of fiction positioned between what he calls the marvellous, fairy tales, myths, and the like which do not pretend to reproduce a recognizable world; and the uncanny, fiction that may present extremely bizarre or strange events but that, nonetheless, never transgress notions of the possible. His definition also hinges on his idea of "hesitation" in which both reader and character should remain in doubt about the nature of perceptions.[6] Henry James's *Turn of the Screw* most thoroughly matches Todorov's concept of a fantastic tale that sustains throughout the ambiguity between marvellous and uncanny, but requires some adjustment to his notion of hesitation. In his *Poetics,* Todorov returns to the analysis of James's tale to clarify that the hesitation resides here only in the reader, whereas in most nineteenth-century fantastic tales, the character and reader share a similar point of view. James creates a character completely convinced about the appearance of ghosts, but the narrative's textual strategies invite the reader to doubt her version.[7] If James locates hesitation solely in the reader, according to Todorov, Kafka's "Metamorphosis" takes the next step in doing away with "hesitation" altogether. Kafka's story marks the apprehension of the fantastic intrusion typical of twentieth-century works where the calm acceptance of the absurd into everyday life defines the modern fantastic and much of the grotesque as well.

If the fantastic suggests the supernatural, the grotesque is more closely allied to the uncanny, the process whereby the author "makes strange" the everyday elements of common life without crossing the boundary into the magical. As twentieth-century fiction increasingly questions the rational and the au-

39

thoritative, but has less interest in the "beyond," the grotesque becomes its dominant aesthetic.[8] My own use of these terms assumes that fantastic events can be one source of the horror of the grotesque, but that they coincide only in part. Each mode, rather, represents a possible subset of the other. The fantastic questions specific events of a narrative's plot, while the grotesque, which may also contain many of the same elements—doubles, nightmares, ghosts, and so on—refers also to its tone of narration in which ordinarily horrifying events are viewed with humor. Both the fantastic and the grotesque promote the essential function of Silvina Ocampo's fiction as an encounter with the absurd. Certain visual images she employs have been universally linked to both the fantastic and the grotesque, and usually suffice to characterize, at the same time, her obsessions: The distorted, estranged world to which she gives life is dominated by an interest in magical transformations; doubles or other shattered personalities; play with time and space; dreams or nightmares; mad or obsessed characters; the mixture of plant, animal, and human elements; the mixture of animate and inanimate qualities as in machines and automatons, puppets, dolls, and masks; and also what Mikhail Bakhtin calls the lower bodily processes of eating, defecation, and sexual life.

Kafka's "Metamorphosis," a work discussed as pivotal by both Todorov in his concept of fantastic fiction and by Wolfgang Kayser in his description of the grotesque, represents the epitome of the twentieth century's interrogation of reality and a fusion of these two modes essential to Ocampo's work as well as to Kafka's. According to Todorov, Kafka's story eliminates both the "hesitation" and the suspense heretofore required by the genre by inverting its traditional ordering of events: The fantastic element, in which the character is transformed into an insect, is presented in the story's first sentence. Kayser adds that the disturbing element of this famous tale, which defines it as grotesque, resides in the cold objectivity of the narrative voice, the flat acceptance of absurdity and horror into everyday life. This chapter will use both Kayser and Bakhtin—though their conceptions of the grotesque are often considered to be contradictory—in order to arrive at a complete understanding of Ocampo's darkly humorous narrations. What we discover is Bakhtin's carnival laughter converted to twentieth-century derision, or, as Lee Byron Jennings describes it, "the fearsome made trivial."[9]

Rosemary Jackson credits Todorov for recognizing the literary evolution in the nineteenth century from what he calls the marvellous to its gradual replacement by the uncanny, a term she uses nearly synonymously with the grotesque.[10] However, by restricting their discussion to structural elements and visual images, neither Todorov nor Kayser can engage the unconscious desire expressed by these fictions nor their ideological issues. Jackson's conflation of fantastic and grotesque—her preferred term is *fantasy* literature—studies these subversive discourses with a psychoanalytic approach. Her enlightening study makes the connection between the terminology of psychoanalysis and that of Bakhtin's carnivalesque,[11] and in so doing indirectly opens the way for recognition of Ocampo's fantastic and grotesque fiction as feminine subversion.

THE FANTASTIC

Rosemary Jackson's study provides a detailed analysis of fantasy literature's rebellion against received notions of reality. Her psychoanalytic approach suggests that fantastic fiction's preoccupation with the problematic positioning of "self" in relation to "world," the "I" to the "not-I," can be viewed as an attempt, at least within the illusions of fictional representation, to reverse human progress through the mirror stage: that is, the human maturation process, described by Freud and elaborated by Lacan, by which the "I" is originally severed from the "not-I." At this point the child enters the symbolic order and perceives himself as a separate object and also as a divided subject with a superego that "watches, judges, measures and condemns the self as it tries to meet the demands of the social order."[12] For Lacan, passage through the mirror stage confers the status of (conscious) Subject but only at the expense of submission to the Law of the Father, that is, the laws of language and the Symbolic Order. The notion that this submission is crippling to the subject lies at the heart of fantasy literature which attempts an impossible return to the bliss of undifferentiated being represented by the Imaginary: "They [literary fantasies] express a desire for the imaginary, for that which has not yet been caught and confined by a symbolic order, yet the self-mutilation, cruelty, horror and violence which they have to employ to return to the imaginary suggests its inaccessability" (ibid., 91). Jackson suggests that fantasy literature is essentially subversive by virtue of its insistent challenges to accepted notions of reality, in its play with time and space, for instance, but that many fantasies conclude by returning to a comfortable stasis, in effect, "neutralizing their own impulses towards transgression." I argue that many of Silvina Ocampo's fantastic narratives represent Jackson's ideal category of fantasy literature which seeks to "remain open, dissatisfied, endlessly desiring."[13]

Jackson's thematic division of fantasy literature into three broad categories—metamorphosis, disintegrated bodies, and the uncanny—proves useful in an approach to the large number of Silvina Ocampo's stories. Metamorphosis, an ancient device that harks back to Classical literature, seeks to blur the difference between self and other by imagining their impossible unity; disintegrated bodies, on the other hand, includes the cluster of fantastic devices with the opposite tendency, the splitting of self into other; and the uncanny, the fiction that suggests but falls just short of the supernatural, merges in her definition with my own concept of the grotesque. No set of organizational categories is intended to be absolute. Quite interesting are Ocampo's stories of metamorphosis, for instance, which occur in combination with themes of the double or with that of the magical object. Jackson concludes that both impulses, splitting and combining of beings, represent attempts to undo ego boundaries which are alien to the Imaginary: "it is precisely this subversion of unities of 'self' which constitutes the most radical transgressive function of the fantastic" (ibid., 83). Ocampo's stories demonstrate quite fanciful combinations of all three of Jackson's categories.

METAMORPHOSIS

Jackson points out that in most post-Romantic fiction, such as Kafka's "Metamorphosis," physical transformations "simply happen" (ibid., 83). The origins of this motif, however, date from ancient Classical tradition in which such transformations explained or imitated natural phenomena. Silvina Ocampo's stories of metamorphosis retain something of this archaic quality. "Sábanas de tierra," for instance, describes an old gardener whose hand becomes literally rooted in the ground and who gradually turns into a shrub.[14] Like Daphne of Ovid's *Metamorphosis,* the protagonist changes by way of an abbreviated but wholly natural process, one that also seems to be implicitly willed: His devotion to his work has allowed him to become the object of his devotion. The intentionality behind Ocampo's tales of magical metamorphoses is more obvious in her story entitled "Isis," in which a retarded girl transforms herself into a strange animal. The child's hidden power is suggested in the story's many details: from her name, Isis, that of the great Egyptian goddess, to the narrator's report that "algunas personas sospechaban que no era del todo idiota, sino que más bien se hacía la idiota" (*I* 63) [some suspected that she was not completely idiotic, but that she pretended to be an idiot]. Her indifference to daily life and insistent staring out the window toward the nearby zoo suggest a secret, inner life, confirmed by the story's conclusion in which the narrator takes Isis for a walk, and finds that she is compelled by the child to enter the zoo. Isis leads her to the cage of a strange animal where the narrator realizes that this particular cage is visible from Isis's window. The dramatic final sentence has an air of inevitability to it:

Comprendí que ése era el animal que ella había contemplado y que la había contemplado. —Dame la mano—dije a Isis. Y me dio una mano que fue cubriéndose paulatinamente de pelos y de pezuñas. (*I* 64)

[I understood that that was the animal that she had contemplated and which had comtemplated her. "Give me your hand," I said to Isis. And she gave me a hand that was slowly becoming covered with hair and hooves.]

The event of metamorphosis exemplifies the repeated triumph of the Imaginary in Ocampo's work. Isis refuses to suffer the mutilation of passage through the mirror stage, to acquire language; her humorous/horrific transformation into an animal liberates her from the constraints of consciousness that throughout the story are presented as irksome and trivial.

The development of this theme through the chronology of Ocampo's stories reveals the moment of metamorphosis as a liberating event, particularly for her female characters. If the issues in "Isis" emphasize questions of language, "Malva" presents a complex rebellion against all elements of the symbolic. This a macabre tale of a woman who, in moments of extreme impatience, bites and mutilates herself. The story begins with a description of Malva's long wait to see an official at her daughter's school, during which she bites off her little finger. Further episodes of brutal self-mutilation explode during stressful moments in ordinary bourgeois life—waiting for an elevator, sitting through a boring party—and the story ends by implying Malva's transformation into a fox or wolf. The narration hints that her metamorphosis was willed, in this case out of exasperation with middle-class urban existence, the rebellion of a radical kind of mad housewife. Finally, in "El automóvil" a jealous husband narrates the circumstances that lead him to believe that his beautiful wife turns herself into a racing car. In despair when he has lost her in traffic, he moans: "Amar en exceso destruye lo que amamos: a vos te destruyó el automóvil. Vos me destruiste . . ." (*Y así* 56) [To love in excess destroys what we love: the car destroyed you. You destroyed me]. The reader of this story, however, may feel that the wife's metamorphosis represents, rather than her destruction, a unique escape from the narrator's smothering kind of love. Ocampo's transformations represent, not "meaningless, absurd acts which cannot signify" (Jackson, 82), but willed, if unconscious, challenges to the established order. These stories present fantasies of escape both from the social order as well as from the symbolic order by way of their impossible return to the imaginary.

DISINTEGRATED BODIES

Jackson's second broad category of fantasy, called "disintegrated bodies," includes the cluster of fantastic devices which function in opposition to metamorphosis: While metamorphosis assumes the impossible unity of self and other, the category of disintegrated bodies represents the split of the self into other(s). The discussion of such a huge category requires some further division, but does allow an appreciation for a fundamental similarity between themes of the double, magical objects and ruptures of time and space.

THE DOUBLE

Ocampo's stories are crowded with doubled characters and every imaginable device for splitting or multiplying the fictional self. C. F. Keppler categorizes many literary doubles as "false" either because they are presented only as objects such as mirrors, portraits, photographs, statues, shadows, and the like; or because they are merely subjective, as in dreams and hallucinations.[15] The true "second self," in Keppler's terms, is neither one nor the other but always both, that is, always both objective and subjective simultaneously. While Ocampo has created characters that fall into his narrow range, I have found it more useful to consider the "false" as well as the "true" doubles that appear in Ocampo's works because they are, in my opinion, all significant and interesting images of the splitting of the self, the examination of the "I" in literary representation. Though Ocampo's interest in the figure of the double spans her entire opus, her first stories of doubled characters are not properly fantastic and will be discussed briefly in the next chapter. Her earliest fantastic doubles are to be found in her second collection, *Autobiografía de Irene* (1948).

The title story doubles its main character in time and in space: Irene's ability to foresee the future creates a temporal splitting, while a physical double who appears in the story's conclusion creates the spatial split. In his review of the collection, González Lanuza described this story as "ese laberinto lúcido" [that lucid labyrinth] since its circular narrative structure traps Irene in an eternal life that seems to approach its end only to start over at the beginning.[16] Though Irene writes her autobiography as an adult, many of the story's events are narrated from the child's perspective. These are the events that reveal her powers to foresee the future: She predicts the arrival of a pet dog, Jazmín, describes in advance the gift of a statue of the Virgin of Luján, and foretells the abundant growth of a vine in the patio before it was ever planted by her father. Later, she horrifies friends and family by readying herself for her father's death months in advance, then reacting with indifference to the actual event. In adolescence she predicts the face of her first love, Gabriel, but starts to distance herself emotionally from him long before his departure from her life.

Not surprisingly, Irene has the feeling she must be causing, not just foreseeing, the future. For a time she tries to avoid unpleasant thoughts: "mis visiones debían ser agradables; debía ser cuidadosa con mis pensamientos, tratar de evitar las ideas tristes, inventar un mundo afortunado" (*AI* 159) [My visions should be pleasant; I should be careful with my thoughts, try to avoid sad ideas, to invent a happier world]. More disturbing eventually than the sense of responsibility is the loss of memory caused by Irene's "gift." Because of so many images of the future, she has no ability to recapture the past: "los acontecimientos, que pueden ser infinitos en el recuerdo de los seres normales, son brevísimos y casi inexistentes para quien los prevé y solamente los vive" (160) [Events, which can be infinite in the memory of normal beings, are brief and almost non-exixtent for those who predict and merely live them]. She yearns for her death because she realizes that as her future diminishes she will regain thoughts of her past. We know from Borges (and Lacan) that memory *is* fiction and that our notion of self is based on this fiction, the fiction of the self. Without memory we have no self; hence, Irene's problem is that of her own constitution as a subject. In the story's conclusion she foresees herself writing her autobiography, which starts with the same words as the beginning of the story thus realizing the "triste destino" [sad destiny] she had feared from the start: "Me aflige sólo el temor de no morir" (149) [I am pained only by the fear of not dying]. As she meets her double on a park bench, Irene realizes that she is a character trapped in representation who cannot "die" and whose story therefore cannot end. Silvina Ocampo's "Autobiografía de Irene" posits immortality as the ultimate absurdity just as Borges's "El inmortal" did at about the same time. While Borges's immortal is encountered in a city far off in an unknown desert, Silvina Ocampo's Irene is figured as an ordinary child/woman placed in an all-too-banal setting.[17] This story introduces elements that become constants in Ocampo's works: the foregrounding of the female as narrator or main character, the importance of the child's perspective, the splitting of the characters or narrator, and a narrative structure which prevents closure or "death."

From the same collection, "El impostor" presents another intriguing story of a double. "El impostor" hints broadly at fantastic intrusions, but eventually terminates in a series of enticing questions that serve to deny a supernatural explanation, a conclusion that Keppler would classify as a "mistake" and that Todorov would term *uncanny*. This ending, which eliminates the possibility of the supernatural, is hardly less shocking to readers than a traditional fantastic ending might be. Since its narrative thrust implies an interrogation of the "self" in a context of linguistic and narrative subversions I include it here.[18]

The principal first-person narrator is young Luis Maidana who is sent on a strange mission by one of his father's closest friends. He is to travel to a decaying cattle ranch, where the friend's son, Armando Heredia, is residing, having abandoned his family and his studies in favor of a mysterious and isolated existence. Luis is to claim a need for rest from his own studies in order to live with Armando for a month and accomplish his real purpose, to assess his mental condition and report to Armando's father. Luis's journal forms the body of the story, and he presents the reader with an almost stereotypical setting for the fantastic: an old, decrepit house in an isolated, rural setting. He portrays Armando Heredia as a withdrawn, violent, and possibly insane young man. Furthermore, he recounts one experience after another of *déjà vu* and of dreams that accurately predict the future. The theme of the double becomes apparent as the two protagonists engage in a relationship of mutual fascination and repulsion, both attracted to the same mysterious young girl. Luis's commentary ends with his decision to flee the ranch. He suspects that Armando is about to kill him because he has learned that Luis is a spy for his father.

Abruptly a new narrator, Rómulo Sagasta, is introduced. He identifies himself as a friend of Armando's father who was sent to the ranch to check on Armando. Upon his arrival he discovers Armando dead. Among his possessions is Luis's notebook which he is directed to read by the grieving parents when they arrive for Armando's funeral. Sagasta tries to locate Luis Maidana in order to learn something about his friend's apparent suicide, but discovers that Heredia's friends and family know of no such person. Furthermore, Armando's other writings clearly prove that the notebook is in his own hand. The journal, evidently written not by Luis but by Armando himself, is entitled, "Mis sueños" [My Dreams]. The anguished Sagasta ends his account with these questions:

¿Por qué, suponiendo que esos relatos fueran sueños, Armando fingía ser otro personaje? ¿Fingía o realmente soñaba que era otro, y se veía desde afuera? ¿Lo obsesionaba la idea de no tener sueños, como lo dice en una de las páginas del cuaderno? . . . Armando Heredia, al suicidarse, ¿creyó matar a Luis Maidana, como creyó matar en su infancia a un personaje imaginario? . . . ¿Quiso, odió, asesinó a un ser imaginario? (*AI* 128–29)

[Why, supposing that those tales were dreams, did Armando pretend to be someone else? Did he pretend or really dream that he was another person, and that he saw himself from outside? Was he obsessed by the idea of not having dreams, as it says in one of the pages of the notebook? Did Armando Heredia, on committing suicide, believe that he was killing Luis Maidana, as he thought in childhood that he killed an imaginary person? Did he love, hate and kill an imaginary being?]

Sagasta's questions reflect those of the disconcerted reader, who at this point is mentally trying to rewrite this story to incorporate the astonishing news of Luis Maidana's non-existence. The fact of his death would not have surprised us. We were prepared for that by the building tensions between the "two" main characters, hints at Armando's madness, violence, and suspicion. The fantastic double has proved to be a doubly fictional representation of the divided self. Ocampo has used an old device, the document which contains a story-within-a-story, to unseat our expectations. The journal forms a mirror in which Armando attempts to describe himself through the eyes of "another" who is at once his own invention.

A retrospective reading reveals Armando Heredia's desperate attempt to escape the father's law, in the literal and in the Lacanian sense. He flees to an isolated, magical place; creates the character of Luis as an image of the ideal son, the son his father would approve and who is imagined as "spying" on his own failure and/as madness; he then strives to kill this image of perfection. He first subverts the image's supposed perfection by attributing cowardice and traitorous acts to Luis, "confessed" in the journal. Then, he apparently attempts to kill him bodily, but ends by destroying himself. Killing the created double represents a futile attempt to repeal passage through the mirror stage into the symbolic. The failed attempt at a return to an undifferentiated imaginary can be viewed as an escape from repressive laws of language and of patriarchy. The "truth" about his identity is revealed by the appearance of a second narrator, a representative of the "real" father. In this case, the truth is more horrifying than the "fiction" and reveals the ferocity and self-destructive character of desire for the imaginary. In Ocampo's most Borgesian collection, both stories of doubles play on categories of the symbolic, that is, readerly expectations of the narrative tradition itself. Both Armando Heredia and Irene, like other authors of doubles, contemplate "self" in relation to "other" who is in reality the same.

The following collection, *La furia y otros cuentos* (1959), produces several instances of the oldest type of literary double, the twin. The narrator of "Nosotros," one of a pair of identical twins, speaks in first-person plural in relating his and his brother's attempt to share a marriage to the same woman. "El vástago" contains two sets of doubles, the brothers from one of whose point of view the narration is told and the grandfather and grandson both of whom are named eventually "Labuelo." This story's subplot, like that of "Nosotros," has the two brothers in love with the same woman, and curiously, the woman in both stories is named Leticia. While in "Nosotros" the brothers eventually decide to sacrifice the woman for the sake of preserving their own relationship,[19] the narrator of "El vástago" is disappointed in love and has to watch his brother's happy marriage from within the same large house. The problem of their shared love for Leticia is overshadowed in this story by their father's domination and abuse. Once a son is born to the young couple, the brothers try to rid themselves of the tyrannical father by teaching the little boy how to shoot a pistol. Although the child succeeds in killing his grandfather, the tyranny continues, for the little boy has inherited his grandfather's personality: "Éste [el padre/abuelo] de algún modo proyectó sobre el vástago inocente, rasgos, muecas, personalidad: fué la última y la más perfecta de sus venganzas" (F 22) [He (the grand/father) somehow projected on his innocent descendant, characteristics, expressions, personality: it was his last and most perfect revenge]. The child "becomes" his grandfather in a story that combines themes of the double with metamorphosis.

A similar combination occurs in "La casa de azúcar," which creates doubled characters who "share" an identity. Though the women in this story, Cristina and Violeta, never meet, their fates are intimately related and they seem to feel a special identification even from a distance. Cristina appears to understand, even if incompletely, the dangers of her own ego fluidity; she warns her fiancé before they are married that she cannot live in a house that has been previously occupied. The young man, the story's narrator, searches in vain for such a dwelling and finally resorts to deception: A clean little house, which Cristina delightedly compares to a lump of sugar, becomes their home on the pretext that it is brand new. Thereafter, the husband constantly guards against his new wife's discovery of there having been a previous owner, another young woman, Violeta. Gradually, however, he becomes aware that Cristina and Violeta are exchanging identities, or rather that Cristina is becoming Violeta: She seems to gain information, habits, and even objects (a dog, a black velvet dress) that she did not possess before. The subtle suggestion that an individual's personal possessions can affect another weaves its way into many of Ocampo's narratives, often, as here, in a combination of referenes to metamorphosis, doubling and magical objects.

The fragmentation of human personality takes several unusual forms in *Las invitadas* (1961). "La vida clandestina," for instance, describes a man who perceives his mirrored self as totally alien to what he identifies as his essential self. In "Las termas de Tirte," a French actor in a luxurious health spa has figured out how to double the useful time of his life by sleeping through his most tedious duties, including conversation with strangers. The self or part of the self continues to function even in sleep. "Cara en la palma" describes an independent body part which functions like a double: It talks, bites, and usually opposes the will of the narrator. These three stories explore extreme representations of the divided self. All have in common the context of a love story. The man with the false reflection tells his tale ostensibly to explain his rejection by his true love, Magdalena; the French actor's amazing sleeping habits are told with great resentment by a man who feels he is losing his own girlfriend to him; and the woman with the hand confesses her dilemma to the man she loves, because the hand hates him and she is considering cutting it off. Ocampo has placed these experiments with disintegrated bodies, then, within what Todorov categorizes as themes of the other, fantastic expressions of sexual desire.[20]

On the story's surface, for example, "La cara en la palma," presents a loathsome double. In reference to her recent past, the woman explains that the hand had convinced her to flee her family and that she was subsequently found wandering the streets half-crazed and begging by her now beloved Aurelio, the story's *tú*. At the moment of the story's present she is engaged in the trade that Aurelio has taught her, the construction of handmade artificial flowers. The hand, already described as an enemy, as an agent for transgressive behavior (fleeing the family), furthermore, hates Aurelio and tries to undermine the skill he has taught: The hand tells her that the flowers she makes look like insects and "para torturarme les pasa la lengua o las muerde" (*I* 91) [it licks them or bites them just to torment me]. By setting up questions about Aurelio himself, the story offers a central ambiguity. The hand describes him as having "paso de soldado" [a soldier's gait] and this barest of hints at the lover's oppressive nature allows for a reading of the hand as representative of female freedom, authenticity and self-determination. In this light the story becomes a gruesome image of the divided self and of the suppression of the unacceptable necessary in order to fit the female into patriarchal society. The long description of the benefit of artificial over natural flowers reflects the inner debate that this narrator describes for herself: To accept herself as she is "naturally," with what she views as a hideous defect, and thus give up the beloved; or to cut off the offending part of her self, make the self into an artificial flower acceptable to the lover. Her dilemma is summed up in the story's final sentence:

> Si me ves llegar un día con la manga del vestido vacía, como esos guardianes lisiados de las plazas, sabrás que estoy dispuesta a casarme contigo; pero si me ves alejarme como siempre, aparentamente normal, con ese guante tejido, en la mano izquierda, entiende que yo, tu enamorada, vivo oyendo en mí la voz de alguien que te odia. (*I* 92)

> [If you see me coming one day with the sleeve of my dress empty, like the crippled watchmen of the plazas, you will know that I am ready to marry you; but if you see me moving away like always, apparently normal, with that knit glove on my left hand, understand that I, your beloved, live hearing in me the voice of someone who hates you.]

The very ambivalence of this story, and the difficulty of knowing how to "read" or interpret the double, makes it an important example of the unwillingness to assign value to the two sides of self seen in much of women's writing.[21]

In other of Ocampo's stories the beloved himself acts as double.[22] Gilbert and Gubar suggest that women writers display greater identification with the Other of their fictions than do male authors, and consequently reveal an unwillingness to view either manifestation of the self as completely evil. The double as lover is an embodiment of the figure which offers such ambivalence. In Ocampo's story "Amada en el amado"[23] the opening sentence clearly describes the lovers as double, a splitting of a single being. As the story continues, the young bride expresses her envy at her husband's ability to dream. One day, after hearing him recount a particularly fascinating dream, she declares, "Quisiera ser vos" [I would like to be you]. They decide to try to experiment with different ways of sleeping in order to allow her to enter his nighttime world. They succeed to a certain point in that she begins to collect objects from his dreams: an insect, a nylon thread, and a vial of magic liquid. The vial emerges from a dream about an ancient Greek sage, who tells him that it is the one drunk by Tristan and Isolde: "'Cuando quieras llevar a tu amada como a tu corazón dentro de ti,' le dijo, 'no tienes más que beber este filtro'" (*Ldn* 24) ["Whenever you want to carry your beloved like your heart inside of you," he said, "all you have to do is drink this"]. When they awake the vial has materialized in the young wife's hand; when her husband drinks the liquid the wife disappears:

> Él la llamó, la buscó. Oyó una voz dentro de él, la voz de ella, que le contestaba:
> —Soy vos, soy vos, soy vos. Al fin soy vos.
> —Es horrible—dijo él
> —A mí me gusta—dijo ella. (*Ldn* 25)

> [He called her, he looked for her. He heard a voice inside himself, her voice, who answered him, "I am you, I am you, I am you. At last, I am you." "It's horrible," he said. "I like it," she said.]

Together with deeply human longing to break down barriers of self and other, this story presents as false the polarities between dream and reality and between abstraction and object.[24] The issues of female authorship and creativity are also disturbingly clear: creative capacity is seen as a male prerogative. The female longs for intimacy, but also for appropriation of creative power.

MAGIC OBJECTS

"Amada en el amado" combines themes of the double and of metamorphosis with another of singular importance in Ocampo's work, the magical object. Sylvia Molloy lists a few of these apparently trivial items in order to suggest their unsuspected importance:

> Simplicidad aparente de Silvina Ocampo. Pensemos en algunos títulos de sus relatos: "El cuaderno," "Las fotografías," "La propiedad," "La boda," "La piedra," "Los objetos." Podríamos seguir: acabaríamos con una lista semejante a aquellas inocuas lecciones de los libros de idioma donde se rozan sin peligro—pero en otra lengua, la que se nos invita a aprender—la lapicera y el pizarrón, el chaleco y el paraguas. La lista de títulos de Silvina Ocampo es sin embargo menos tranquilizadora que esos ejercicios. Entre el cuaderno y las fotografías, entre la propiedad y la piedra, se insinúan crímenes perfectos, pecados mortales, razas inextinguibles, expiaciones y liebres doradas.[25]

> [Apparent simplicity of Silvina Ocampo. Let us consider a few story titles: "The Album," "The Photographs," "Real Estate" "The Wedding,"

"The Stone," "The Objects." We could go on: we would end up with a list similar to those innocuous lessons in language books where things rub harmlessly together—but in another language, the one we are invited to learn—things like pencil and blackboard, vest and umbrella. The list of Silvina Ocampo's titles however is less comforting than those excersises. Between the album and the photographs, between the real estate and the stone, she insinuates perfect crimes, mortal sins, inextinguishable races, expiations and gilded rabbits.]

Molloy's random listing of titles obeys the same impulse as Ocampo's own, to reveal the importance of such trivial items, whether fantastic or not, in the lives of characters. Many of Ocampo's stories create objects with magical powers; but even in nonfantastic tales, ordinary household objects are rarely ordinary in her world. At times the magical objects represent a veiled version of the splitting of the subject, similar to the doubles described above. In other cases they relate more closely to psychic states such as dreaming, foretelling the future or telekinetic powers.

The importance of unsuspected objects is first suggested in "La enemistad de las cosas." While a man wears a sweater vest that his mother had given him, his girlfriend rejects him, or at least seems to reject him; when he removes the vest he feels an unexplained relief, and just at that moment his girlfriend telephones to apologize for their quarrel. The barest hint is given that the garment had effected some evil influence over the man's life. "Los objetos" repeats the theme of the magical power of ordinary things when a woman suddenly begins to find articles that she had lost over fifteen years before. At first, the objects are valuable—a gold watch with ruby flowers, a dove of rock crystal—but the items begin to appear more and more frequently, date from farther into her past, and have less and less value until she begins finding toys from her childhood. Finally, she starts to see faces in the objects and goes mad, haunted by *things*.

Certain objects appear with regularity: Black velvet dresses have particularly potent magic and appear not only in "La casa de azúcar," as we have seen, but in several others.[26] Photographs, portraits, and statues fall easily into Keppler's category of "false" doubles, by which he refers to a nonhuman object which acquires certain aspects of human personality. An early story, "La inauguración del monumento," allows a man's statue to take a posthumous revenge on his lifelong enemy.[27] In "El cuaderno" and in "El goce y la penitencia," a painting predicts the appearance of a newborn baby. A photograph in "La revelación" confirms the magical powers of a young retarded boy. The fantastic event of "El novio de Sibila"—Sibila is magically cured at one point by a *curandero* [popular healer, usually specializing in herbal remedies] who swallows three fleas—is not as memorable as the web of lies revealed at the protagonist's death. The photograph that she had always claimed depicts her lover, turns out to be a photo of a handsome nephew. The lover, who appears at her funeral, is a married man, "feo, de rasgos mezquinos, enlutado" (*I* 68) [ugly, wretched, dressed in mourning]. The falsely identified photograph and the life she had attributed to it are revealed as fabrications. The mistaken identity of a photograph in "El novio de Sibila" also becomes an issue in "El enigma." In this case, the photograph's capacity to disengage physical identity from the body is coupled with the telephone's ability to do the same to the identity of the voice. Two people talk accidentally by phone and never properly identify each other thereafter in a series of deceptions and mistakes. Curiously, "El enigma" is not properly a fantastic story: It uses all the conventions of the fantastic to demonstrate the "magical" aspects of technology. The play with representation and referent made possible by way of a photograph (or telephone) makes it unnecessary to "add" magical elements to an object of everyday reality magical in and of itself.

Ocampo is particularly inventive in the array of objects that she puts to supernatural purposes. The title character of "Magush" uses the windows of a vacant building to predict the future; the salesman of "Paradela" inherits the good or bad characteristics of the previous owners from their used furniture; the little girl of "La hija del toro" constructs voodoo dolls to get rid of irritating family members; "Ulises" discovers a potion for eternal youth; "Amancio Luna, sacerdote" works cures for illness with special stones. Whereas these objects are presented as overtly powerful in themselves, other stories contain objects less directly responsible for the magical event. "Amada en el amado," for instance, with its physical relics of dreams, relates to an earlier story with a similar premise, "Los sueños de Leopoldina," in which an old woman awakes from her dreams with small tokens, a pebble if she has dreamed of walking along a stream, a feather, or perhaps a twig. Like the bride of the later story, the dream world produces concrete remnants for those with powerful sensibilities.

RUPTURES OF TIME AND SPACE: FORETELLING THE FUTURE

Ocampo disrupts notions of linear time in her fiction in two directions: The usual barrier between present and future is crossed by characters who can foretell the future, while that between present and past disappears in her various ghost stories. Her child narrators, the most likely to see and communicate with ghosts, are also the most likely to possess the power to predict the future. Many of these child characters, like Irene of "Autobiografía de Irene," feel that their knowledge of the future grants them control over it. Irene relates this belief as an adult aware of a childish error in judgment, but seven-year-old Cornelio of "Los amigos" remains convinced that his "prayers" for floods and epidemics are answered by a higher power. Most of Ocampo's children with this special power feel, like Irma Riensi of "La divina," that their cursed ability ("maldita vocación") brings them nothing but unhappiness and misunderstanding. Two stories of *Los días de la noche,* "La muñeca"[28] and "La divina," might almost form a single story, the first depicting the young child's early life in which her gift is discovered, and the second, narrated by the adult, describing later stages in childhood and her subsequent professional practice as a soothsayer. Both characters are united with Irene in considering their special power as more of a problem than a gift, subject to misunderstanding or even punishment:

> —¿Qué me pasará hoy, Irma?—le preguntaba una hermana mayor.
> —Te plantará tu novio.—Penitencia por la respuesta.
> —¿Qué me pasará hoy, Irma?—preguntaba la madre.
> —Papá te mandará a freír papas a otra parte.—Penitencia por la respuesta. (*Ldn* 152)

> ["What's going to happen to me today, Irma," asks her older sister. "Your boyfriend is going to ditch you." Punishment for the reply. "What's going to happen to me today, Irma," asks her mother. "Dad's going to tell you to get lost." Punishment for the reply.]

The wistful sadness of many of Ocampo's characters who foresee the future is evoked in her story, "Magush," whose title character reads fortunes, not in cards or in the lines of hands, but in the windows of a vacant building. Once Magush has told him his destiny the young friend who narrates this story finds living out his future less exciting. He tries to give his own future away to other of Magush's clients; then he and Magush contemplate trading destinies, but always back out at the last moment. Children (and sometimes women) are the only characters depicted as having this particular skill. Their unsuspected power is revealed in "Exodo" in which the entire animal population and finally the children all silently and secretly escape from a town, which subsequently burns to the ground destroying all its adult inhabitants. Again, in "Tales eran sus rostros," a group of deaf school children all seem to know some sort of secret, which the teachers suspect but cannot deduce. At the end of the story, all the children escape from an airplane with wings of angels.

Rosemary Jackson's conclusion associates both broad categories of fantasy, metamorphosis and disintegrated bodies, in a struggle within fiction to eliminate ego boundaries that are alien to the Imaginary:

> "Fantastic" character deformation suggests a radical refusal of the structures, the "syntax" of cultural order. Incoherent, fluid selves exist in opposition to precious portraits of individuals as whole or essential. They break the boundaries separating self from other, leaving structures dissolved, or ruptured, through a radical open-endedness of being. The fantastic makes an assault upon the "sign" of unified character and this has far-reaching consequences in terms of interrogating the process of character construction.[29]

Ocampo's fantastic fiction repeatedly questions the integrity of individual personality and depicts the unacknowledged influence of the object world on the human. The power of objects relates to the mental process of projection, a totalizing impulse of the imaginary. In general this fluidity and multiplicity of identities mimics the "spatial syntax" of the imaginary realm in which a child has no clear sense of the boundaries between self and other. Ocampo represents this unconscious play of categories as intruding on conscious thought, as breaking through the repressions of adult rationality. The transgression and violence often depicted in this world replicates the "aggressivity" that characterizes the rivalry between self and other "in a period that precedes the very elaboration of a self or the construction of an ego."[30] Ocampo's closest associates, Bioy Casares and Borges, take the reader into labyrinths of the mind in elaborate plays with categories of the symbolic itself, with what Jameson calls "perpetual alienation." Ocampo's vision, on the other hand, is found within the ordinary, intimate minutia of everyday life, within the flexible spatial categories of the imaginary. Jameson argues generally against the "overestimation of the Symbolic at the expense of the Imaginary" in Lacan's work and provides, with Jackson, an association between the imaginary and more overtly political subversion.[31]

NARRATIVE STRUCTURE

If twentieth-century writers in general have seen the necessity to challenge basic narrative patterns, fantasy writers, including Borges and Cortázar, can be found at the cutting edge of this tendency. Ocampo's fantastic fiction has experimented with various structural configurations which accomplish the ruptures within everyday apprehensions of reality which her stories' thematics pose so insistently. Here I would like to discuss briefly her strategies to avoid closure and to maintain important elements of ambiguity. Ocampo's fictions challenge the notion of a unified subject in their incessant dramatizing of split, fragmented or multiplied fictional characters. The structural implications of such fragmentation occur when attributed to the narrative voice itself. The multiplicity and shifting positions of the narrator undermine the authority of the narrative voice, leaving the reader to create meaning from the disperse elements of the text.

Todorov's observations about narrators of the fantastic suggest that, at least in nineteenth-century fiction, the reader must usually identify and react with the main character, who, along with the reader, experiences a hesitation with regard to the events reported. For that reason, narrative perspective within the fantastic is usually focused closely on the protagonist. Ocampo's stories, as we have already observed (in "El impostor," for example), create multiple narrative voices and in other ways create the possibility of disparity between what the character sees and feels and what the reader believes. Ocampo's stories with multiple narrators, in particular, ask the reader to decipher a version of truth from two differing accounts. "El impostor," as we saw earlier, contradicts the version of the main narrator and forces the reader to retrospectively reconstruct an entirely different version of the events narrated. "La red," a tale from the same collection also contains dual narrators and, like "El impostor," ends by setting up questions about the original narrator. The reader may conclude that the fantastic element, that is, the monstrous butterfly, was simply an hallucination, a result of Keng Su's guilt-induced madness. The principal narrator raises questions about her own account, too, when at the end she says, "Cuando pienso en Keng-Su, me parece que la conocí en un sueño"(*AI* 31) [Whenever I think of Keng-Su it seems to me I met her in a dream]. The problems of vision and interpretation are never completely resolved and, thereby, focus attention on issues of narration as such rather than on the events narrated.

Ocampo's narrators generally demonstrate an insistence on the artifice of the text, which serves to distance the reader from the mesmerizing entrance into the text as world. The female narrator of "La cara en la palma," for instance, says "Si adviertes cierta incoherencia en mis palabras no te asombres" (*I* 90) [If you detect a certain incoherence in my words don't be suprised], a statement that foregrounds indeterminacy of the entire narrative for it ends completely unresolved: the dilemma is the climax of the story. Many of Ocampo's narrators break the rules regarding a coherent position; as in the works of Proust, her stories represent a "scandal" of focalization.[32] "Epitafio romano" and "La última tarde" contain mysterious first-person verbs that intrude on a third-person account. The latter, narratated entirely in third-person, ends with this sentence: "Subió al caballo y nadie, salvo yo, pudo oír aquel galope, que se alejaba en la noche" (*F* 105) [He got on the horse and no one, except me, could hear that gallop which disappeared into the night]. "Las esclavas de las criadas," on the other hand, introduces a first-person narrator who trips over an embalmed tiger and breaks a candy dish in the first paragraphs, engages in dialog with the main character, but then seems to become invisible during the rest of the story, reporting on conversations that no embodied character could realistically be expected to overhear.

Both "Malva" and "La vida clandestina" contain narrative voices that flaunt the conventions of "person." "Malva"'s narrator says at the beginning of the story, "Cuando pienso en esta historia creo que soñé, pero la prueba de que no sueño está en los comentarios y chismes que oí a mi alrededor" (*Ldn* 105) [Whenever I think of this story I think I was dreaming, but the proof that I am not dreaming is in the comments and gossip that I heard around me]. As the story concludes, the careful reader will have noticed that everything that is narrated is based on the so-called proof of gossip and hearsay. The narrator admits at the end that she does not know what finally happened, but offers a volley of speculations. The narrator's stated sympathy with Malva in the face of such gossip, at the same time repeating every word of it as true, creates the hypocrisy on which the story's humor is based. The ambiguity of its unresolved conclusion may actually add to the story's effectiveness as a horror tale, for it undercuts readerly expectations of closure.

The "yo" of "La vida clandestina" has a similar relation to the narrative. The man whose reflected images, both auditory and visual, do not match his own inner concept of them, is reported by a first-person witness narrator who admits in the opening paragraph that he really does not know him very well. The ending describes the friend's escape to the desert:

> Rendido, se acostó a dormir. Luego vio su impronta en la arena, que no guardaba relación alguna con su cuerpo; le dibujó ojos y boca, y le modeló una oreja, donde susurró el final de esta historia, que nadie sabrá." (*I* 100)

> [Exhausted, he lay down to sleep. Later he saw his imprint in the sand which had no relation to his own body; he drew eyes and mouth and molded an ear into which he whispered the end of this story which no one will know.]

This lack of narrative "logic" and refusal of closure are the most subversive elements of Ocampo's fantastic fiction. Not only do her fantastic "themes" question normal constructions of reality (and offer fantasies of escape from the symbolic), but her characters and narrators, the very structures themselves, undermine reader expectations of what it means to "know."

IMAGES OF THE GROTESQUE

The fantastic stories discussed earlier have already provided numerous vivid examples of grotesque imagery. For instance, the hideous hand of "La cara en la palma" demonstrates classic grotesque motifs of deformed characters and of animation of parts of the body; the transformation of "Isis" into a mysterious animal, the doubles of "La casa de azúcar" and other stories utilize images which all commentators list as grotesque. Each of these stories also views the fantastic event with a measure of either humor, irony, or resignation which jars the reader's ordinary perception of reality, producing the mixture of humor and horror, fear and fun, characteristic of literary grotesques. Kayser's global examination of grotesque art and literature stresses its paradoxical nature as a mixture of opposites. He begins his analysis with the first appearances of the term around

the time of Raphael's ornamental sculptures. Even in these playful creations, which mix animal and plant forms, there lies a
sinister destruction of natural laws which, according to Kayser,
foreshadows the more ominous visions of Bosch and Bruegel.
In the literary grotesque, particularly of the nineteenth century,
the mixture is of the horrible with the ludicrous. The grotesque
is the estranged world, our word that has been inexplicably
transformed, and that produces in the reader a reaction of awe,
horror and "overwhelming ominousness." Furthermore, the
source of these feelings should remain unknowable (Kayser's
theory of the impersonal "it"), for to assign a source, such as the
devil, to our horror destroys the essential quality of the grotesque, which should remain "a play with the absurd."[33] In the
same spirit, Lee Byron Jennings describes the grotesque world
as one "devoid of pervasive purpose and of warmth and understanding, a world in which even horrors are denied the grandiosity that would give them sense."[34] Bakhtin's analysis of the
grotesque in Rabelais, in marked contrast, stresses its origins
in folk humor in which the grotesque image serves as a counter
to official ecclesiastical and high culture. His chief objection to
Kayser lies in the historical limitations of Kayser's study, which
identifies the first grotesque images in the Renaissance and concentrates on their development in German Romantic literature.
Bakhtin links the grotesque to the feasts and spectacles of popular medieval ritual which can be traced to pre-Christian tradition
and are intimately linked to time and the cycles of nature. The
comic images of grotesque realism consist in great part of what
Bakhtin calls "the material bodily principle, that is, images of
the human body with its food, drink, defecation and sexual
life."[35] Its images of "impossible" mixtures reflect abundance,
the fullness of life: old age and birth, life and death. Though the
laughter evoked by these images is gay and playful, Bakhtin
views it as subversive in a deeply positive sense.

Bakhtin corrects Kayser's version of the grotesque in his am-
plification of its sources backwards in history. In doing so, he
describes the positive, essentially healthful conceptions of its
medieval and ancient origins. However, in Bakhtin's discussion
of nineteenth-and twentieth-century grotesque, he agrees with
Kayser that here the grotesque image has been severed from
the totality of the medieval vision and becomes, instead of a
joyful symbol of life's wholeness, a sinister, truncated image of
fear. Both critics agree that by the nineteenth century the grotesque had become associated with evil, with the repulsive, un-

acceptable aspects of life, and that the humor inevitably connected with the grotesque rather adds than subtracts from the basic reaction of horror or disgust. Both critics treat the grotesque as a visual phenomenon, though Bakhtin concentrates on folk art, masks, costumes, rather than fine art. Nevertheless, Bakhtin's primary focus on the literary grotesque exemplified by Rabelais provides an account of the subversive potential of grotesque humor.

I will trace briefly the themes of the grotesque that coincide with the term *uncanny*: ghosts and monsters, dreams and madness, and certain objects; then examine elements of Ocampo's fiction that are best explained by Bakhtin's concept of grotesque realism, bodily images of eating and sexuality. I then turn my attention more directly to the source of the stories' humorous tone, the narrative voices who relay their tales with such detachment and derision. Those narrative voices provide the key to Ocampo's feminine subversion.

THE UNCANNY

Though fantastic events are viewed as one possible source of grotesque horror, the uncanny, by which both Kayser and Todorov mean anything strange and inexplicable that falls just short of the supernatural, is actually more typical of the genre. Some of Ocampo's best stories allow enough coincidence to interact with a presumed magical event that the story becomes quite ambiguous, in the manner Todorov so admired in James. "El vástago," for instance, hints at a magical connection between grandfather and grandson, a metamorphosis of sorts. "El árbol grabado" conflates a child's guilt over a family tragedy with her association of magical powers inherent in her devil costume. The greedy adult children of "El almacén negro" sell their father's possessions and then wonder afterward if their subsequent financial ruin is attributable to magical properties of his eyeglasses, purchased by their business rival. The child character of "La sibila" seems to predict the death of the narrator, a thief, by reading his future in cards. Each story upholds both a supernatural and a realistic reading, and maintains the ambiguity considered ideal by Todorov to the fantastic genre.

Todorov identifies the uncanny as one of the boundaries for the fantastic, but which itself has no clear limits: it "dissolves" into the general field of literature. Jackson gives extensive attention to Freud's essay, "The Uncanny," which provides a two-tiered definition of the word.[36] As in English, the German word is negative; the positive form, "das Heimlich" means "homey" and "familiar" on one level, "hidden" and "secreted" on the other. Its negated version, "das Unheimlich," indicates a revelation of the familiar which is normally hidden: "It uncovers what is hidden and, by doing so, effects a disturbing transformation of the familiar into the unfamiliar."[37] The association of fear with the term depends on hidden anxieties that Freud argues are projected from within the subject. Though Freud focuses on repressed sexual desire, Hélène Cixous's study of Freud's essay argues that the uncanny represents an encounter with death. Death is pure absence, what Cixous designates as a "signifier without signified"; she continues, "the immediate figure of strangeness is the ghost." The attempt to replace absence with presence is fantasy's attempt to discover a secret "which should stay hidden, for if manifested to me, it means I am dead; only the dead know the secret of death."[38] The fluidity of definitions is chaotic at this point, for what Todorov would classify as fantastic, a ghost, Cixous describes as uncanny. Ocampo's ghost stories coincide so intimately with issues of madness or dreams that the uncanny seems the appropriate place to discuss them.

GHOSTS

Ocampo's ghosts seem to have an aesthetic more than a fantastic function. Rather than make strange the already familiar, these stories transform something generally considered beautiful into an object of horror. "La red" retains a classic horror-story tone in its portrayal of an avenging ghost or monster in the form of a butterfly. The delicate creature was killed by a collector and stuck with a pin; it disappears only to haunt its captor by filling the books she is reading with tiny pin pricks. The narrator, a close friend of the besieged woman, never sees the monstrous butterfly herself thereby permitting a multitude of interpretations. The reader may conclude that the protagonist is mad or perhaps suffers vivid nightmares. In any case, the transformation of something gentle and beautiful into a source of fear is a strategy of the other ghost stories as well. For example, the parents of "La familia Linio Milagro" are haunted by piano music, the piece their daughter had been practicing when she was killed in a fire; "El fantasma," in a complex plot twist, creates a ghost from a delicious perfume. Again the narration allows for a many-layered reading, but the intent of the latter is more obviously humorous than the previous stories. This fundamental attitude of smiling at death is the basis for the grotesque in Ocampo's works.

"El siniestro del Ecuador" exemplifies the ambiguity of the uncanny and the subversive humor of the grotesque. The story is situated in an ordinary locale, a neighborhood restaurant, and has none of the fear and awe associated with classic ghost stories. Its lighthearted spirit derives in great part from its vantage point, the gleeful delight expressed by a young boy at the consternation of his parents. The family, a father, a mother and two young boys, do nothing more exciting than go out to dinner at a favorite restaurant. As it happens, the restaurant has recently been reopened after a fire that supposedly killed all the waiters. Once the family is seated, however, their usual waiter, Isidro Ebers, appears to take their order. The family gradually becomes aware that the waiter is a ghost, but tries to maintain proper decorum:

> —Tiene cara de muerto—dijo mi hermano, mirando para el lado donde había desaparecido el mozo. Vamos a preguntarle si es cierto que ha muerto o si es una calumnia.
> —Mañana no irás al cine—dijo mi madre—. ¡Mal educado! (*I* 78)

> ["He has a dead man's face," said my brother, looking in the direction where the waiter had disappeared. "Let's ask him if he's really dead or if its a lie." "Tomorrow you can't go to the movies," said my mother. "How rude!"]

The parents and later the *maitre d'hotel* try to enforce polite behavior as their response to the "dead" man. In the face of the supernatural the adults desperately cling to the known and the routine; the two boys are the only ones who can admit the miracle. The dead man breaks the rules of restaurant policy by sitting down with the family to talk about the experience of dying in the fire. In the conclusion he writes his address on a card, and instead of giving it to the father, hands it to the young narrator. His mother grabs it from him, but not before he notes the address. The brothers vow to visit Isidro Ebers "aunque estuviera muerto" [even though he might be dead]. The subversive elements of grotesque humor emerge from the child's point of view, which provides both the humor and the destablizing force against the status quo.

The word *monstrosities* is one of Kayser's synonyms for the grotesque, and deformed or monstrous creatures are an important source of Ocampo's grotesque vision. So often, Kayser tells us, the grotesque situation starts out playfully and then gets out of hand to become frightening or horrifying. In "La casa de los relojes" a little boy describes a party given by his parents in which the guests become drunk, and conceive the idea of ironing a hunchbacked watchmaker's wrinkled suit. They leave the house for the dry cleaner's shop (the proprietor being one of the drunks), where they decide to iron the little misshapen man as well as his suit. At the point when the men lay Estanislao, the hunchback, under the steaming industrial iron, the child narrator, who has dipped into plenty of the wine himself, gets sick from the heat and the crush of people, and leaves. The next day, he realizes that the watchmaker has disappeared. The deformed character, the situation that begins playfully and ends as tragedy, and the child's uncomprehending and, therefore, detached point of view, all create the tragicomedy of the grotesque. The trivializing elements of the story occur throughout, but are particularly evident in the last paragraph in which the boy's mother evidences more concern for objects in the house that were destroyed during the party than for the guest who disappeared:

> Cuando pregunté a mi madre dónde estaba Estanislao, no quiso contestarme como era debido. Me dijo, como si hablara al perro: "Se fue a otra parte," pero tenía los ojos colorados de haber llorado por la carpeta de macramé y el adorno y me hizo callar cuando hablé de la tintorería. (*F* 41)

> [When I asked my mother where Estanislao was, she didn't answer me as she should. She said, as if talking to the dog, "He went away," but she had eyes reddened from crying about the macrame bag and the figurine and she made me shut up when I talked about the dry cleaners.]

The wistful sadness of the child's voice contrasts with the apparent indifference of his mother. The tragic made trivial is one defining characteristic of Ocampo's grotesque. The subversive quality of the grotesque, articulated by Bakhtin, is evident here and in "El siniestro del Ecuador" by way of a marginalized view which disrupts the usual hierarchy of family and town.

MADNESS

While the two child narrators above seem perfectly sane, many of Ocampo's monster and ghost stories can also be read as the hallucination of an unbalanced character. Whereas Kayser considers madness as one way of depicting the alienation of the human spirit, Bakhtin's vision of it as an escape from false official truth seems more in keeping with Ocampo's purposes. And, of course, the "loco cuerdo" has a longer tradition in Hispanic literature than in perhaps any other.[39] Ocampo's gothic thriller, "El impostor," is one of several stories that illustrate a classic Kayserian approach to the grotesque. However, its surprise ending privileges the greater truth of the madman, as suggested by Bakhtin. I return to this key story to explore its grotesque dimensions.

The story's themes of the double (discussed as part of the fantastic), magical dreams and nightmares, together with the isolation and danger of its setting, the mysterious events, which hint of ghosts, sadistic cruelty, and madness, all contribute to the oppressive terror that Kayser associates with the grotesque vision. The theme of madness implicates both characters; the question of Armando's sanity is the one that motivates Luis's journey in the first place, and indeed, Luis portrays Armando Heredia as a withdrawn, violent, and increasingly insane young man. Luis's own mental condition seems to deteriorate during his narrative. He agonizes over his potential betrayal of Armando's friendship on two accounts, that he may unknowingly have fallen in love with his girlfriend and that his first obligation to write to Armando's father conflicts with his loyalty to Armando himself. His fear that they both love the same girl is tied to the trail of deceptions and lies that Luis suspects throughout. On the train he meets a beautiful young girl whose mother addresses her as Claudia but who wears a pin spelling the name "María." Attempts to discover whether she is the María Gismondi of whom Armando speaks occupy much of Luis's attention. This plotline is never resolved, but turns out to be the story's red herring; it is ultimately irrelevant. The desperation Luis expresses over this issue becomes increasingly hysterical and confused, and relates to his problem of deciding Armando's sanity because it raises the questions of false identity and deception. Luis's commentary becomes more convoluted as he attempts to see Heredia's actions from every conceivable vantage. Luis finally writes to the father and says, "temería volverme loco yo mismo, por contagio" (*AI* 111) [I think I may be going crazy myself, by association]. The possibility of deception by all the characters of the story leaves no ground firm.

The story draws attention to the dream as a problematic element of psychic life. The detailed realism of Luis's first section, the overnight trip by train, changes upon his arrival at the decrepit old house. Luis's account loses coherence almost immediately, and the short sections into which the rest of the story is divided have no obvious connection to each other. They do seem to be narrated in a roughly chronological order, but the gaps in time and space indicate a different mode of narration from the earlier section. Though a few of the events are overtly identified as nightmares, others not so clearly marked have the same absurd quality. For instance, in one section Luis describes taking several books to a shady spot and lying down to read. Suddenly he is attacked by a huge bee whose monstrous characteristics recall the mad butterfly depicted in "La red" from the same collection. The improbable episode concludes abruptly without clarifying its reference to "mi pesadilla" [my nightmare] near the end. This ambiguity permits two readings, as metaphorical—this event was like a nightmare—or literal—what I am describing was (only) a nightmare.

Luis's narration includes increasingly nightmarish occurrences and one experience after another of *déjà vu* (noticed in connection to strange objects: a vase and an old rocker, for example, as well as to certain faces) and of dreams that accurately predict the future. Toward the end of his journal it is impossible to distinguish his narration of "real" events from dreams. Later, of course, his entire account will fall under the title "Mis sueños" and be attributed to Armando himself. Early in "Luis's" journal, Armando describes to him a session with a psychiatrist who recommended that he keep a record of his dreams. Though apparently wishing to comply, he says that he never dreams, and adds, "No soñar es como estar muerto. La realidad pierde importancia. . . . Cometería un crimen si ese crimen me permitiera soñar" (54) [Failing to dream is like being dead. Reality loses importance. I would commit a crime if this crime would permit me to dream]. In the same conversation he gives this notebook to Luis who promises to write his own dreams in it. The association of dreams with creative power takes on a special urgency:

Evidently a failure to dream is not only a failure to create and imagine, but a failure to live.

The madman, Armando, we later discover, is himself the "author" of the journal. His vision of the father's ideal son reveals that what is hidden behind that ideal is a coward and a hypocrite, a person capable of betraying a friend both in love and in matters of survival. The greater truth of the madman, who has dropped out of normal society, lives with the lower classes, and attends to his dreams instead of to the Law of the Father, makes Ocampo's surprise at the conclusion of "El impostor" particularly satisfying. Though the ending seems to recuperate the story's transgression by a return to reality and to law, the uncertainty expressed by the father's emissary, Rómulo Sagasta, allows it to remain at least partially open:

> Todavía siento un profundo malestar cuando pienso en este cuaderno. El misterio que envuelve sus páginas no ha sido totalmente aclarado para mí, ya que la muerte selló para siempre los labios del autor y actor, de la víctima y del asesino de esta inverosímil historia. (*AI* 129)

> [I still feel a profound unease when I think about this notebook. The mystery that surrounds its pages has not been totally clarified for me, now that death has sealed forever the lips of its author and actor, the victim and assassin of this strange story.]

The play of documents recalls several other stories that will be discussed shortly. The questioning of identity, of authorship and authority, of dream and reality is extreme in this case, for the doubled self is not killed but, in fact, never "existed" in the first place.

OBJECTS

Objects are a particularly powerful menace in both the fantastic and grotesque stories. In "La enemistad de las cosas" and "Los objetos" the trivial items of everyday life—vest in the first and a host of ordinary objects, including childhood toys, in the second—control the lives of characters. A friendship goes aground over a pen in "La pluma mágica" while an entire family is wiped out fighting over eyeglasses in "El almacén negro." Themes of the double and madness combine with a most ordinary object in "La piedra," in which the main character, Valerio, encounters a beggar on the street and steals from him an unusual stone. When he gets it home, Valerio discovers that the stone breathes and sweats, has a heartbeat and, at night, two blinking eyes. Terrified, he tries to return the stone to the beggar, but the story ends with the beggar's taking over his apartment and Valerio out in the vacant lot where he first encountered the beggar. The conclusion suggests a process of metamorphosis by which one character is transformed into another. It also hints that there is some magical property to the graffiti on the building walls surrounding the property where the beggar sits. The stone serves equally as an image of madness, of guilt, and as a magical implement of poetic justice. "La piedra" illustrates the truly subversive nature of Ocampo's fantasies, not only of the individual subject but of the social order more generally. Here, the beggar takes over in a very obvious reversal of social hierarchy. Ocampo's texts clearly evidence the kind of subversive quality that Bakhtin insists is present in one form or another in all grotesque fiction.

Kayser lists dolls along with puppets and other kinds of inanimate human forms as alienated images of humanity. Dolls, like masks, have faces and personalities, and a long history of use as literary (and filmic) images of fragmented, alienated human beings. Almost all the dolls of Ocampo's stories are associated with magical powers to control the future. Irene predicts receiving a kind of doll, a statue of the Virgin of Luján, as a gift just as the child narrator of "La muñeca" predicts a more typical childhood toy. In both cases, the appearance of the predicted images confirms the child's divinatory powers. Amalia of "La hija del toro" makes voodoo-like images of family members and throws them into a vat of boiling oil. Not only does she predict the future for troublesome family members, she seems to cause it. The title character of "Icera" attempts to become a doll herself. She succeeds in remaining the size of a doll by the force of intense concentration, by repeating the phrase "no debo crecer" [don't let me grow], as a kind of prayer. The narrator makes the overt connection between the fantastic event and religion: "Su fe obró un milagro. Icera no creció" (I 125) [Her faith worked a miracle. Icera did not grow]. What becomes apparent in this sad story is that the little girl wants to be in the place of dolls, to use their luxurious furniture, wear their clothes, and finally, to sleep in the beautifully decorated box in which one of the dolls was packed. The suggestion that this invented doll world is better than reality is confirmed by the brief description of Icera's mother, which implies that she too may be a dreamer after better worlds: "La madre de Icera era como todas las madres, un poco más pobre y más apasionada, tal vez" (125) [Icera's mother was like all mothers, a bit poorer and more passionate, perhaps]. The association with time and the future is made by the revelation at the story's end that the "child" Icera who climbs into the packing box has just turned forty years old. The doll frequently serves as a narrative element to redeem a child character, to confirm abilities denied by adult versions of "reality," and in the case of "Icera" to offer a critique of women's expectations in which life in a dollhouse might seem a better option than that of the real world.

Costumes are a category of objects, which like masks always have special significance. Bakhtin claims that the mask for medieval man is "connected to joy of change and reincarnation, with gay relativity and with the merry negation of uniformity and similarity; it rejects conformity to oneself," whereas by the nineteenth century masks "hide something."[40] Both the playful and more sinister qualities of costumes are visible in Ocampo's story "El árbol grabado." The narrator describes a family celebration of carnival in which all the guests wear costumes and are, as a result, more animated than usual. The narrator herself is dressed as a devil, and makes the fateful, and certainly devilish, suggestion to her friend Clorindo that they hide ants in the cake that will be served as dessert. Clorindo's humilliation at the public punishment for the misdeed induces him to stab his grandfather with a table knife. In the story's conclusion, the narrator feels responsible for the disaster: "'Por aquí pasó el diablo, que se apoderó del alma de Clorindo' dijeron las personas, después del crimen. . . . Y yo me sentí culpable" (I 149) ["The devil passed through here and took control of Clorindo's soul," people said after the crime. . . . And I felt guilty]. The young narrator takes the general reference to the devil as a personal accusation of her costume's and, therefore, of her own complicity in the deed.

Other stories develop the connection between a devil costume and a supernatural force. "Clotilde Ifrán" seems to use exactly the same costume as the one described in "El árbol grabado." Both stories occur at the time of carnival and describe the devil costume as smelling of "aceite de ricino" [castor oil]. The seamstress named in the story's title is apparently herself a kind of devil since she died eight years before the story's action.[41] Ocampo's depiction of Clotilde Ifrán as the embodiment of the devil coincides with a statement made by the young narrator of "La muñeca": "Por una aberración, a mi juicio vergonzosa, contrariando la enseñanza que me habían dado, imaginaba que el demonio pertencía al sexo femenino y no al masculino" (*Ldn* 133) [Through an aberration, shameful in my view, and contrary to the teachings I had received, I imagined the devil as pertaining to the feminine sex and not the masculine]. The devil in several of Ocampo's stories is envisioned as a kindly seamstress who makes costumes for lonely children.[42] This image is consonant with Bakhtin's notion of the playful inventiveness of the grotesque.

BAKHTIN'S GROTESQUE REALISM

A recognition of the origins of the grotesque within ancient and medieval traditions of carnival allows for closer attention to the humorous and subversive side of this mode. For Bakhtin, the grotesque is always a positive force, even in its nineteenth-century manifestations described by Kayser in terms primarily of horror and fear: "The relative nature of all that exists is always gay; it is the joy of change, even if in Romanticism gaiety and joy are reduced to their minimum."[43] Bakhtin's emphasis on the importance of change, the cycles of nature and bodily processes, what he calls the material bodily principle, sheds new light on several thematic categories of Ocampo's stories, allowing a view of their sometimes discomfitting humor as subversive of a kind of polite discourse required of women.

The fluidness of Bakhtin's grotesque and its ultimately subversive quality can be seen in Ocampo's story "Sábanas de tierra," in which the old gardener metamorphoses into a shrub. The story's calm, poetic language evokes the positive mixture of death with rebirth and the cycles of nature. Its subversive social message appears, though subtle, in its depiction of the beautiful, wealthy woman who does not notice the gardener's transformation. For her, the humble employee was already less worthy of attention than the shrubs themselves. Kayser speaks of human and plant/animal mixtures as part of the grotesque, but for him the combination is horrific. Ocampo's story invites a reading of the gardener's metamorphosis as an escape from imprisoning human life. This playful, positive attitude is even more apparent in her approach to animal transformation, as we have seen. Her stories of metamorphosis have already been viewed as fanciful escapes from the reality principle. She has no story that matches Kayser's image of frightening or alienating transformations; though "La peluca" and "Malva," for instance, are quite menacing, the metamorphosis itself is treated with irony and humor. Humans have animal characteristics or become animals, either through supernatural intervention as in the examples noted, or by way of direct characterization: "Los ojos de lebrel, la boca de anfibio, las manos de araña, el pelo de caballo, hacían de ella un animal más que una mujer" (*Ldn* 69) [The eyes of a greyhound, the mouth of an amphibian, the hands of a spider, the hair of a horse, all made her more an animal than a woman]. If many of her stories suggest that humans are animal-like, others such as "Fuera de las jaulas," "La gallina de membrillo" and "Carl Herst" play with the opposite notion, the human-like characteristics of animals. The first tells of a schoolmaster and his students who decide to free the animals at the zoo and end in cages themselves being observed by the escaped animals. Carl Herst, a dog trainer, has a house filled with photos of dogs, while his dog has a house filled with pictures of humans and popular sayings about them that invert dog/human cliches. Yet another story, "La soga," blurs the distinction between animante/inanimate as a little boy's rope is transformed by virtue of the child's imagination into a snake which "bites" and kills him. "La soga" illustrates especially well the ambiguity of language to evoke the power of childish imagination and the ways in which adults, in this case the adult narrator, become drawn into a world in which anything is possible. The supernatural is artfully suggested, but the story "works" either as a tale of the fantastic or of the uncanny, and its exuberant fantasy captures the playful tone of Bakhtin's grotesque without mitigating the horror of its tragic conclusion.[44]

The "degraded" bodily processes of eating, defecation, and sexual life are used by Ocampo to humorous effect in several stories.[45] "La venganza" introduces the feud between Mercedes de Umbel, a prim, upper middle-class woman, and the doorman of her apartment building, who resents her careless habits with keys and elevator doors and her fondness for feeding the pigeons. The doorman's feelings about this particular woman are illustrative of his attitude in general toward wealthy women, "Tonio Juárez comparaba las palomas con las mujeres elegantes.—Están cubiertas de plumas, con la pechuga llena, pero roñosas, ensuciando lo que otros limpian con el sudor de su frente—decía a quien quisiera oírlo" (*I* 64) [Tonio Juárez compared pigeons to elegant women. "They are covered with feathers, with a full breast, but mangy, dirtying what others clean with the sweat of their brow," he would say to anyone who would listen]. One day Mercedes is accidentally locked in the elevator with the garbage; the doorman deliberately leaves her there to suffer for several hours. Her vengeance is inspired by the pigeons of which she is so fond: she defecates each day on the stairway. The doorman lies in wait and when he finally catches her in the "postura prevista" [expected posture] he gives her a kick, "un certero puntapié descargó su venganza contra palomas y señoras elegantes" (66) [a sure kick discharged his revenge against pigeons and elegant ladies]. Perhaps the most Rabelaisian of Ocampo's stories, its grotesque humor invites a critique of class privilege easily identifiable as positive in Bakhtin's sense.

"Los amantes" deals with two other bodily processes, eating and sex, but is more difficult to view as a positive image of life's wholeness. Two lovers are described as engaged in a lengthy, ritualistic encounter in which they meet at a pastry shop, buy eight pastries, slowly eat them in synchrony and then spread a blanket on the ground and make love. The story describes each pastry with care, and then the certainly grotesque process of eating each one. The introductory statements to the story even more strongly reinforce its overtly carnivalesque nature since the lovers are each described as carrying photographs of the other in costume, he as a conscripted soldier, she as a Turkish concubine. Despite its comic overtones, the story as a whole is not essentially humorous. The two lovers are shown to be slaves in life just as much as their costumes suggest in play. They do not control their lives, and even in moments of recreation seem governed by some unconscious force. In spite of superficial resemblances to Bakhtin's notion of the carnival, this story rather denies its true essence. It is not a laughter that communicates the participant with the universe but rather illustrates the isolation and impotence of common man in our twentieth-century world.

If it is difficult to find in "Los amantes" that curative laughter which Bakhtin describes in the medieval grotesque, two other stories use the bodily process of eating to true comic effect. "Mimoso" and "Amelia Cicuta" both describe female protagonists who avenge themselves on men by feeding them poisoned pet animals. "Mimoso," in particular, with its gleeful attention to certain macabre details and its fanciful plot, uses just the right combination of horrible and humorous elements that Bakhtin would have approved. These and other stories descend into the truly repellent realm of the grotesque. "Malva," discussed earlier, describes in detail the vicious self-mutilation of the main character. The comments of the unnamed first-person narrator provide the trivializing humor of the grotesque by relaying horrifying episodes in the context of chatty gossip. The fantastic is suggested at the end of the story when Malva is said to have died, but no corpse is present at the wake. The narrator finds animal paw prints and animal hair in her bedroom. Is Malva, like a fox caught in a trap, ready to bite off a limb in order to free herself? Has she succeeded in transforming herself into an animal and thus in escaping from the traps of middle-class city life and propriety? Here Ocampo's story borders dangerously on satire, something Kayser has forbidden the grotesque; but its salient features, the extremely macabre mutilations in contrast to the narrator's ironic concern for social decorum, provide just the exaggeration of reality that Kayser claims as the essence of the true grotesque and the subversion of official culture important to Bakhtin.

Blas Matamoro's long chapter on Silvina Ocampo analyzes her work in a way easily reconciled with Bakhtin's view of grotesque realism as subversive of dominant cultural norms. Though he does not employ the word *grotesque* or refer to Bakhtin, Matamoro rightly observes that Ocampo's narratives reveal the mortal struggle that lies beneath the surface of conventional social and family life. Essentially a Marxist approach to Ocampo's works, Matamoro's analysis identifies certain elements—servants, children, lumpen, animals and objects—as occasionally allied with each other against oppressive governesses, parents, and more generalized forces of culture. Matamoro notes the sympathy of Ocampo's narrations with these groups; her recognition of their usually unacknowledged power. His list of subversive marginals repeats in part that of theorists of the grotesque, but adds two which deserve further comment, servants and children.

Since the homes of "la gran burguesía" (Matamoro's phrase) provide the setting of many stories, the presence of servants is the norm. "La propiedad," "El crimen perfecto," "Clotilde Ifrán" and "Esclavas de las criadas," among many others, illustrate the dangerous powers that servants in a house may exercise. The first two hint that the cooks have poisoned their employers; the kindly seamstress steals children; and finally, a servant kills the abusive relatives of her ailing mistress. At least two of Ocampo's stories imply that the mistress of the house is being sexually blackmailed by her dependence on servants ("El crimen perfecto" and "Voz en el teléfono"). The servants, in other words, are a lethal force whether for selfish or unselfish ends. The alliance between children and servants or the possibility that servants might be preferred to parents is suggested repeatedly. The narrator of "Voz en el teléfono" speaks of the family cook as a powerful force within the family and as a figure of admiration and affection; the child of "El pecado mortal" likes to visit the servants in the room where they do the ironing; Amalia and her brothers of "La hija del toro" spend happy hours with one of the ranch hands.

While the motivation for violence and hostility on the part of servants is obvious, Matamoro argues that the violence of "los nenes terribles," is also motivated by revenge incited by "los padres terribles."[46] The parental violence of certain stories, even if presented as unintentional, creates obvious child victims in Ocampo's works: "Fulgencia era única hija, por eso sus padres la mataban de cuidados que transformados en penitencias involuntarias despertaban venganzas aviesas" (*Vo* 134; quoted in Matamoro, 196) [Fulgencia was an only daughter, so her parents killed her with care which, transformed into unconscious punishments, inspired sinister vengeance]. The indifference, neglect, or simple misunderstanding of parents, from the child's point of view, are forms of aggression that deserve a defense. In "Autobiografía de Irene," as we saw earlier, the child character who possesses supernatural powers is herself the victim of her own force. Her powers go unacknowledged in her family, however. Her frustration at not being heard or understood is drawn with humor in one episode when, after having long predicted the appearance of her dog, Jazmín, Irene receives from her uncle a dog of exactly the description she had made. Irene's mother, instead of recognizing her daughter's gift, says, "Tu tío es adivino" [Your uncle is a soothsayer]. Other characters also suffer from misunderstanding by adults, the most poignant being perhaps the narrator of "Los amigos" whose adult relatives persist in believing in the saintliness of his friend Cornelio. The ironic narrator of "Cartas confidenciales" best expresses the child's point of view: "La pucha que son locos los padres que uno tiene; parece que lo odiaran a uno de puro cariño" (*Ldn* 34) [Damned if one's parents aren't crazy; it seems they hate you out of pure affection]. Parental overcontrol, neglect, and the inability to credit a child with the authority of speech are childhood frustrations of particular interest to this author.

Matamoro portrays the oligarchical heads of household in Ocampo's fiction as surrounded by threatening elements, including their own children. The majority of Ocampo's commentators have noted the menacing quality of her child characters, who shock the reader with their uninhibited cruelty. Miss Fielding, for instance, the victim of one of Ocampo's most unforgettable little villains, Porfiria Bernal, says: "No suponía que los niños fueran capaces de infligir desilusiones más amargas que las personas mayores" (*I* 155) [I didn't imagine that children were capable of inflicting disappointments more bitter than those of adults]. Matamoro does take up gender difference in Ocampo's work when he suggests that the male children are marginalized only temporarily by their status as child, but that, in their turn, they will come to dominate just as their fathers do. The double marginalization of the little girl makes hers a particularly subversive position since she is not destined to rule. Matamoro's chapter title, "La nena terrible" [the incorrigible little girl] while overtly referring to Ocampo herself, identifies the evil girl child as the character most emblematic of her fiction.[47] These "nenas terribles" form part of the permanent underclass constantly poised for rebellion.

"El vestido de terciopelo" illustrates the children, servants, animals, and things which collaborate to threaten the oligarchy. It also demonstrates many of the elements of Ocampo's grotesque fiction in which a child narrator provides the sardonic, marginalized point of view that introduces the fantastic element, a black velvet dress, in a context of humor and horror. The first paragraph of the four-page story relates the arrival of a little girl and her friend, a seamstress, from the poor outer neighborhoods of Buenos Aires to the wealthy *Barrio Norte* in the center of the city. The day is quite hot, and they have come a long way by bus and on foot to deliver a dress to a woman who has ordered it for her impending trip to Paris. The contrast between the wealth and privilege of the customer and the world of necessity and hard work of the two working-class characters makes almost everything the woman says unintentionally ironic. Throughout the fitting session she resists the need to try on the dress, engaging in conversation alternately frivolous and petulant, while the seamstress urges her patiently. The suppressed hostility between the two working-class characters and the overbearing, insensitive, and condescending client is clear despite the apparent neutrality of the child narrator.

Sinister elements quickly accumulate: the repeated sardonic refrain of the young narrator, "¡Qué risa!" [What a laugh!]; the special, almost mystical properties the wealthy woman attributes to the black velvet fabric of the dress; the shining, sequined dragon embroidered on its front; the mention of the lily, a flower the seamstress describes as "sad," as the *señora's* favorite;[48] and her repeated efforts to get into the heavy dress, impeded by her own hot, sticky body. The child's fascination and the underlying danger of the situation are visible in one of the final paragraphs:

En la calle oí gritos de los vendedores ambulantes. . . . No corrí a la ventana, para curiosear, como otras veces. No me cansaba de contemplar las pruebas de este vestido con un dragón de lentejuelas. La señora volvió a ponerse de pie y se detuvo de nuevo frente al espejo tambaleando. El dragón de lentejuelas también tambaleó. El vestido ya no tenía casi ningún defecto, sólo un imperceptible frunce debajo de los dos brazos. Casilda volvió a tomar los alfileres, para colocarlos peligrosamente en aquellas arrugas de género sobrenatural, que sobraban.
—Cuando seas grande—me dijo la señora—te gustará llevar un vestido de terciopelo, ¿no es cierto?
—Sí—respondí, y sentí que el terciopelo de ese vestido me estrangulaba el cuello con manos enguantadas. ¡Qué risa! (*F* 108)

[In the street I heard the shouts of vendors. . . . I did not run to the window to see as usual. I couldn't get enough of the fittings of this dress with its sequined dragon. The woman got to her feet again and stood swaying before the mirror. The sequined dragon also swayed. The dress now had almost no other defect, only an imperceptible wrinkle under the arms. Casilda once more took up the pins to place them dangerously in those folds of supernatural cloth. "When you grow up," the woman said to me, "you will want to wear a velvet dress, won't you?" "Yes," I said, and felt that the velvet of that dress was strangling my neck with gloved hands. What a laugh!]

The child's usual interest in the busy street scene below is suspended in favor of the scene being enacted within. The narrator's declared "sí" contrasts sharply with her unspoken reaction of horror and dislike, causing the reader inevitably to associate the woman's fate with the suppressed desires of the child. In the rapid conclusion, all these elements come together in the strangulation of the woman by the writhing "dragon dress." The story's wicked humor, reinforced by the narrator's repeated "¡qué risa!," illustrates the menacing quality of Ocampo's wicked little girls. This child's comic tone creates a sense of horror or at least ominousness for the reader, at the same time that the carnivalized laughter offers a glimpse of gleeful satisfaction at the overturning of an unjust status quo.

NARRATORS OF THE GROTESQUE

Silvia Molloy discusses the dispassionate narration of Ocampo's stories without naming this attitude as grotesque: "Ni acercado ni alejado por la compasión, ni condenado por la indiferencia manifiesta. . . . no hay desdén, no hay patetismo, no hay resentimiento en estos textos" [Neither drawn closer nor distanced by compassion, nor condemned by their obvious indifference . . . there is no disdain, no pathos, no resentment in these texts].[49] This "unimpassioned view" both dispels and creates horror for the reader. The humor of the grotesque not only fails to mitigate its horror in many cases, but rather serves to increase the reader's discomfort. When I suggest that Ocampo's grotesque vision contains a positive aspect I hope not to deny the repulsion that may also be felt. The very contradictions of Ocampo's work validate both Kayser's and Bakhtin's approaches to the grotesque. Kayser's word "unimpassioned" and Bakhtin's concept of carnival laughter suggest that the manner in which grotesque images are represented is more important than the images themselves. In fiction it is the language used to describe events that make these events grotesque for the reader. As Kayser and others have said, the grotesque lies in its reception. While implying a certain subject matter, the grotesque emerges primarily from our attitude toward it. The delicate balance between the horrible and our perception of it as ludicrous depends on two elements common to Ocampo's fiction, both of which distance the voice of the narration from the events themselves: trivializing elements that undermine the "seriousness" of an event or a narrator who fails to understand completely the import of what is being narrated.

One of Ocampo's earliest stories illustrates the use of language in creating the grotesque situation. "El retrato mal hecho" could attain the high tragic implications that its plot involving infanticide suggests, but because of its narrative voice, becomes a source of grotesque humor. The story focuses on two characters, Ana, a trusted servant, and Eponina, the mistress of the house. From the first, Eponina is said to despise her children as "ladrones de su adolescencia" [thieves of her youth], while it is Ana who saves her from having to deal with them: "Los brazos de Ana, la sirvienta, eran como cunas para sus hijos traviesos" (*Vo* 64) [The arms of Ana, the servant, were like cradles for her mischievous children]. Eponina spends her time reading fashion magazines which are quoted extensively with their special vocabulary of objects and colors: "Traje de visita para señora joven, vestido verde mirto . . . Las hojas se hacen con seda color de aceituna . . . las venas y los tallos color albaricoque" [visiting gown for young matron in myrtle green . . . The leaves are made with olive green silk, the veins and stems with an apricot color]. The last of these phrases she repeats to herself several times and transforms them in the story's final lines to chilling effect. In the conclusion, the servant Ana murders one of the children in her charge. The child's mother, Eponina, reacts by embracing the murderess and describing the dead child in terms of the fashion magazine she had just been reading:

> Eponina se abrazó largamente de Ana con un gesto inusitado de ternura. Los labios de Eponina se movían en una lenta ebullición: "Niño de cuatro años vestido de raso de algodón color encarnado. Esclavina cubierta de un plegado que figura como olas ribeteadas con un encaje blanco. Las venas y los tallos son de color marrón dorado, verde mirto o carmín." (*Vo* 66)

> [Eponina embraced Ana with a long and unusual gesture of tenderness. Eponina's lips moved in slow motion: "Four-year-old child dressed in blood red satin. Cape covered by a pleat shaped like waves trimmed with white lace. Veins and stems of guilded purple, myrtle green and crimson.]

The reaction of horror produced by this concluding paragraph is compounded by surprise and the kind of laughter induced by sick jokes. The careful description of the dead child in terms of fashion and sewing vocabulary trivializes the moment beyond any kind of readerly expectations. One of Ocampo's most richly suggestive stories, its power to shock has hardly diminished in the fifty years since its publication.

"Las fotografías" offers a narrative perspective with both characteristics of Ocampo's grotesque, a voice which trivializes events that it only partly comprehends. The fretful voice of the narrator gradually reveals her position as a kind of hanger-on, perhaps a distant relative, who relates events leading to what under other circumstances would certainly be a poignant death of a young girl, unwittingly tortured beyond endurance during a family celebration. The first-person narration directs itself to an implied listener, who without being addressed directly, is assumed to know the various guests at the party and the family in question. The narrator's monolog draws the reader without preamble into the intimacies of a family gathering, a birthday party for fourteen-year-old Adriana. The narrator's informal "speech" assumes "the listener's" prior familiarity with the particulars of the family situation, that Adriana has been recovering in the hospital from a serious accident and was released specifically for the occasion of her birthday party.

The first four paragraphs set the scene with a description of the table carefully prepared with sandwiches, cake, and flowers, Adriana's stiff, formal attire, her orthopedic shoes ("botines ortopédicos"), and a long list of guests, referred to by often unflattering nicknames; attention turns repeatedly to "un rubio que nadie me presentó" [a blonde guy no one introduced to me] and "la desgraciada de Humberta" [that pathetic Humberta]. The gossipy indifference of the narrator's tone turns to peevishness when the greedy account of the banquet table is followed by her undisguised irritation at having to wait in order to eat for the arrival of the photographer. The narrator's preoccupation with the food and her jealous obsession with Humberta become the motivating concerns of her own discourse as she describes the taking of seven formal photographs of Adriana by a professional photographer, subsequently known as "el pobre Spirito" (poor Spirito). The narrator's unacknowledged (to herself) flirtations with the photographer and the unknown blonde man and the consequent rivalry for their attention with Humberta occupies most of her attention. The reader, however, learns to be more concerned about Adriana:

En el dormitorio, que medía cinco metros por seis, había aproximadamente quince personas, enloqueciendo al pobre Spirito, dándole indicaciones y aconsejando a Adriana las posturas que debía adoptar. Le arreglaban el pelo, le cubrían los pies, le agregaban almohadones, le colocaban flores y abanicos, le levantaban la cabeza, le abotonaban el cuello, le ponían polvos, le pintaban los labios. No se podía ni respirar. Adriana sudaba y hacía muecas. El pobre Spirito esperó más de media hora, sin decir una palabra; luego, con muchísimo tacto, sacó las flores que habían colocado a los pies de Adriana, diciendo que la niña estaba de blanco y que los gladiolos naranjados desentonaban con el conjunto. Con santa paciencia, Spirito repitió la consabida amenaza:

—Ahora va a salir un pajarito.
Encendió las lámparas y sacó la quinta fotografía, que terminó en un trueno de aplausos. Desde afuera, la gente decía:
—Parece una novia, parece una verdadera novia. Lástima los botines. (*F* 64)

[In the bedroom, which measured five meters by six, there were approximately fifteen people, driving poor Spirito crazy, giving him instructions and advising Adriana about the poses she should strike. They arranged her hair, they covered her feet, they added pillows, they placed flowers and fans around her, they lifted her head, they buttoned her collar, they added powder, they painted her lips. You couldn't even breathe. Adriana was sweating and grimacing. Poor Spirito waited more than half an hour without saying a word; then with great tact he removed the flowers that had been placed at Adriana's feet, saying that the child was dressed in white and that the orange gladioli clashed with the overall impression. With saintly patience, Spirito recited the well-known threat, "Here comes the birdy." He turned on the floodlights and took the fifth photograph to a thunder of applause. From outside, the people said, "She looks like a bride, like a real bride. Too bad about the shoes."]

The asphyxiating heat of the day, which eventually kills Adriana, mirrors the suffocating nature of the gathering, its hypocrisy, its callousness, and finally its cruelty. The delicious ironies of what could also be called an unreliable narrator make the reader laugh, but it is an uncomfortable laughter. The humor resides in the colloquial language, the humorous names, and in the narrator's focus away from the tragic event onto details of comparative insignificance. Although the enunciating act relates events of the recent past, there is no retrospective understanding on the part of this narrator, no sign that she has reconsidered her own priorities in light of events. She is still concentrated on "that pathetic Humberta" and "poor Spirito" to the end. The advantage of such a narrator, of course, is that the unintended violence and cruelty of family life are viewed without mitigating pity or sympathy. A more sympathetic view can be read between the lines of the narrator's version, for the love and care lavished on Adriana are demonstrated by the expensive dress, the elaborate party food, the professional photographer, and the large concerned family. The power of the grotesque to uphold contradiction is at its most effective here.

In a later story, "Cartas confidenciales," a "friend" again provides a grotesque perspective on a family tragedy. As the title's plural indicates, two different narrators write one letter each.

The first narrator, Paula, tells of a man who lived his life in reverse, from old age to infancy, as in Carpentier's "Viaje a la semilla." The old man, don Toni, simply appeared in their house one day, gradually became younger and younger, evolved into the child, Tomi, and then one day, as a tiny infant, disappears. Paula's tone is one of great distress as she relates this mysterious process. In her reply, Prilidiana comments on the events narrated in the first letter with a personality similar to that of the jealous female narrator of "Las fotografías." She provides a humorous contrast in perspective. Her indifference to a fate most people would find astonishing combine with the exaggerated colloquialisms of her language to produce the distanced trivialization of the grotesque and an example of Ocampo's infallible ear for popular speech:

> Querida Paula:
> Leí tu carta ¡como si me hablaras en chino! ¡Y pensar que somos tan amigas! Te complicás por nada, eso es lo que a mí me parece.... Para mí que hay gato encerrado, porque decime en qué cabeza cabe que un hombre aparezca en una casa de la noche a la mañana sin que lo echen y sin que a nadie se le ocurra llamar a la policía para ver si es un asaltante, un leproso, un ladrón o un loco escapado de un manicomio. ¿No se dieron cuenta tus papis, Nena, del peligro en que ponían a toda la familia? Qué querés que te diga, yo nunca soñé que algo así podía suceder en tu casa, con lo severos que han sido siempre con vos. (*Ldn* 33)

> [Dear Paula, I read your letter, and I just couldn't believe it! And to think we are such good friends! You are making mountains out of mole hills, I say. I smell a rat, because who would believe that a man could appear just like that, and no one would think to call the police to see if he is a thief, a leper, a murderer or some lunatic escaped from an asylum. Didn't your parents realize, Girl, what danger they risked for the whole family? What can I say? I never dreamed anything like that could happen in your house with as strict as your parents always were with you]

The humor of this abrupt change of narrative tone accomplishes more than the creation of grotesque laughter: The declared intent to discredit the first narrator ironically provides corroboration for the original version. It is also an illustration of what Kaja Silverman notes in discussing cinematic voices as a "corporeal encroachment," i.e., "a regional accent or idiosyncratic 'grain.'"[50] In her analysis of cinema Silverman argues that this quality of the voice causes it to lose its association with phallic power, the power to transcend the body. This observation allows us to see that Ocampo's narrative tilts readerly sympathies toward Paula's version not only by what Prilidiana says but by how she says it.

In all of Ocampo's stories with multiple narrators, one narrator provides the ironic distance necessary for the "unimpassioned view" of the grotesque. Frequently this second narrator represents what is perceived as a more realistic appraisal of a situation that simultaneously establishes a contrast to a more innocent truth. These distanced narrators often confirm key points in a fantastic narration, giving it more, rather than less, credibility. The fact that the distanced, ironic, and "realistic" voices of the grotesque confirm in their version fantastic events frequently related by others demonstrates a fascinating second function for the narrators of grotesque realism. They affirm, (apparently) unwittingly, the subversive impetus of their more credulous counterparts, narrators of the fantastic.

The interplay of narrators is best demonstrated by "El diario de Porfiria Bernal," which employs all of Ocampo's favorite fantastic themes—metamorphosis, doubling, magical objects and foretelling the future—together with the wicked humor of the grotesque. My extended reading of the story will introduce more systematically many issues of gender that have already been suggested throughout this chapter. The story exemplifies the consistent subversion in Ocampo's fiction of the notion that passage through the mirror stage represents, in Jackson's terms, a "civilizing process." The story reads as a fantasy about the human subject in which the struggle to resist the repressions of the symbolic triumphs.[51]

Like Henry James's novella, *The Turn of the Screw,* Ocampo's short story plays an English governess, Miss Fielding, against a child, Porfiria Bernal, and also frames the narration within a document. Ocampo's text invites a reading of her story with James's when Ana María Bernal, Porfiria's mother, says to Miss Fielding, "Estoy segura de que la vida de usted debe ser como una novela muy romántica, como las novelas de Henry James" (*I* 157) [I am sure that your life must be like a romantic novel, like the novels of Henry James]. Like James's governess, Miss Fielding is steeped in literature and spends much of her time reading; like James's character, she carries out her duties with zeal, admitting for instance that she herself studied in order to teach Porfiria. Silvina Ocampo's Miss Fielding, however, becomes a caricature of the English governess, and not, in the words of James's character Douglas, "the most agreeable woman

I've ever known in her position." In her description of herself, Miss Fielding consciously admits her enthusiasm and naivete (characteristics shared by James's governess) even as she reveals her vanity and narcissism:

> Me llamo Antonia Fielding, tengo treinta años, soy inglesa y el largo tiempo que pasé en la Argentina no modificó el perfume a espliego de mis pañuelos, mi incorrecta pronunciación castellana, mi carácter reservado, mi habilidad para trabajos manuales (el dibujo y la acuarela) y esa facilidad que tengo para ruborizarme, como si me sintiese culpable Dios sabe de qué faltas que no he cometido (esto se debe, más que a timidez, a una transparencia excesiva de la piel, que muchas amigas me han envidiado). (*I* 155)

> My name is Antonia Fielding, I am thirty years old, English, and the long period I spent in Argentina did not change the lavender perfume of my handkerchiefs, my incorrect Spanish pronunciation, my reserved character, my ability with fine handiwork (drawing and water color) and that tendency to blush, as if I felt guilty about God knows what error that I have not committed (which is due, rather than to timidity, to the excessive transparency of my skin which many friends have envied.)

Shoshana Felman reads James's story as the history of a document and its transmission from one narrator to another.[52] Ocampo's story consists of two documents, one supposedly embedded in the other, the first acting as frame. Miss Fielding's account encloses, figuratively and literally, Porfiria's diary. Her opening paragraph seeks an odd authority for her version of events even as it questions the nature of truth and belief:

> Pocas personas creerán este relato. A veces habría que mentir para que la gente admitiera la verdad; . . . Soy modestamente, torpemente honesta. Si llegué al borde del crimen, no fue por mi culpa: el no haberlo cometido no me vuelve menos desdichada.
>
> Escribo para Ruth, mi hermana, y para Lilian, mi hermana de leche, cuyo afecto de infancia perdura a través de los años. Escribo también para la conocida *Society for Psychical Research;* tal vez algo, en las siguientes páginas, pueda interesarle, pues investiga los hechos sobrenaturales. (*I* 154)

> [Few people will believe this tale. At times one must lie in order for people to admit the truth; . . . I am modestly, awkwardly honest. If I came to the brink of crime, it was not my fault: the fact that I did not commit it fails to make me less miserable.
>
> I write for Ruth, my sister, and for Lilian, my foster sister, whose childhood affection has lasted through the years. I write also for the

well-known Society for Psychical Research; perhaps something in
the following pages may interest them for they investigate supernatural occurrences.]

Miss Fielding's mysterious statement of purpose is followed by
a lengthy description of her first impressions of the Bernal
household, in which her remembered enthusiasm of the past is
punctuated with the foreboding imposed from the perspective
of the enunciating moment, the greater knowledge of the story's
present. She remembers the door knocker at the street entrance
as an announcement of the danger within: "La súbita aparición
del llamador en la puerta de calle oscureció por un instante mi
alegría. En los objetos leemos el porvenir de nuestras desdichas.
La mano de bronce, con una víbora enroscada en su puño acana-
lado, era imperiosa y brillaba como una alhaja sobre la madera
de la puerta" (156) [The sudden appearance of the knocker on
the street door darkened for a moment my happiness. In objects
we read the future of our unhappiness. The bronze hand, with
its snake coiled around its furrowed fist, was imperious and
shone like a jewel on the wood of the door]. The richly appor-
tioned rooms and startling artifacts of the house coincide with
the narrator's striking appraisal of its mistress, Porfiria's mother,
Ana María Bernal: "Parecía una reina egipcia del *British Museum,* de esas que me asustaron en la infancia y que admiré
más tarde, cuando aprendí que hay bellezas que son muy desa-
gradables" (157) [She seemed like an Egyptian queen from the
British Musuem, one of those that used to frighten me as a child
and that I later admired when I learned that there are types
of beauty that are very disagreeable]. The ensuing encounter
between Ana María Bernal and Miss Fielding sets up a trap for
poor Miss Fielding and perhaps for her reader.

As in Henry James's story, the essential dilemma of Miss Fielding's letter resides in the child, in what the child "knows." The
governess of Bly convinces herself that the beautiful, innocent
appearance of her charges disguises their complicity with evil.
Miss Fielding's story is about another beautiful and innocent
child and about what powers or knowledge may lie behind such
a facade. The mother, Ana María Bernal, describes her child with
the phrase, "hija de rigor," which she then defines as "volunta-
riosa" (wilful). This description, together with the little girl's
name, sets up a series of expectations about her for Miss Fielding
and for the reader: "Su nombre, que me recordaba una apasionada poesía de Byron y la conversación que yo había tenido con

su madre habían formado en mí una imagen resplandeciente y muy distinta" (158) [Her name, which reminded me of a passionate poem by Byron and the conversation which I had had with her mother had formed for me a resplendent and quite different image]. Miss Fielding expects Porfiria to be a younger version of the girl's exotic mother. This expectation, which will be proved true in every detail as the story continues, nevertheless is nearly forgotten by Miss Fielding once she sees Porfiria for the first time: the child's outward appearance of innocence erases the mother's description and her warning about the daughter's "wilful" nature:

> Pálida y delgada, con modestia se acercó para que le besara la frente.
>   Porfiria no era hermosa, no se parecía a su madre, pero hay una belleza casi oculta en los seres, que presentimos difícilmente si no somos bastante sutiles; una belleza que aparece y desaparece y que los vuelve más atrayentes: Porfiria tenía esa modesta y recatada belleza, que vemos en algunos cuadros de Botticelli, y esa apariencia de sumisión que me engañó tanto en el primer momento. (158)

> Pale and slim, she approached with modesty so that I could kiss her forehead. Porfiria was not beautiful, she did not look like her mother, but there is an almost hidden beauty in some people which we perceive with difficulty if we are not sufficiently subtle; a beauty which appears and disappears and which makes them more attractive: Porfiria had that modestly shy beauty which we see in some paintings by Boticelli, and that appearance of submission which fooled me so in the first moment]

The last phrase only partially prepares the reader for the contents of Porfiria's diary. An abrupt change of style reflects the contrast between Miss Fielding's sentimentalized account of the child and Porfiria's own forthright reflections on the same subject a few pages later in the first diary entry:

> Miss Fielding piensa que no soy hermosa, pero que tengo una expresión fugitivamente hermosa. "Es la expresión de la inteligencia," me ha dicho. "Es lo único importante." Me parezco a los ángeles de Botticelli que usan cuellitos bordados y que tienen "las caras viejas de tanto pensar en Dios," como dice Miss Fielding. Yo no pienso en Dios, sino de noche, cuando nadie ve mi cara; entonces le pido muchas cosas y le hago promesas que no cumplo. (162)

> [Miss Fielding thinks that I am not beautiful, but that I have a fleetingly beautiful expression. "It is the expression of intelligence," she has said. "It is the only thing that matters." I look like those Boticelli

angles who wear little embroidered collars and have "old faces from thinking so much about God," as Miss Fielding says. I do not think about God except at night when no one sees my face; then I ask for things and make promises which I don't keep.]

The difference in tone between the two voices, Miss Fielding's admiring and somewhat tentative language and Porfiria's more direct simplicity, functions similarly to the dual narrators discussed above. Miss Fielding's naive and innocent version introduces the fantastic element, which will be corroborated by Porfiria's "unimpassioned" view. Though Porfiria's version differs from that of Miss Fielding's in some essential points, each confirms the other regarding the fantastic event that ends her diary.

Porfiria's second diary entry returns to the issue of her name: "Soy la esclava de mi nombre" [I am a slave to my name], she writes. Corominas gives a three-layered definition to the word "porfía:" 1) "obstinación" [obstinacy]; 2) "el que jura en falso, engañador" [perjurer, deceiver]; 3) "que en los Padres de la Iglesia tomó el sentido de 'herejía'" [in works by the Church Fathers came to mean "heresy"].[53] All three levels of signification of this name will come into play: Miss Fielding's own account hints at the first meaning, obstinate, by describing the determination with which Porfiria insists that she read the diary; the second meaning, deceitful, is clear from Miss Fielding's first description of Porfiria; and the third level of meaning, heretic, is suggested in this first diary entry, and confirmed when Porfiria writes: "28 de marzo: He inventado esta oración: Dios mío, haced que todo lo que yo imagine sea cierto, y lo que no pueda yo imaginar no llegue nunca a serlo. Haced que yo, como los santos, desprecie la realidad" (165) [28 March: I have invented this prayer: Dear God, make whatever I imagine come true, and whatever I can not imagine never be. Make me, like the saints, disdain reality]. Porfiria's name confirms magical, heretical powers, the capacity for deceit, and obstinate, stubborn resistance. That Porfiria feels herself to be "slave" of her name plays humorously with Lacan's theory that naming is an act of repression.

Slowly Miss Fielding—who twice interrupts the reading of the diary with anguished commentary—begins to realize that Porfiria's record is not of the past but of the future. In the first interruption, Miss Fielding tells that she had confronted her pupil about the discrepancy in the dates of the diary, and Porfiria responds: "Escribir antes o después que sucedan las cosas es lo mismo: inventar es más fácil que recordar" [Writing before or after events happen is the same: inventing is easier than remembering]. Both Porfiria and Miss Fielding, like other Ocampo protagonists who foresee the future, seem to believe that Porfiria is causing future events not just predicting them. Porfiria writes: "29 de septiembre. Miss Fielding me ve tal vez como a un demonio. Siente un horror profundo por mí y es porque empieza a comprender el significado de este diario, donde tendrá que seguir ruborizándose, dócil, obedeciendo al destino que yo le infligiré, con un temor que no siento por nada ni por nadie" (168) [29 September: Miss Fielding sees me perhaps as a demon. She feels a profound horror toward me and it is because she begins to understand the significance of this diary, where she will have to go on blushing, docile and obedient to the destiny I will inflict on her, with a fear that I feel for nothing and no one]. Porfiria's chilling and pitiless version of events nevertheless always feels genuinely childlike and truthful, so much so that she becomes more believable than the governess herself.

The discrepancies between them are significant. The optimistic, naive Miss Fielding of her own version becomes a vicious hypocrite when seen through Porfiria's eyes by way of her diary. The child expresses her contempt for Miss Fielding's attraction to wealth, an assessment she then modifies to imply that Miss Fielding sees only the surface of things: "La riqueza es como una coraza que Miss Fielding admira y que yo detesto" (165) [Wealth is a protective shell which Miss Fielding admires and which I detest]. Porfiria's diary repeatedly describes Miss Fielding as a cat, even relaying various episodes in which she is scratched to the point of bleeding. The hatred between Porfiria and Miss Fielding, as recorded by Porfiria, rises to a climax until on 24 December, Porfiria describes with some ambiguity a fall from the roof of the house that she feels was Miss Fielding's attempt to kill her, a notion confirmed earlier by Miss Fielding herself when she mentions having come close to committing a crime. Finally, the last entry in the diary reads:

Por la puerta entreabierta veo que Miss Fielding prepara el chocolate. Hierve la leche en un calentador. Ya no podrá traerme la taza. Se ha cubierto de pelos, se ha achicado, se ha escondido; por la ventana abierta da un brinco y se detiene en la balaustrada del balcón. Luego da otro brinco y se aleja. . . . Ahora Miss Fielding es inofensiva y se perderá por las calles de Buenos Aires. Cuando la encuentre, si algún día la encuentro, le gritaré, para burlarme de ella: "Mish Fielding, Mish Fielding," y ella se hará la desentendida, porque siempre fue una hipócrita, como los gatos. (*I* 172)

[Through the half-opened door I see that Miss Fielding is preparing the chocolate. The milk is boiling in the heater. She can no longer bring me the cup. She has become covered with hair, she has grown smaller, she has hidden; through the open window she hops and pauses on the railing of the balcony. Then with another hop, she is gone. . . . Now Miss Fielding is harmless and will be lost in the streets of Buenos Aires. When I run across her, if someday I run across her, I will shout, to make fun of her: "Mish Fielding, Mish Fielding," and she will pretend not to hear, because she was always a hypocrite, like a cat.

The crime finally is committed not by the governess, but by the diabolical child. James's tale of innocence corrupted is turned on its head.

James's Miles, according to Felman, is emblematic of the unconscious which is repressed, and finally killed, by his governess in her attempt to "master meaning," to "dispossess" the child of contradictory "readings": "At its [the story's] final, climactic point, the attempt at *grasping* meaning and at *closing* the reading process with a *definitive* interpretation in effect discovers—and comprehends—only death" (Felman, 174). Felman equates reading with seeing, and places both of these activities of the governess on the order of the signifier; knowing—always associated with the child—she places on the level of the signified. By analogy, then, the governess represents the repressive impulses of the symbolic (signifier) over the child who figures as the unconscious imaginary (signified). Using Felman's analogy to read Ocampo's story makes it clear that Porfiria Bernal successfully defends herself against her own governess's attempt at murderous repression.

The two documents of Ocampo's narrative, read as an allegory of the drama of the subject, place Miss Fielding, the image of the symbolic order, in mortal combat with Porfiria Bernal, the "child who is presumed to know," symbol of the unconscious.[54] All Miss Fielding's repressed desires, transgressive sexuality, and murderous impulses, appear in the story of the unconscious. Porfiria's discourse involving indifferentiation between subject and object, magical and "timeless" elements, along with the extreme ferocity of emotions suggest Lacan's imaginary realm. Further, psychoanalysis recognizes the many images of cutting and scratching as moments of castration and entrance into the symbolic. To dramatize further the unconscious's reluctance to pass through the mirror stage, Porfiria says on 20 December: "Me he contemplado largamente en el espejo, para decirme adiós, como si los espejos del mundo fueran a desaparecer para siempre. Creo que existo porque me veo" (*I* 171) [I have contemplated myself at length in the mirror to tell myself goodbye, as if the mirrors of the world were about to disappear forever. I believe I exist because I see myself]. Porfiria's document as diary reinforces the notion that she is caught in the mirror stage, for a diary is another kind of mirror. The letter in Felman's analysis, as in Lacan's theory, signifies language itself: It is a message from a sender to a receiver. A diary, however, is a message whose sender and receiver are one: It is a message to the self about the self. When we remember that Miss Fielding was the one who insisted on the diary, it now seems to "mean" that Miss Fielding wants to reduce Porfiria Bernal to discourse as she reduces everything else. But Porfiria's magical diary refuses to be bound by the rules of discourse.

If Porfiria's diary is the story of the imaginary, Miss Fielding's account figures as the symbolic. Miss Fielding's discourse insists on representation itself, reducing all nature to "art." We have already seen that she describes Ana María Bernal as a statue from British Museum, and Porfiria as an image by Boticelli; she herself, in turn, is described in terms of a character (a romantic heroine) from fiction (Henry James). Miss Fielding declares early on that she "knows" Argentina itself from the novels of William Henry Hudson. Later, on a vacation with the Bernal family, the governess meditates on the passing scene:

> Por la ventanilla del tren veía todo el campo incendiado por el poniente; ni un árbol lo interrrumpía; los animales parecían juguetes recién pintados. . . . He venerado siempre la naturaleza; sus diversas manifestaciones me traen a la memoria versos, frases enteras de algunas novelas, . . . reproducciones de cuadros pintados al óleo por Turner, . . . ciertas canciones de Purcell (*I* 159)

> [Through the train window I could see the whole countryside inflamed by the sunset; not a single tree interrupted it; the animals looked like recently painted toys. . . . I have always respected nature; its diverse elements bring to mind poetry, whole passages from certain novels . . . reproductions of oils by Turner, . . . certain songs by Purcell]

The reduction of all reality to language (or art) in Miss Fielding's account, the exaggeration of the inevitable disparity between signified and signifier, is the essence of her character, the essence of the symbolic, which the child sees and labels *hipócrita*.

According to Felman, "As an object of suppression and of repression, the knowledge of the child itself becomes thereby the very emblem of the unconscious; of the unconscious which is always, in a sense, the knowledge of a child about to die and yet immortal, indestructible; the knowledge of a child dead and yet which one has always yet to kill" (Felman, 166). James's story imagines the subject's painful entrance into the symbolic order by means of repression of the knowledge of the child (the unconscious) to a position below the bar, which leaves only a simulacrum, a corpse, a signifier above the bar (173). Ocampo's story, by contrast, imagines the failure of the symbolic. In this fantastic tale, as in so many others by Ocampo, the child/unconscious triumphs over repressive forces of adult reality. Porfiria Bernal destroys the governess/ symbolic by sending her back through the mirror to the death of consciousness into a future of timeless, animal imaginary. At this point the story ends, and in this reading of the two characters as essential parts of the same subject, Porfiria Bernal has also killed herself as a conscious subject. Viewed in the context of Ocampo's other stories of metamorphosis, we can understand the note of triumph in this self-destructive act.

Though Shoshana Felman's analysis does not take up the issue of gender, her reading does allow us to see how James's text expels the female. The governess's story, as Felman points out, is framed and reframed in the introduction by two different male narrators, Douglas and the story's first "I." Though this framing device overtly invites the reader to place confidence and authority in the governess's account, its ultimate effect is to open this account to question. Furthermore, little Flora, who might also represent a "child presumed to know," exits with the housekeeper, Mrs. Grose, before the story's climax. Therefore, the child as Other who is presumed to know (emblem of the unconscious) in James's text is only the idealized male child, Miles. He, in turn, of course, as "the little master" is inevitably associated with the absent Master of Bly, the hidden force behind the narrative. The governess's attempt to "master meaning" by "killing or stifling the silence within him" (195) obeys the rule of the Master and Law of the Father as James's tale (or Felman's analysis) so neatly illustrates. The painful closure of this work exemplifies the ways in which fantasy literature tends to (paraphasing Jackson) neutralize its own impulses toward transgression. In this respect, Ocampo's two narrators have a significantly different position with regard to the narration than do James's. The framing device in James's and Ocampo's texts, though presupposing the end, are read at the beginning; the "story" itself then follows its frame, leaving the framed narrator with the final word. In spite of this structural similarity an important difference can be observed. James's narrators, Douglas and the "I" listening around the fire, relay events that "actually" occurred earlier. Even though we read their account first, the governess's tale is framed in literary time by theirs. Ocampo's narration, however, resolves itself in a perpetual future since Miss Fielding writes her version only on the supposition, based on good evidence, that Porfiria's prediction will, in fact, come true. Miss Fielding sends both documents to their intended recipients only in expectation of an event yet to come. The story ends with an eternal question mark, imposed structurally, rather than thematically. "El diario de Porfiria Bernal" illustrates the two structural characteristics of Ocampo's fantastic narratives at their best: the problemetizing of the narrator in terms of authority and unity, and the resistance to closure.

Ocampo's text, furthermore, recuperates the female at every level. The two documents both relay female voices (thus constituting a female subject, however resistant!). The all-powerful Master who confers authority on the governess of James's story is reenvisioned in Ocampo's text as the mother, who haunts this text as a kind of witch. Miss Fielding describes her first encounter with Porfiria's mother with portents of hidden powers:

> Nunca pude saber . . . la edad de Ana María Bernal . . . En un mismo día podía ser joven y envejecer con elegancia. . . . Frente a esta desconocida mujer argentina me sentí desamparada. Me sentí transparente. . . . El color de mi piel, el oro gastado de mi cabello . . . me parecieron . . . una *maldición* inexplicable. El color oscuro de la piel suele dar a los seres una jerarquía, un *poder oculto,* que admiro, desprecio y temo secretamente . . . (*I* 156, emphasis mine)

> [I was never able to discover Ana María Bernal's age. . . . In one day she could be young and age with elegance. . . . Before this unknown Argentine woman I felt defenseless. I felt transparent. . . . My skin color, the tired gold of my hair . . . seemed an inexplicable *curse.* Dark skin color gives status, a sort of *hidden power,* which I admire, disdain and fear secretly.]

Porfiria and her mother are associated with magical powers and heresy. Though Porfiria relays ambivalent feelings about both

Miss Fielding and her mother, the identification between mother and daughter, originally denied in Miss Fielding's letter because of Porfiria's outwardly angelic appearance, is reinforced in the diary itself by the repeated refrain, "Se lo dije a mi madre" [I told my mother about it]. Porfiria seeks rescue from the mother particularly after incidents of cutting or scratching that earlier are identified with castration. The authority figure is clearly Ana María Bernal, and her heir is her daughter Porfiria, the female equivalents of James's Master and "little master."

The notion that separation from the mother is necessary for passage from the imaginary to the symbolic makes the alliance between Porfiria and her mother an essential ingredient to her refusal of the mirror stage. The element which forces the splitting within the mirror stage in Freudian theory is the father (phallus for Lacan). Ocampo's story embodies the splitting mechanism in the person of Miss Fielding an ineffectual, hypocritical, sterile entrance to the symbolic. On the other hand, Porfiria's father, a shadowy figure barely mentioned in either document, becomes a second mother figure in Miss Fielding's account: "Mario Bernal era un hombre tranquilo y bondadoso y sentía por su hija una ternura casi maternal" (159) [Mario Bernal was a tranquil, kindly man who felt for his daughter an almost maternal tenderness]; while in Porfiria's he is oddly irrelevant: "Veo muy poco a mi padre o más bien lo miro muy poco" [I see very little of my father or rather I look at him very little]. Miss Fielding's document is addressed, furthermore, not to an absent Master (who embodies Lacan's Law of the Father in Felman's analysis) as are the various letters of *Turn of the Screw,* but to two females, the two sisters mentioned in her first paragraph, and two males: "Escribo también para la conocida *Society for Psychical Research ;* . . . el primer presidente de esta sociedad, el profesor Henry Sidwick, fue uno de los mejores amigos de mi abuelo" (154) [I also write for the well-known Society for Psychical Research; . . . the first president of this society, Professor Henry Sidwick, was one of my grandfather's best friends]. The receivers of the message are a split female character, Ruth and Lilian, and an even more splintered male figure, the Society for Psychical Research, and its president, a friend, not of the father, but of the grandfather. Finally, Miss Fielding admits that her own document, like Porfiria's, is really one more mirror, a story of the self for the self: "Escribo sobre todo para mi misma, por un deber de conciencia" [I write above all for myself, as a duty to conscience]. The gender implicit in

Lacan's law of the father has been expelled here by making the distant authority plural, feminized, and eventually powerless, and by having a female character stand in for what, in Lacan's theory, would be the phallus. Ocampo has succeeded in the struggle, articulated by Jane Gallop, to depict the law of the father as other than a "biologistic reduction . . . to the rule of the actual living male."[55] "El diario de Porfiria Bernal" is a story of female power and knowledge, a story whose characters enact a drama in which all aspects of the subject, the imaginary, the symbolic, and the law (of language and culture) are vividly imagined as female.[56] Furthermore, the child character may stand as the epitome of the "*nena terrible*," the "perverse," "impure" little girl who has been recognized as the core of Ocampo's fiction.[57] Readers' fascination with these stories can now be better understood if we "read" their admittedly strange characters as images of a particularly female unconscious, the *female* child who is presumed to know.

"El diario de Porfiria Bernal" has been read here as a fantasy of the subject in which the split between being and meaning, in Lacan's terms, is represented by two fictional characters who each speak differently about similar events. Miss Fielding represents the order of meaning, the invented persona forever alienated from the essence of "being," the inevitable product of the repression necessary for entrance into articulated language. The unconscious as a second text, usually inaccessible to the first, is presented in Porfiria's diary. That Porfiria's account has the final word, that her version seems more genuine, reflects Lacan's refutation of *cogito ergo sum,* paraphrased by Anika Lemaire: "Freud's discovery, Lacan points out, obliges us to recognize that . . . I 'am' more surely there where 'I' do not 'think.' The contents of the unconscious form the very heart of our being."[58] This hidden heart of being is the essence of fantasy literature, so successfully explored by Silvina Ocampo. What is new is her insistent exploration of the "I" identified as female.

In conclusion, I would like to return to Matamoro. His analysis does differentiate between the gender of both adults and children because he observes that women remain part of the permanent underclass. The little girl is a powerful element of subversion partly because, unlike her male counterpart, she cannot expect to become one of the ruling forces and, hence, even as an adult, may be expected to identify more thoroughly with marginalized elements of society. Furthermore, she is nearly always assumed to be weak, innocent, and ignorant, so that her acts of violence come as a surprise. The boys, in contrast, are unfettered and frequently remorseless. Claudio, of "La oración," kills one of his playmates; Cornelio, of "Los amigos," "prays" for epidemics and earthquakes; the little boys of "Voz en el teléfono" burn down the house with stolen matches. The narrator of "Los amigos" and the two friends of "Magush" are notable exceptions, but in general, the boys of Ocampo's fiction seem to be practicing for the all-powerful role they will enact as adult men of the ruling class; in other words, to dominate the system already in place. Interesting, then, that even though the little girls only observe or predict terrible things, while the boys actively commit murder and mayhem, readers have found the girls more shocking. Violence in the male is nothing new, no doubt, whereas even the suppressed wish for violence on the part of a little girl is considered surprising, even horrifying. There is more to the little girls, however; I argue in the subsequent chapter that Ocampo's little girls are acting against an entire system of oppression, whereas the boys are just acting up.

Matamoro compares Ocampo's frequent themes of revenge and betrayal to the "ley de gallinero" [pecking order] which incites underlings to fight each other instead of the oppressive authority. While he speaks here of children in general, this remark contradicts his earlier assessment of the boys who fight the fathers for control; clearly, it is the girls who frequently fight each other. Ocampo's "nenas terribles" lash out in desperation and many times get it wrong, but the very depiction of this struggle, the pain at the margins of the patriarchy, is vastly illuminating. Only a few escape their condition as oppressed beings by way of criminality, sex change, change of social status, or transformation into animal or object. But, Matamoro continues, that escape remains a fantasy, and marked within the fiction as fantastic: "Pero la renuncia a la identidad sexual y social no pasa de mera fantasía y queda, dentro del contexto del relato, como un rasgo de inverosimilitud, aun para el mismo relato" [But the renunciation of sexual and social identity does not go beyond mere fantasy, and remains an unbelievable element, even in the context of the story itself].[59] As we grow to understand just how stubborn are even our fantasies with regard to feminine positioning, the importance of Ocampo's "mere fantasies" of female transformation and power belie Matamoro's faint praise.

The complexity of motivation surrounding the little girls and their position as wild card can already be glimpsed in terms of the fantastic and grotesque. It seems to me that theories of carnival and grotesque realism cannot uncover what they acknowledge as hidden in the recesses of these narratives. Neither is it revealed completely by way of ideology of class struggle. If there is a redemptive quality to Ocampo's horrific laughter, it is available only through a different kind of reading. Matamoro comes to a similar impasse in his concluding assessment of Ocampo's fiction as caught up in concern with evil rather than with revolutionary change. He argues that identifying with evil depends on confirming an image of goodness as its opposing term, and is therefore a conservative gesture.[60] For a woman writer, however, a reassessment of evil is of primary importance, and, as Gilbert and Gubar have shown, is an essential first step in the creative act itself. Viewed from the perspective of women's writing, Ocampo's fantasies of female evil and rebellion seem much more important than they do viewed in the context of her talented male contemporaries.

At this juncture it is clear that discussion of the fantastic and grotesque fails to uncover the "unseen" (Jackson's term) of culture which Ocampo's fictions address. Matamoro finds that Ocampo's work differs slightly from her male counterparts in its ideology of class struggle, but that "Esa parcial contradicción con su clase, que la enriquece, no alcanza a elevar la obra al nivel de lo revolucionario" (220) [That partial contradiction with her class, which enriches her work, does not elevate it to the level of the revolutionary]. My reading of Ocampo's work in subsequent chapters offers a lengthy disagreement. The oddness and cruelty of her stories have no parallel in those of Borges, Bioy Casares or Cortázar. Theories of the fantastic and grotesque argue that their subversion of normal constructs of reality provides a glimpse of a different kind of world. Ocampo's little girls are not just subversive images, they represent speaking subjects identified as female. Mary Russo's call for a grotesque female subjectivity discusses the critiques of carnival theory which have noticed that carnival is structurally conservative. I agree with her, however, that, "The extreme difficulty of producing lasting social change does not diminsh the usefulness of these symbolic models of transgression."[61] Ocampo's stories offer one response to Russo's concluding question: "I imagine . . . [feminists] shifting the terms of viewing, so that . . . there will be a new question, the question that never occurred to Bakhtin in front of the Kerch terracotta figurines—Why are these old hags laughing?"[62] The remainder of this book will explore potential

answers to the question, what are Ocampo's evil little girls laughing at/rebelling against? Matamoro's insightful analysis of
Ocampo's work introduces many of the elements of discussion:
the theme of betrayal, the marginalization of the female, the
locus of the family as arena of conflict. Most important of all,
the smiling evil of her young protagonists with its mixtures of
opposites, innocence and power, laughter and horror, become
Matamoro's emblem—and mine—for Ocampo's entire opus.

2

The Feminine: Subverting the Master Plot

INTRODUCTION: "BREAKING THE SEQUENCE"

IF THE FANTASTIC AND GROTESQUE HAVE OFFERED BOTH MALE AND female authors the possibility of questioning dominant modes of discourse, the appearance of the woman writer as speaking subject itself has been identified as a wholesale subversion of the structures of language.[1] This chapter focuses the study of Ocampo's plot structures on modifications to conventional narrative patterns necessitated by the expression of a female subjectivity, and depends on psychoanalytic theories which posit narrative plot as a mechanism of desire.[2] Virginia Woolf predicted that women writers would "break the sequence" of inherited patterns.[3] More recently, Peter Brooks clarifies the importance of doing so: "Narrative is one of the ways in which we speak, one of the large categories in which we think. Plot is its thread of design and its active shaping force, the product of our refusal to allow temporality to be meaningless, our stubborn insistence on making meaning in the world and in our lives."[4] Brooks's study, which relates Lacanian psychoanalysis to literary forms, mentions women writers and the "woman's plot" in passing, but his "we," in the context of works by male writers and unrevised Lacanian theory, makes no attempt to account for the strategies of either women writers or women readers. My readings of Silvina Ocampo's stories depend on feminist revision of Lacan's theories in an effort to understand how she has modified conventional plot structures to "make meaning" in accordance with a female psychology. Lacan's theories prove useful in connecting gendered psychic life with fictional narratives; however, while Lacan would deny the possibility of female desire or of full female subjectivity I argue that Silvina Ocampo joins a legion of modern women writers who have sought to transform the "grammar" of plot structure in order to make a space for a feminine "I."

97

Coupled with the twentieth century's generalized suspicion of plots and plotting and wariness toward endings that "move toward full predication of meaning,"[5] twentieth-century women writers face a double problematics with respect to plot: As modernists they experience a need to revise and revitalize the predictable machinations of plotting, and as women writers they frequently express the need to rewrite and break out of the standard woman's plot. Chapter 1 of this study provides insight into the several ways that Ocampo's fiction seeks to transform narrative conventions: The refusal of closure, subversion of authority of the narrator, the ruptures in the logic of point of view, and other modernist techniques visible in the discussion of Ocampo's fantastic stories become part of the arsenal of feminine subversion as does the trivializing language associated with the grotesque. It is no surprise to discover that as a woman writer Ocampo chooses various distortions of the romance plot in order to put subversive elements into fictional motion. The fantastic and grotesque subvert dominant discourse's logic of phemonenology and conservative ideology, while the feminine subversion of romance seeks to unseat the usual positioning of gender in the subject/object relations of plot.

Rachel Blau DuPlessis utilizes Peter Brooks as a starting point to articulate various strategies which twentieth-century women writers have employed in order to position the female as subject of her own discourse. DuPlessis argues that women writers of Western tradition must contend with two inherited patterns governing the feminine in fiction, the romance plot which typically ends with the marriage of the female character or the quest plot which ends in her death. DuPlessis equates marriage and death as endings that firmly (re)situate the female within a patriarchal order that considers love and quest (vocation) irreconcilable choices for women characters. Twentieth-century women writers consciously disrupt these structures in a process that DuPlessis calls "writing beyond the ending." They consciously avoid plots which either privilege the formation of a heterosexual couple by the heroine's marriage or punish by death the girl-hero's quest for "more."[6] This chapter begins with a study of Ocampo's ironic exaggerations of the conventional romance plot; its insistence on doubling is then reconsidered in light of Gilbert and Gubar's by now well-known discussion of female doubles in women writers.[7] The mother and child, key figures of Ocampo's fiction and of contemporary feminist theory, position the female as subject rather than object of narrative desire.

The sexually transgressive mother and wicked little girl provide plot elements that disrupt the expected flow of narrative and lead Ocampo finally into her most disturbing questions. Her recently published works take up overtly what always has lurked as latent in her narratives, the issues of perversion.

The Language of Love

Ocampo's ironic humor becomes one strategy for her unwriting of romance. Several stories present romantic situations as humorous accidents, in which one or both parties become entangled in a love plot against their will. Nevertheless, once placed in the situation they react according to the expected script. In spite of all evidence to contradict them, the narrators conclude their tales by utilizing the language of deeply felt romantic love to explain their situations. "El almacén negro," for instance, describes life in a small town in which the narrator is forced to marry a young woman because she fainted in his arms. Similarly, the main character of "La boda" finds herself engaged to a man because her aunt misinterpreted his pose one evening as he knelt beside her to untangle her long hair from the cane chair in which she was sitting. Both stories begin with marriage as the antithesis of true romance, and both narrators describe marriage with the fellow prisoner of convention as a most negative experience: In the first, the young Ema is described as an avaricious monster of a wife, finally imprisoned for murder; in the second, the bride spends her engagement terrified and disgusted by her husband and the first year of marriage in a mental hospital. Nevertheless, both narrators, one male and one female, conclude their tales with romantic phrases jarring in the context. The narrator of "El almacén negro" bemoans the absence of his terrible wife with endearing phrases such as, "¡Pobre Ema de mi corazón!" [My poor beloved Ema], and the narrator of "La boda" ends her tale with violent images of revenge and death over the discovery of her husband's affair with another woman. Although their marriages are far from ideal and neither has made any pretense throughout of any loving feelings, both characters conclude by situating themselves within the conventional expressions of romantic love.

Both "El almacén negro" and "La boda" convert the discourse of romance into hollow nonsense. In one way, however, the characters demonstrate a truth explored elsewhere in Ocampo's work, that desire operates through lack. Popular lore and Lacan's theories coincide with regard to marriage: Desire, fundamentally insatiable, arises from lack; consequently, the attempt to live a life of continuous desire for something (someone) already possessed is impossible.[8] Ocampo situates many romantic narratives in the early stages of a marriage, thereby utilizing the institution itself as a means to discuss the mechanism of desire. The two characters above both fall back on shop-worn expressions of passion or tenderness with the absence, either real or threatened, of the marriage partner. Jealousy, inspiring the fear of loss, becomes the strategy of choice for recreating the lack essential for the operations of desire.

The young bride of "Amor," for instance, describes her honeymoon cruise as a series of psychological duels and bitter quarrels in which both husband and wife deliberately attempt to inspire the jealousy of the other. The ship hits an iceberg and begins to sink, but the young pair stays on deck arguing until the last possible moment. The wife laments their eventual rescue, suggesting that she would have preferred to die in her husband's arms than continue to live in a world of conflict. The compelling force of the romance plot and its dangers are clearly demonstrated by this story's exaggerations. Closure, even a false one, is preferable to the decidedly unromantic life lived to an inconclusive end. The story begins with the honeymoon, almost ends with death, but manages to break away from either of the traditional fictional endings for women characters.

"El asco" describes the fluctuations of romantic desire between a newly married husband and wife, but curiously introduces as narrator a third party, a hairdresser, a distanced narrative positioning that creates the story's essential ambiguity. The story's title refers to the fact that the wife, Rosalía, finds her husband physically repulsive. Since there is no explanation for the marriage in the first place, one can assume perhaps that Rosalía and her husband find themselves married by "accident." The unnamed husband attempts to overcome his wife's aversion to him by providing her with every domestic comfort and by showering her with gifts, all to no avail. A conversation in the beauty parlor about this couple reveals an unexpectedly profound truth:

—¿Qué le pasa a esa señora? El marido anda loco por ella, ¿qué más quiere?

—Ser amada no da felicidad, lo que da felicidad es amar, señora— yo le respondía (*F* 158).

["What is wrong with that woman? Her husband is crazy about her, what more does she want?" "Being loved does not give happiness, what gives happiness is loving, ma'am," I responded.]

It is not enough to be the object of desire; the subject attains not only happiness through desire, but its very being.

When at last Rosalía conquers her aversion for her husband, she is transformed by relief and happiness. However, just as she makes this change, depicted as a willed transformation accomplished with effort, her husband changes too: He begins to neglect her, comes in late at night drunk, and chases women. The narrator implicates herself in his adventures if only by what she does not say, the self-serving hypocrisy of her account condemning her finally in the reader's mind far more completely than the wandering male. Rosalía's despair at her husband's behavior manifests itself in a neglect of household duties. Among the dirty dishes and dead plants, her jealousy turns her metaphorically into a piece of bad stitching: "Los celos la trabajaban todo el día, como ella a su costura, con puntadas largas y cortas, con pespuntes torcidos, pues era mala costurera" (158) [Jealousy worked on her every day, like she did on her sewing, with long and short stitches, with twisted backstitching, since she was a bad seamstress]. Eventually Rosalía makes every effort to undo the love she had worked to create in herself and again the process is described in terms of sewing stitches, now painstakingly torn out. Oddly, the mechanism of romantic love attributed to Rosalía implies that it can be consciously motivated, willed, as an act of laborious creativity. The notion of desire as something that can be consciously either created or destroyed is, of course, completely at odds with all theories.

While Rosalía may seem more in control than her husband, her behavior is dependent on the all-powerful male and motivated as a response to his desire. At the story's conclusion the couple has returned to the original situation: Rosalía has recovered her revulsion, and her husband has returned to the fold as adoring (because) unrequited lover. The narrator observes, "después de todo, no es tan malo. Es como todos los hombres" (160) [After all, he is not so bad. He is just like all men]. The male's desire, based in lack, can be firmly directed toward his wife as long as she rejects him, continues to provide a space for desire. When she responds fully to him, the lack has been filled, and desire directs itself toward a new object. The map of female sexuality in this story is far less clear, either in terms of the wife or of her friend/rival, the hairdresser. Some clues to female sexuality may lie in the first paragraph where the narrator describes the husband in curiously religious terms:

> Para cumplir con una promesa, durante la internación de Rosalía, se dejó crecer la barba. Gracias a esa circunstancia el fotógrafo Ersalis, sin cobrarle nada, para propaganda, lo fotografió y expuso en el escaparate de la tienda la fotografía cuya copia en un marco de madera, está colgada sobre la cabecera de la cama matrimonial. Cuando Rosalía, de noche, se arrodillaba a rezar, la presencia de ese cuadro le parecía un *sacrilegio;* ahora, como si el marido fuera un *santo,* la aceptaba como algo natural. Es claro que al rato de mirar el retrato, a pesar de la barba sedosa y negra que llama la atención como un adorno *religioso,* la mujer más desprevenida o depravada advierte que el barbudo tiene cejas de *demonio* y probablemente olor a sapo o a culebra. (156, emphasis added)

> [In order to fulfill a promise, during Rosalia's internment, he let his beard grow. Thanks to that circumstance the photographer Ersalis photographed him free of charge as advertisement and displayed the photograph in the shop window, a copy of which in a wood frame is hanging over the headboard of their double bed. When Rosalia at night would kneel to pray, the presence of that picture used to seem like a *sacrilege;* now as if her husband were a *saint,* she accepts it as natural. It is clear that after looking at the portrait for a while in spite of the silky black beard that calls attention to itself as a *religious* adornment, the most incautious or depraved woman notes that the bearded man has the eyebrows of the *devil* and probably the smell of a toad or a snake.]

The beard, obviously a symbol of male difference, elevates this man's photo to the level of religious icon not only for his wife but for the town where his picture hangs in a photographer's shop window; henceforth the narrator identifies him as "el barbudo." The worship of maleness is one way religion has been defined, and Ocampo's ironic association of a bearded man with God appears in other stories as well.[9] The reference to the divine moves to its opposite pole in this passage, becoming first sacrilegious and then diabolical: the photograph's flaunting of male privilege appears as a sacrilege for the wife because of its positioning in the place (literally, above the bed) of religious icon, while for the narrator its religious overtones reveal the demonic character of this man and his probable reptilian smell. Jane Gallop makes much of the olfactory sense in one of her most audacious chapters of *The Daughter's Seduction,* pointing out that Freud's discussion of sexual difference relies in part on the degradation of smell in our culture.[10] If male desire depends on the visible, the female is more responsive to the other senses, particularly those of touch and smell. The impossible attribution of smell to the photograph suggests the diabolical nature of the male, but also perhaps to the narrator's arousal.

That her arousal, or the photograph that occasions it, is evil seems further corroborated in the two adjectives used to describe the photograph's potential female viewers: "desprevenida" means "incautious" or just "unprepared," and "depravada" means "depraved" or "morally bad, corrupt." The two female characters, the innocent wife and the treacherous narrator, may provide illustrations of the adjectives in question. In any case, they present two oppositions constantly at work in Ocampo's world, a duo we will have occasion to study in detail below. Here, as elsewhere, they are rivals for a male whose desire for each is seen as "algo natural" and at the same time, demonic: arbitrary, bewildering, and cruel. The male is crazy-making in the vacillation of his desire as observed here in Rosalía's pain and domestic disorder. Rosalía is surrounded by a demonic husband and deceitful friend. Of the two, the female comes off even worse than the revolting, philandering husband. As the narrator herself says, he is not so bad because he is "just like all men."[11]

The mechanism of desire in "El asco" finds its parallel in a later story, "La boda." Both stories begin with a similar premise, that a young woman marries a man for whom she feels physical disgust, and again, the narrator of "La boda" describes her aversion to her intended husband in terms of masculine difference. Instead of the luxurious beard of the first story, the man's body hair makes him too grossly masculine for her taste: "Parecía, por más que no lo fuera, siempre sucio" (*I* 38) [He seemed, although he was not, to be always dirty]. Here the wife's hospitalization for insanity is mentioned explicitly. One word from the first sentence of the earlier story, "El asco," now strikes the reader as significant, "internación": for what and for how long was Rosalía committed? The story never answers this question. Of course in Spanish the word may mean that she was hospitalized for a physical illness, but, as in English, the suggestion of insanity is unmistakable. The husbands of both stories attempt to please their wives with gifts, to no avail. The one gesture that occasions a conversion to "true love" is the appearance of a rival for the husband's affection. Ocampo represents sexual difference here and elsewhere as extremely subtle. Her stories validate several theoretical speculations regarding the female's lesser reliance on the visual field, her greater responsiveness to touch and smell. Unlike theorists of psychoanalysis however, Ocampo's fiction insists that feminine sexuality, like male sexuality, operates according to the basic mechanisms of desire. If their psychic motivation is the same, why do the fictions so often forgive the male for behaving "just like all men" while the female characters are polarized between the foolish innocents and the conniving hypocrites, between "desprevenida" and "depravada?" Ocampo's works suggest that conventions of romance dictate each character type.

"La paciente y el médico" contains two first-person narrators, the first a young woman who feigns illness, and the second, the doctor who treats her. Their contrasting account of the same events illustrates important points at issue here. The female speaks first and describes the workings of her own sexual response on the register described by Gallop of touching and smell: "Detrás de un biombo me desvestí para que me auscultara. Anotó mis datos personales y mi historia clínica sin mirarme. Cuando colocó su cabeza sobre mi pecho, es cierto que aspiré el perfume de su pelo y que aprecié el color castaño de sus rizos" (*F* 125) [Behind a screen I undressed so that he could examine me. He made note of my personal and clinical history without looking at me. When he put his head on my breast, it is true that I breathed in the perfume of his hair and appreciated the brown color of his curls] . Later, the doctor gives his version of the same moment: "Cuando entró en mi consultorio y la vi por primera vez me interesó" (129) [When she entered the examining room and I saw her for the first time she interested me]. In that first moment, male desire is initiated by sight, the female's by smell; the male acknowledges his desire, the female only hints at hers.

The curious use of a photograph as religious icon, as in "El asco," is here transformed into a fantastic device. The attraction of the first scene leads patient and doctor to a brief flirtation, but the doctor quickly tires of it, and in order to get rid of this adoring patient he presents her with his portrait. Her version recalls that he gave it to her saying that she could hang it above the bed and ask the picture for advice, adding, "Puedes rezarle, ¿acaso no rezas a los santos?" (125) [You can pray to it, after all, don't you pray to saints?]. The photograph becomes a hidden camera in the girl's room that he is powerless to shut off; the doctor can see and hear her every movement, a situation he describes as "una suerte de castigo" [a kind of punishment]. After years of sending him gifts and feigning illness, she plans a faked suicide attempt to force him to attend to her at home. The doctor, who already knows her scheme thanks to the magical photograph, delays his arrival in order to give the drug she has taken plenty of time to kill her.

Many of Ocampo's female narrators demonstrate an acute awareness of themselves as objects (or not) of male desire despite their status in the narrative as subjects of their own discourse. This narrator summarizes toward the end of her account: "Me trató como los niños tratan a sus juguetes: los primeros días los miran con avidez, les besan los ojos cuando son muñecos, los acarician cuando son automóviles, y luego, cuando ya saben cómo se les puede hacer gritar o chocar, los abandonan en un rincón" (128) [He treated me like children treat their toys: the first days they look at them intensely, they kiss their eyes if they are dolls, they caress them if they are cars, and later, when they know how to make them cry or crash, they abandon them in a corner]. The female describes herself readily as object, while the male who has ill used her is compared with a child whose violence and abandonment are viewed as normal. She has much more trouble acknowledging even to herself the manipulative operations of her own desire. This narrator attempts, like the male characters of previous stories, to woo the object of her affection by giving gifts; when that effort fails, she attempts the opposite tack, threatening him with loss of herself. Occasionally, in other stories at least, that tactic proves effective as the loss of the lover inspires unexpected passion. Here, it seems, her stratagem will not work. In her final paragraph, however, she attempts to persuade herself not that she loves him with what is clearly an unreasonable and masochistic passion, but that he loves her: "Yo no me resigné a ese abandono porque sospecho que Edgardo tuvo que librar una batalla consigo mismo para abandonarme" (128) [I refused to resign myself to that abandonment because I suspect that Edgardo had to battle with himself in order to abandon me]. Again, the reader is allowed little sympathy with the female speaker. Ocampo's narrative judges both male and female characters harshly, but if anything, the petulant, fantasy-ridden female is even less attractive than the cynical doctor, who is at least honest with himself if not with his patient. The inability of the romance plot, and language in general, to express female desire necessitates a hypocrisy on the part of female characters which becomes one of Ocampo's most important critiques of conventional gender positioning.

If the female is frequently depicted as hypocritical because of her inability to acknowledge (sexual) desire, the male has the opposite problem: He is overwhelmed by its irrational power. The inexplicable nature of love's object, its accidental quality, especially for the male is a constant source of humor in Ocampo's works. Several of Ocampo's stories seem to take up Lacan's theory of metonymy as the mechanism of desire, and by exaggerating the notion of the part for the whole, poke fun at the romance plot.[12] The male narrator of "Mi amada," for instance, focuses on his beloved's beautiful hair, and eventually has to ask himself: "Cómo podría comprender que yo amé (aparentemente) una parte de ella más que a ella misma?" (*Ldn* 123) [How could she understand that I (apparently) loved a part of her more than herself]. The sensuous long hair of "Mi amada" is reduced to a wig in "La peluca." The female narrator accuses her lover of falling for another woman because of his fascination with her wig, suggesting that the part does not even have to be an integral one in order to initiate the mechanism of desire; once desire is started it has a momentum of its own which fails to reevaluate in the face of logic or new information, because it lies outside the control of consciousness.[13] Desire in Ocampo's works, like other magical occurrences, is a completely irrational and unexplainable force, more irrational, uncontrollable and inexplicable than fantastic or grotesque events which often accompany it in Ocampo's stories.

Female desire is made visible in "La gallina de membrillo" even if it can be expressed only indirectly. The story depicts a fantastically manipulative female character, but concludes that men not only tolerate but demand the kind of deception she practices. Rosaura Pringles uses fairly normal feminine wiles, such as perfume and false eyelashes, but also flirts with men in a most unusual way by speaking as if she were her dog Blanquita Simara:

> No sólo expresaba lo que Blanquita hubiera dicho en tal y cual circunstancia, sino que remedaba la voz que le atribuía: una voz de acuerdo a su idiosincrasia, que era mezcla de niño mimado, de negro de las Antillas y de viejito provinciano tartamudo. ¿Qué mujer, cuando vale algo, no es juguetona? Ella misma decía "Soy Blanquita."
> (*I* 117)

[Not only did she express what Blanquita would have said in such and such a circumstance, but she modified the voice she attributed to him: a voice in accordance with her idiosyncrasy, which was a mixture of pampered child, Caribbean black, and little old provincial man with a stammer. What woman worth anything is not playful? She herself would say, "I am Blanquita."]

This story's exaggerations make it particularly revealing as a study of female posturing and of male desire. The central episode relates her lover's violent insistence that Rosaura come away with him. He threatens, revolver in hand, to kill her and then himself if she refuses. At first she responds in the voice of Blanquita about the practical impossibilities of this scheme: She would have to leave her shop, they would have no money, her tastes run to expensive things, and so forth. If her voice is ridiculous her words, for the most part, are not. When he continues with renewed urgency and more physical directness she is frightened into taking up her own voice and at the same time a litany of romantic clichés. At the conclusion of this second speech, the man has disappeared. Frightened at the sound of Rosaura's real voice, does he flee from her because of the discovery of so much artifice or, as Ocampo's story hints, at the idea of her ceasing to use any? One phrase confirms that Rosaura's procedure was a deliberate strategy to frighten him off: "respondió . . . aterrada, con su propia voz, por primera vez, para asustar al hombre" (119) [she responded . . . terrified, with her true voice, for the first time in order to frighten the man]. Her subsequent self-satisfaction at the escape further reinforces the impression of conscious calculation. She straightens her hair and clothes, then says:

—Si no vuelve tu mamá a casa le comerán toda la sopita y van a dejarla sin postre. La voz divina de Blanquita Simara resonó en sus labios con la misma gracia de siempre; Rosaura se encaminó a su casa llevando consigo ese Sésamo ábrete de los corazones, que le permitiría gozar aún del amor. (*I* 120)

["If your mommy doesn't get home they are going to eat all the soup and leave her without dessert." The divine voice of Blanquita Simara resounded on her lips with same charm as always; Rosaura headed for home carrying with her that open, Sesame, of hearts which would permit her to continue to enjoy the pleasures of love.]

Rosaura may seem like a dumb broad, but she knows what she is doing. She seems to understand that the male cannot tolerate a direct expression of female desire, hence, she veils her "self" in an affected voice and an array of female adornments. Ironically, when she wants to get rid of the man, she has nothing more to do than to use a sincere voice, to express a direct (but insincere) passionate feeling. The fulfillment of desire kills it completely—the lover gets what he desired, and instantly no longer desires it. Rosaura's little piece of theater recalls Mary Ann Doane's discussion of masquerade as one way in which "to effect a separation between the cause of desire and oneself."[14] Doane quotes Michelle Montrelay's argument in which she suggests that this kind of ploy, the body as disguise, serves the woman as a means to evade masculine law. Rosaura utilizes the stratagem of the masquerade, "the excess of femininity," to inspire and then confound male desire and hence permit herself to "gozar aún del amor," i.e., to follow the directions of her own desire.

Rosaura began both her more conventional flirtatious activities and the odd stratagem of speaking as her dog only upon the reappearance of her husband who had abandoned her without explanation twenty years previously and at the beginning of the story had just as inexplicably returned. Though his return initiates the narrative and serves as its motivation, he remains a somewhat minor figure in a story that concentrates on the portrait of Rosaura, her relationship to the dog, and to other men of her acquaintance. The only description provided of the husband is, in fact, filtered through the dog's impression of him, or rather, the narrator's speculation of the dog's reaction: "Rómulo Pringles llegó con un cargamento de valija, con menos pelo, pero mayor mandíbula, lo que le confirió un aire feroz que no desagradaba a Rosaura, pero sí a Blanquita Simara, que descubrió en el hombre, así lo sospecho, pretensiones de animal" (116) [Romulo Pringles arrived with a load of luggage, with less hair, but larger jaw, which conferred on him a ferocious air which was not displeasing to Rosaura, but was to Blanquita Simara, who discovered in the man, I suspect, pretensions to animal status]. As the story progresses, it is equally the case that Blanquita Simara has pretensions to being human.

The first phrase that Rosaura says in her new pose as voice-of-dog is a plea to her tenant, Manuel Grasín, to move out to allow the husband to return:

—¿Manuel Grasín, que es tan bueno, no nos dejará el cuarto, para que podamos alojar a papá? Por difícil que sea conseguir alojamiento, Manuel Grasín lo encontrará y vendrá a visitarnos y a traernos huesitos de la confitería, y alguna vez, para mamá, una gallinita de membrillo. (*I* 117)

[Manuel Grasín, who is so sweet, won't he let us have his room so that we can house Papa? Even though it may be difficult to find lodging, Manuel Grasín will find it and then he will come visit us and bring us bones from the deli and once in a while, for Mama, a little quince candy in the shape of a chicken.]

The linguistic complications of this speech are evident: Rosaura pronounces them in direct address to Manuel Grasín, but grammatically, the speaker is the dog speaking to Rosaura *about* Manuel Grasín. As silly and affected as this may seem, the success of the tactic in the case of Manuel Grasín assures her continued use of it. The story's title and its concluding line, which again refers to the "gallina de membrillo" [quince chicken] confirm his, and by extension, other men's approval of her ploy. Rosaura's use of "mamá" and "papá" in speaking for the dog inevitably places Blanquita Simara in the position of child. The all-female shop workers also take up the position of children with respect to this "family" and respond with sibling-like jealousy to the special privileges accorded to the dog. The Oedipal competition in this "family" is acted out one night when Rómulo Pringles tries to strike the dog and Rosaura defends him. This is the last mention in the story of Rómulo Pringles. Rosaura begins to flirt openly with men and to speak through the male/child/dog once her husband has returned. The sequencing of events suggests that she seeks revenge for the twenty years of disgrace his absence had inflicted on her and possibly for his aggression against Blanquita Simara. Desire, then, has its impetus from a source that remains partially covered over. And it is set into motion by the reappearance of the father's/law's representative. The husband was more effective as law when absent.[15]

The narrator's impossible positioning is particularly complex in this story. The voice speaks in first person, defines himself as masculine—"soy testigo" [I am witness]—and can be read as one more of Rosaura's besotted admirers by virtue of the positive adjectives used to describe behavior that the reader will view as either silly, manipulative, or both. The intimate information that he divulges about Rosaura's activities finally make his observations difficult to attach to a single character: He becomes another "scandal" of point of view since some of the positions he occupies are clearly incompatible according to narrative conventions. For instance, the interplay of pronouns in one dialog suggests either that the *yo* and the character Manuel Grasín are both present during the conversation or that they are one and the same person:

> *Yo* temía que la vida de Blanquita Simara estuviera en peligro y se lo dije a Rosaura, que respondió, con voz adorable:
> —Tiene siete vidas. Tenemos un Dios aparte.
> Al oír esto, *Manuel Grasín* se tranquilizó.
> *Yo* la seguí aquel día. (*I* 118, emphasis mine)

> [*I* was afraid that Blanquita Simara's life was in danger and I told Rosaura, who responded with her adorable voice: "He has seven lives. We have our own special god." On hearing this *Manuel Grasin* calmed down. *I* followed her that day.]

In any case, the judgments this narrator makes in describing Rosaura's behavior form part of the humor and irony of this story: words like *divina, adorable, irresistible, encanto* [enchantment] and *gracia* [charm] impart a validation of behavior the reader is unlikely to share. I would also argue that these are words that derive from a feminized discourse unlikely to be utilized by a male speaker. The impossible positioning of the narrator within the plot together with these verbal slips associate "his" perspective with that of Rosaura herself, making the male-voiced description a particularly narcissistic mirroring. The sliding of identity and even of gender categories with respect to the narrator draws attention to the dog's sexual ambiguity: He is male, but is referred to by a feminine name because "no parecía un macho, sino una hembra" (116) [he didn't look like a male, but rather a female]. Rosaura speaks through a male dog who appears to be feminine, while the narrator speaks with masculine pronouns but describes events from a female perspective, that of the main character, in feminine language. "La gallina de membrillo" represents a complex destablizing of gender surrounding romance in which the calculation attributed to the female is countered equally by the absurdity of the males in falling for it.

Another story explores the fantastic and grotesque aspects of male desire, this time narrated overtly in first-person by the "object" herself. "La expiación," presents a grotesque version of the romance plot which contains elements crucial to Ocampo's narrative practice, including a narrator described by Silvia Molloy as having "esa curiosa mezcla de comprensión

y de narcisismo que tan frecuentemente caracteriza a los per-
sonajes femeninos de estos relatos" [That curious mixture of
comprehension and narcissism which so frequently characterizes the female characters of these stories].[16] The unnamed
narrator begins her story with the final moments, providing
background information in the form of extensive italicized
flashback segments. These relate the couple's friendship with
Ruperto whose insistent, finally pornographic, stare haunts both
the narrator and her husband, Antonio: "Ruperto no era un
hombre: era un par de ojos, sin cara, sin voz, sin cuerpo; así me
parecía" (I 105) [Ruperto was not a man but a pair of eyes without face, without voice, without body; that is how he seemed to
me]. Ruperto represents an exaggeration of the male gaze, whose
obvious expression of desire elicits Antonio's jealousy. Antonio
abandons the marriage bed to sleep in a back room of the house,
an absence that reignites the narrator's desire. Her wish to relive
their first passionate moments is fulfilled, however, when Antonio returns to the bed during a night of carnival when his friend
Ruperto is invited to sleep over with them and occupies the
extra room. At this point, the narrator assumes life has returned
to normal, and she recognizes what other Ocampo characters
only intuit, that the third party is essential to the continuance
of their passion: "se hubiera dicho que aquellas miradas eran
indispensables para nuestro amor" (112) [one could have said
that those glances were indispensable for our love].

The directions of desire in this bizarre story are complicated
by the obvious doubling of the two men, who have been friends
since childhood. The narrator admits to feeling jealous because
of their friendship. Jealousy and desire circulate in all directions
here culminating in a climax which spells tragedy for all. Antonio blinds his friend Ruperto and then attempts to do the same
to himself. The narrator explains her husband's motivations in
terms consistent with Lacan's theories of the gaze: "Comprendí
el dolor que él habría soportado para sacrificar ... los ojos de
Ruperto, su amigo, y los de él, para que no pudieran mirarme,
pobrecitos, nunca más" (112) [I understood the pain that he
must have borne in order to sacrifice ... Ruperto's eyes, those
of his friend and his own, so that they could not look at me,
poor things, ever again]. Once the tension of Ruperto's unful-
filled desire is eliminated—and his desire is eliminated by
blinding—the mechanism of desire is cut off for the other two
as well. Antonio's final gesture seems destined not to the extinc-
tion of his own desire, which was snuffed simultaneously with

Ruperto's, but as an expiation (as the title indicates) for the damage to his friend.

"La expiación" repeats themes of masquerade and narcissism as mechanisms of female *modus operandi*. Like Rosaura of "La gallina de membrillo," this narrator operates with keen awareness of her position as object of the men's desire. The trivializing commentary regarding preoccupations with her personal appearance contribute to the grotesque, rather than the tragic, feel of this narrative. In the moment of Ruperto's blinding, for instance, she expresses a concern about getting her hair rolled while it is still wet; in the final scene, she wants to look in the mirror instead of attending to Antonio's confession. As narrator, she speaks her position as object, but in declaring her desire for her husband, fully constitutes herself as subject. She narrates as subject her position as object of their desire. Doane claims that the "masquerade doubles representation."[17] As Doane suggests, the dual perspective of the narrator of "La expiación" calls into question the absolute opposition of the two categories "subject" and "object." This story's narrator undoes the "syntax" of the narration itself in collapsing subject and object. The intensity of doubling in "La expiación" reflects Ocampo's obsessive use of this trope in her work as a whole. I return to it now, not as a fantastic or grotesque device, but as a specifically feminine one. Ocampo's stories of female doubles further destabilize the image of the feminine as undesiring.

THE MAD DOUBLE

I have chosen to return to this admittedly obsessive figure in Ocampo's work because I consider its grotesque and fantastic implications secondary to its significance as part of her reevaluation of the feminine.[18] Ocampo's doubles construct a code not broken by the numerous studies of the *doppelganger* but understood more effectively by works attentive to a specifically feminine mode. The studies of Rank, Rogers, Keppler, and others cannot be applied fully to female-authored fiction simply by rewriting their definitions or conclusions in nonsexist language. Feminist literary theory has had much to say about the very different dynamics to be observed in women writers's use of this device.[19] Naomi Schor defines feminine literary difference itself as a double consciousness which manifests itself in the linguistic dimension of subject-object and on the level of ideology in which, for instance, women perceive themselves as both part and not part of a given social class. Many of Ocampo's narratives depict tales of sexual desire centering, like "La expiación," on the complex relationships of three people. These romantic triangles speak intimately to issues of subjectivity, because they enact an allegory of the individual psyche, which Lacan describes as constituted through a split and activated by desire.[20] The intensity of these narratives indicates that more is at stake than the simple romantic tale. These stories deal with feminine imaging and identity, and the very functioning of the unconscious.

The romantic triangle is explored in Ocampo's works from every conceivable vantage. Several stories depict a pair of male doubles in pursuit of a single female ("El impostor," "El vástago," "Nosotros," and "El rival"), all narrated by one partner of the doubled character. "La expiación," as we have just seen, permits a female narrator's perspective on the dynamics of male doubling. The opposite vantage, in which a male voice describes his complex relationship with dual female characters, is operative in "La casa de azúcar," "El fantasma" and "Casi el reflejo." Ocampo's stories that focus on female pairs, narrated by one of the doubled characters, present the female version of Lacan's split subject. The narrator no longer positions herself as object, but as a doubled subject of desire. Ironically, perhaps, these are some of Ocampo's most violent and painful stories.

Ocampo's first volume, *Viaje olvidado,* contains a series of stories preoccupied with the most primitive type of double, what Keppler calls the "Twin Brother." Even though the tales may not present biological twins (and in several cases are "sisters" rather than brothers), they do depict characters with "a special closeness, . . . each constituting one of a pair or dual unit, the inseparable and also inescapable half of a single whole."[21] Ocampo's first dual protagonists, two little girls, one rich and the other poor, are further fragmented into still other doubles. In "Las dos casas de Olivos," each girl, so like her "twin" that their parents do not notice when they switch places, has, in addition, her own guardian angel. In "La siesta en el cedro," one of the spiritual twins has a biological twin as well. These early stories embody the identification associated with doubles; their differences, always those of social class, are imposed externally by the enemy, the uncomprehending adult world bent on maintaining difference. The accidents of social and economic difference succeed in separating the twins of the early stories except the two girls from Olivos who after death ascend to a heaven without economic divisions: "No había casas ni grandes ni pequeñas, ni de lata ni de ladrillos" (83) [There were no houses, neither big nor small, neither made of tin nor of brick].[22] The other "twins" of Ocampo's fiction appear in *La furia y otros cuentos* and are male. None of the doubled adult female characters can be considered twins in the sense Keppler describes, characters united by their similarity. Rather, they are the more common kind of doubled character, antagonists.

In Ocampo's fiction this relationship viewed from within, that is, from the perspective of one of the female characters, is extremely troubling. Among the narratives most noted for their violence and grotesque cruelty are several that involve an intense hatred between two women, a hatred marked by a lack of motivation.[23] One of Ocampo's narrators, herself a short story writer (and doubled character), comments upon the process of developing a fictional character who has decided to commit suicide and her own lack of interest in the issue of motivation: "¿Qué es lo que motiva su resolución? Nunca llegué a determinarlo, porque me parecía superfluo, fastidioso de escribir" (*F* 13) [What was it that movivated his resolution? I never succeeded in determining it because it seemed superfluous, tedious to write]. Like her character, Ocampo as author works and reworks the theme of female hostility without seeming to examine its origins. That her female doubles have no "reasons" for their extreme reactions makes the power of their emotions all the more perplexing and ominous. The reader reacts to these stories with a degree of horror that places them within the world of the grotesque. They can be better understood, however, by reading them as part of a dynamic recognized by Sandra Gilbert and Susan Gubar as a recurrent one within women's literature throughout the nineteenth and well into the twentieth centuries. Gilbert and Gubar show that the woman writer has had to "come to terms with the images . . . , those mythic masks male artists have fastened over her human face. Specifically, a woman writer must examine, assimilate, and transcend the extreme images of 'angel' and 'monster' which male authors have generated for her. Before we women can write, declared Virginia Woolf, we must 'kill the angel in the house'."[24] An analysis of Ocampo's stories involving female doubles reveals that the rage they express does have a "reason," however buried, and that by exploring these works in light of Gilbert's and Gubar's perceptions one may trace the ways in which Silvina Ocampo has examined, assimilated, and finally transcended the extreme images embedded in her own creative imagination.

Gilbert and Gubar argue that the image of woman as domestic angel (passive, silent, and possessing no "story of her own") absolutely denies the possibility of artistic creativity.[25] Since a female writer could not, by definition, adhere to the ideal of the "angel in the house," her act of writing necessarily amounted to a "poetic presumption intimately connected with madness, freakishness, and monstrosity." Not surprisingly, the female artist who deals with the mad double in literature identifies herself with the mad half of the pair. "What this means . . . is that the madwoman in literature by women is not merely, as she might be in male literature, an antagonist or foil to the heroin. Rather, she is usually in some sense the *author*'s double, an image of her own anxiety and rage."[26] Or to put it in Keppler's terminology, male authors identify themselves with the "good" double, the one who represents society's version of the ideal, while female authors identify with the "evil" double, what Keppler describes in terms surprisingly apt for Lacanian terminology as the "menacing real."[27] In their long analysis of Grimm's fairy tale "Little Snow White" Gilbert and Gubar point out that the evil queen and the innocent princess are two parts of the same person, and the prototype of the mad double in women's literature: "The Queen is a plotter, a plot-maker, a schemer, a witch, an artist, an impersonator, a woman of almost infinite creative energy, witty, wily, and self-absorbed as all artists traditionally are. On the other hand, in her absolute chastity, her frozen innocence, her sweet nullity, Snow White represents precisely the ideal of 'contemplative purity,' . . . an angel in the house of myth."[28] The evil queen's actions ultimately result in her own destruction, a danger that explains literary women's urgency to work their way through and ultimately to abandon both these images of themselves.

Ironically, Ocampo's first story to display the female plot pattern is "El impostor" whose male antagonists act out a set of female identifications. Armando Heredia as the monstrous author creates the narrator, Luis, who acts as an emissary of the father, and represents Armando's notion of the father's ideal. The ending takes the reader so by surprise not just because the presumed writer of the text is fictional, but because Ocampo has inverted a familiar pattern: the monstrous double, Armando, ends by killing off his ideal invented self, Luis, instead of the reverse. The self-destruction of the process is highlighted because the two characters are ultimately revealed to be one and the same: The murder is really a suicide. A retrospective reading uncovers the hidden plot of human agony about individual inability to live up to an ideal (or, in Lacanian terminology, to represent the phallus).[29] I do not want to suggest that the story does not work as a study of male characters; on the contrary, it imagines an anxiety inherent to the human condition regardless of gender that male writers seldom contemplate so poignantly. As already discussed in chapter 1, the critique of the patriarchal order itself is also more evident here than in classic male-authored texts. A female author writes feelingly about the possibility of killing off our culture's ideal, an ideal which is far more harmful to women than to men. What "El impostor" demonstrates so graphically, even if in male guise, is that killing the angel in the house means for many women writers killing off part of themselves.[30]

Ocampo's work following the 1948 publication of "El impostor" produces a number of female doubles which follow a roughly chronological path in resolving the Snow White plot pattern dominated by the monster/angel duo. *La furia y otros cuentos* (1959) and *Las invitadas* (1961) contain several narratives which perfectly reproduce the Snow White model as well as others which modify the pattern in significant ways. Finally, two stories of *Los días de la noche* (1970) produce female doubles which no longer repeat the destructive, hate-filled patterns of previous narratives.

"Carta perdida en un cajón" fully reproduces the Snow White plot constellation of madwoman/author, obsessed with passive angel, and terminating in the self-destruction of the former. Here the first-person narrator describes her intense loathing for a woman which dates from their childhood together. The irrational obsession is motivated in part by jealousy, first of the popularity with other children and later of the interest of a man. But, as the narrator admits, she never really had any interest in either of them except to deprive the girl, the unnamed *tú*, of other friends. The story, simultaneously a confession and a suicide note, plots the ultimate destruction. The narrator believes that her irrational hatred has brought the narrator and her lover together, that their love is sustained by her envy and loathing. Her suicide is, in her own mind, a form of murder:

Quiero que sepas que debes tu felicidad al ser que más te desdeña y aborrece en el mundo. Una vez que ese ser que te adorna con su envidia y te embellece con su odio desaparezca, tu dicha concluirá con mi vida y la terminación de esta carta. (*F* 94)

[I want you to know that you owe your happiness to the being who most disdains and hates you. Once this person who adorns you with her envy and beautifies you with her hatred disappears, your happines will end with my life and the end of this letter.]

She will most effectively destroy her enemy by destroying herself. The notion that a loving couple is held together by the desire and jealousy of a third person repeats elements of "La expiación" and other stories, while the conflation of murder and suicide, as in "El impostor," signals the flimsy boundaries between self and other, their status as double. The point of view centers on the "monstrous author," who, as Gilbert and Gubar suggest, is seen as infinitely creative. She is engaged in writing (the suicide note/short story) and has created with her very hatred the happiness of two other people. The angelic double in this story is appropriately remembered as a child throughout much of the narrative, and appears to remain innocently unaware of the narrator's machinations. The ending perpetrates a complicated revenge, but its salient characteristic is its self-destruction of the author/narrator. The ferocity of her language as evidenced in the passages quoted at no time seems justified by the events she narrates. This disparity between language and events prohibits any sympathy with her, and hence, creates one of Ocampo's most horrifying monsters.

"La continuación," like "Carta perdida en un cajón," presents itself as a sort of suicide letter, but its ambiguous ending creates an important modification in the Snow White plot. The narrator is a professional writer who becomes so involved with her invented story that she begins to live it out in her own life. Events lead to her hatred of another woman, to her creation of a love relationship between this woman and her own lover, and ultimately to her suicide or disappearance. She had intended to rid herself of all that she cared about in the world, and then kill herself, but she found unexpectedly that life without encumbrances (presumably lovers, children, friends), viewed from the perspective of imminent death has become unexpectedly precious. The letter concludes with an ambiguous farewell, leaving the suicide in doubt. The narrator's absorption in her work, her desire for exile from a normal life, are elements recognizable in women's dilemma of creativity. The story's insistence on the writing process underscores Gilbert's and Gubar's argument that the author herself identifies with the monster of her own fiction. In "La continuación," the "angel" figure, always somewhat shadowy in all literature, scarcely appears; the woman creator/narrator looms in the story's foreground as a self-described monster. She equates her activities in divesting herself of roles as lover, nurturer, and friend to crimes.[31] Most readers will concur with this assessment, for her descriptions of the betrayal of friendship and love, particularly her deliberate humiliation of a young boy, are morally abhorrent, if not strictly illegal. But, significantly, this character's activities, even crimes, though they clearly denote her as monstrous in her own mind, do not necessarily imply her destruction. The suicide is left as one possible resolution, not absolutely inevitable.[32]

A suicide has already occurred when "Rhadamanthos" opens, but in this story the angel figure is the woman who died. In contrast to "Carta perdida en un cajón" and "La continuación," where suicide is threatened by the evil narrator, the victim here is the unnamed and despised "friend." Her death, or at least the attention surrounding her funeral, illustrate to the demented narrator, Virginia, the dead woman's potential power as angelic figure even beyond the tomb, for now she can become a kind of family saint. To forestall such an eventuality, Virginia creates false love letters, twenty of which she writes in one night, in order to destroy even more fully the image of the "angel in the house." The letters are addressed to the suicide victim and attributed to a non-existent lover, "revelando en ellas, con toda suerte de subterfugios, la vida monstruosa, impura, que le atribuía" (*I* 144) [revealing in them, with all kinds of subterfuge, the monstrous, impure life that I attributed to her]. The last lines of the story describe Virginia's success in secreting the letters into one of the dead woman's dresser drawers. She attempts to destroy the angelic quality of the dead woman by attributing to her a sexuality that defies one crucial element of the angel myth, chastity. Ocampo's madwoman of "Rhadamanthos" deviates from the Snow White model by avoiding self-destruction. Except in her isolation from the warm and loving family group, she remains healthy and intact and associated with mythical gods, the unmerciful judge of Greek mythology, Rhadamanthos, in the magnitude of her evil. The issue beneath the surface of all these narratives, however, is the hidden menace of the angel figure. Shadowy, sometimes dimly hidden in the margins of the text, she powerfully obsesses the monstrous narrators. Even the excesses of a Virginia cannot truly eliminate her influence.

The hidden power of the passive angel figure finds its expression in "El lazo," where both characters appear to be equally mad and equally evil, the bitter hatred between them completely mutual. The narrator murders a victim who has become a truly diabolical version of the "angel in the house." Though seen (through the eyes of the first-person narrator, of course) in many stances of domestic activity, she is now far from innocently unaware of the fierce emotion she inspires in the "monster." She is keenly cognizant of her power, and actively flirts with her doom, daring the narrator to lose control and lash out at her. The conclusion describes the narrator, goaded beyond endurance by one of her insults, slitting Valentina's throat with a surgical scalpel. The final sentence, "Muerta, su voz furiosamente alegre continuaba resonando por las salas y corredores del dispensario" (*I* 133) [Dead, her voice furiously happy continued resounding through the rooms and corredors of the clinic], reads like a classic horror story. The narrator presents herself as a kind of victim in her attempt to do what the story depicts as impossible, to eliminate the manipulative angel figure. The latter, dispossessed of her childlike passivity, exposes her potential malevolence. In fact, the hidden aggression of the angel figure has been long suspected in literature: "Finally, the fact that the angel woman manipulates her domestic/mystical sphere in order to ensure the well-being of those entrusted to her care reveals that she *can* manipulate; she can scheme; she can plot—stories as well as strategies."[33] In "El lazo," the two sides of the woman myth are conceived of as equal adversaries and equally destructive. No longer is the creative half of this duel unto death presented as self-destructive in her impotent rage or as a murderous Rhadamanthos, but as an unwilling actress in an absurd and grotesque drama from which she cannot escape.

"El lazo" represents a pivotal point in Ocampo's creative activity, for after its appearance the stories of rage and cruelty between women undergo one more metamorphosis before finally disappearing. In her subsequent story collection, *Los días de la noche,* the strange story, "Las vestiduras peligrosas," takes up the angel/monster dichotomy, but with the images blurred in significant ways. The monstrous creator, Artemia, is a beautiful and sensuous artist, a dress designer whose works destroy other women and ultimately herself. Despite her association with the powerful and destructive goddess, Artemis, however, Artemia fails to elicit the same kind of unmitigated revulsion experienced with Ocampo's other monstrous females. The story, as perverse and disturbing as any Ocampo has written, does present a self-destructive artist, but she is no longer the narrator. The story is told by an unappealing domestic "angel" whose hypocritical, self-serving commentary signals her hidden hostility. Furthermore, the "angelic" half of this double, as an "author" in her own right, leads Artemia, if only indirectly, to her death. The angel and monster figures here are impossibly blurred, setting the conditions for their disappearance altogether.

Two stories put a new twist on the angel/monster dichotomy. "Las esclavas de las criadas" and "Keif" contain female doubles which eliminate the animosity evident in previous stories. Both present powerful, creative female characters, but within relationships notable for loyalty and support. "Las esclavas de las criadas" focuses on a servant who magically defends her dying mistress from abusive, hypocritical friends and relatives. Herminia's fantastic powers avenge the mistress and restore her to health. The odd insistence on Herminia's devotion to the mistress's personal belongings, especially to her embalmed wild animals ("fieras embalsamadas"), finds an echo in the subsequent story, where one of the animals seems to have come to life. "Keif" describes the exotic Fedora's life with the tiger named in the story's title. Fedora involves the narrator, a female friend, in a plan that is to transform the lives of both women. In the conclusion, Fedora commits suicide and is reincarnated as a young circus performer, while the narrator inherits Fedora's house and estate. Fedora orchestrates her own fate and that of her friend and is credited with fantastic powers, but there is no suggestion here of "monstrosity." The absence of female hostility in both stories signals another difference, another absence. In all the narratives discussed previously, the competition for favors from the male is either quite overt as in "Carta perdida en un cajón," "La continuación," and "Las vestiduras peligrosas," or is partially hidden as in "Rhadamanthos," "La furia," and "El lazo." The two stories of adult female friendship present women economically and emotionally allied only to each other.

Both "Esclavas de las criadas" and "Keif" suggest that at least one of the characters is independently wealthy. The former simply eliminates the male altogether, while the latter transforms the male presence in a most unusual way. The story's title refers to Fedora's pet tiger, but in effect delays revealing exactly what Keif is (the reader knows only that he is large and dangerous,

and likened to a dog in several descriptions), while its first sentences clearly lead the reader to think he is a man: "Keif era
misterioso. Conservo una fotografía de cuando era muy joven. . . . Lo conocí una tarde de enero . . ." (*Ldn* 190) [Keif was
mysterious. I keep a photograph of when he was very young . . .
I met him one afternoon in January]. Later when Fedora explains his name she says, "Keif en árabe quiere decir 'saborear
la existencia animal sin las molestias de la conversación, sin los
desagrados de la memoria ni la vanidad del pensamiento'" (192)
["Keif" in Arabic means to savour animal existence without the
bother of conversation, without the unpleasantness of memory
nor the vanity of thought]. Still part of the first encounter, Fedora confesses her love for Keif as well as her troubling loss of
independence since acquiring him. In order to explain further,
"como si quisiera que no la entendiera" [as if she didn't want
him to understand her], she switches into English, and among
other things, warns the narrator, "He is jealous" (193). In the
story's conclusion, a four-year-old "tamer," the reincarnated Fedora, comes to inquire about Keif. She will use the tiger, a beautiful and fascinating symbol of masculine sexuality, as an intimate
part of her "art," lion taming, but will not herself be subjugated
to him or destroyed by him. The sympathy between the two
main characters, Fedora and the unnamed narrator, allows the
story to unfold and, unlike any of Ocampo's preceding narratives, leaves them both healthy and happy and artistically productive in the end. Fedora has given birth to herself as artist,
while her unnamed friend is the story's "author."

Doubling and multiplying of characters never ceases to appear
in Ocampo's works, but the later collections contain no narratives easily reducible to that old master plot of angel versus
monster. Chronologically, Ocampo's treatment of female doubles
goes to extremes in depicting the self-destructive pattern before
transforming and finally eliminating it. As her stories validate
the monstrous author of female creativity, they face the hidden
dangers of the passive-aggressive angel figure. Both parts of the
woman myth are viewed as victims of their seething hatred, occasioned by a patriarchal system which pits women as competi-
tors for male favor. In accepting ambivalence on both sides of
the doubled character, Ocampo avoids the easy relief accorded
to opposites and holds onto the tension inherent in what Jessica
Benjamin calls intersubjective recognition, the difficult balance
of recognizing a separate person as "like us yet distinct."[34] In
"Keif" Ocampo imagines a remarkable resolution, very close to

the image Benjamin offers, to the dilemmas of female subjectivity. Benjamin argues that the negation of female desire in our culture makes love between male and female as equal subjects impossible under current gender arrangements. Only two males can meet as subjects, as *like,* in mutual recognition, and she posits the father/son relationship just before Oedipus as a prototype of ideal love.[35] Ocampo's story offers a complex female version of Benjamin's vision. Fedora has created herself anew in the figure of the four-year-old tamer, but she has also fabricated an ideal mother in the person of her friend, the narrator. In the final scene, the narrator recognizes the child and accedes to her demand for the tiger. However "impossible" the scenario, it provides a unique image of the artist giving birth to herself and finding validation in her desire for "more."

Benjamin calls for subject to subject interaction/recognition while Gallop calls for a desire of a true Other; each in her different way argues for recognition of difference without debasement. Ocampo's female equivalent of ideal love challenges, among other things, Lacan's notion that there can be no desire for a true Other. The child/Fedora desires Keif and recalls Gallop's recommendation for a way out of the "vicious circle" of the daughter's submission to patriarchy: what is needed is "to rediscover a feminine desire for a masculine body which does not obey the Father's Law."[36] The association of Keif with a human male makes him an element surprisingly close to Gallop's proposal for female subversion of the father's law: an image of pleasure. The female child embodies the best hope for a female subjectivity in Ocampo's work, but there is another figure that must precede her. The difficulty for female subjectivity, according to Benjamin, lies with the mother, with a denial of the mother's desire. The woman of pleasure whose desire lies outside (re)productivity and hence subverts the father's law, ironically, must be the mother. Ocampo's many stories about desiring mothers brings us, therefore, into the heart of issues surrounding female subjectivity.

LA MADRE TERRIBLE

Jessica Benjamin points out, "The mother is a profoundly desexualized figure. . . . Her own sexual feelings, with their incipient threat of selfishness, passion, and uncontrollability, are a disturbing possibility that even psychoanalysis seldom contemplates."[37] One of Benjamin's important conclusions indicates that the lack of subjectivity in the mother is one of the most significant formative elements in the subjectivity of both male and female children.[38] The mother's desire, her subjectivity, is a question that has only recently occupied psychoanalytic theory. Silvina Ocampo, however, waded into these dangerous waters more than fifty years ago, and the figure of the mother in her works is one of the most transgressive and disturbing in all her fiction. Ocampo's mothers express desire for what is beyond family, father or child.

A most horrific story of mothering gone wrong is among Ocampo's earliest works, "El retrato mal hecho," discussed in chapter 1 as an example of Ocampo's use of language to create the grotesque. The transgressive desire of the main character, Eponina, is expressed as a narcissistic regret at the disappearance of her own physical attractions and frustration at the static and empty life of the traditional upper-class woman. The resentment of the mother produces an *alter ego* in the form of her agent and substitute, the servant Ana, who in the end acts for her and carries out her barely hidden wishes. Ana, the obedient, sacrificing figure of the perfect woman, the rescuing angel of this troubled household, turns out to have the same transgressive impulses as the more obviously cold-hearted mother. After Ana kills one of the children and Eponina embraces her in an acknowledgement of complicity, the boy is identified by the narrator, chillingly, without naming him, simply as "el que más había ambicionado subir sobre sus faldas: ahora estaba dormido sobre el pecho de uno de sus vestidos más viejos, en busca de su corazón" (*Vo* 65) [the one who had most desired to climb onto her skirts: now he was asleep on the breast of one of her oldest dresses, in search of her heart]. But the heart is precisely what has been controlled out of Eponina's stultifying existence. The horrified family members gather in the doorway while Eponina embraces Ana with tenderness. Both servant and mistress are exploited and repressed by a patriarchal system which puts them in the service of this child of the patriarchy. Instead of viewing each other as enemies, they embrace in an intimate understanding of mutual suffering. The list of family members who witness the post-murder scene includes an abundance of relatives, but at no time is the child's father mentioned directly. One feels his presence in the number of children that torture Eponina and by the opulence of the life she lives. But his existence is limited to a supposition, a powerful textual silence. In

Ocampo's work as a whole, there are male characters of various
kinds, sons, lovers, friends, uncles, servants, but very few fathers.[39] Ocampo's critique of motherhood hardly lets the fathers
off the hook, however. Their absence at the center of her narratives becomes one element of her critique.

Ocampo's stories complexly deconstruct the two extremes of
mothering, the sin of overcontrol and the sin of neglect, often
defining them as two aspects of a single process. The mothers
of her stories are often wealthy, upper-class women whose interests beyond mothering result in neglect of various degrees of
seriousness while the control is delegated to servants. The title
story of *Las invitadas,* for instance, situates the small son
Lucio's initiation into the world of sin at his sixth birthday,
party. His parents are absent, away on a vacation. They had originally planned to take him, but the child becomes ill with the
measles just before the journey, so the parents decide to leave
him in the care of a servant, who receives instructions to buy
the boy a cake on his birthday, even though his friends will not
be able to come to the party. Seven unknown girls and their
mothers visit Lucio the day of his birthday. Their odd behavior
and names that rhyme appropriately, identify them as the seven
deadly sins. Alicia/avaricia [avarice] brings Lucio a present
which she refuses to give him; Livia/lujuria [lust] presents him
with a pair of magnetized kissing dolls, gifts quickly broken by
Irma/ira [anger]. The mothers of these naughty girls chat with
the household servants and each other while the children enjoy
the party by quarreling over the gifts and cake. Milona's/ comi-
lona [glutony] mother comments that she has no trouble getting
her daughter to eat, while Teresa's/ pereza [sloth] mother expresses her contentment that her perpetually sleepy daughter
leaves her in peace. On their return Lucio's parents are puzzled
by the tale of these mysterious guests and surmise that their
little son has a secret life: "que su hijo tenía relaciones clandesti-
nas, lo que era, y probablemente seguiría siendo, cierto" (176)
[that their son had secret relationships, which was, and probably
would continue to be, true]. This humorous morality play lightly
pans the mothers who discuss their children in terms of conven-
ience to themselves, and suggests that Lucio's parents, by placing
their own pleasure before attention to their child (sick on his
birthday, no less), opened the way to his corruption.

The same collection contains another, much more horrific
story of childhood initiation into the world of adult sin. "El pecado mortal" also utilizes religious symbolism to make a similar

point about the secret life of children, but the story of female initiation contains none of the humor of "Las invitadas." At the other extreme of narrative tone, it is one of Ocampo's tragic tales, the dark accusation of neglectful parenting lingering at its margins. The details of parental preoccupation are omitted, but the child is left in the care of a trusted servant because of "fiestas y muertes (se parecían mucho)" [parties and deaths (they were very similar)]. This story depicts the life of a wealthy child as a complex combination of neglect and overcontrol. What is described at length in several of the "twin" stories of *Viaje olvidado,* the limitations imposed on wealthy children, is summarized in one paragraph here, with overtly Christian implications:

Oíste decir en un sermón: "Más grande es el lujo, más grande es la corrupción": quisiste andar descalza, como el niño Jesús, dormir en un lecho rodeada de animales, comer miguitas de pan, recogidas del suelo como los pájaros, pero no te fue dada esa dicha: para consolarte de no andar descalza, te pusieron un vestido de tafetas tornasolado y zapatos de cuero *mordoré*; para consolarte de no dormir en un lecho de paja, rodeada de animales, te llevaron al teatro Colón, el teatro más grande del mundo; para consolarte de no comer miguitas recogidas del suelo, te regalaron una caja lujosa con puntilla de papel plateado, llena de bombones que apenas cabían en tu boca. (*I* 138)

[You once heard in a sermon, "The greater the luxury the greater the corruption": you tried to walk barefoot, like the baby Jesus, sleep in a broken down bed surrounded by animals, eat breadcrumbs off the floor like the birds, but that happiness was not to be yours: to console you for not walking barefoot, they dressed you in an iridescent taffeta dress and shoes of *mordoré* leather; to console you for not sleeping in a bed of straw, surrounded by animals, they took you to the Colón Theater, the largest in the world; to console you for not eating breadcrumbs off the floor they gave you a luxurious box with silver paper edging filled with chocolates that would hardly fit in your mouth.]

This child is protected from the wrong things and neglected in ways that expose her to unforeseen dangers. Both "El pecado mortal" and "Las invitadas" depict bad parenting in terms uncomfortably close to what passes as good parenting. The gender difference between the two is notable. Whereas the little boy's corruption is viewed with amusement, the girl's is portrayed as tragedy. Whether comic or tragic, the overt association of sin with the feminine is constant.

"El goce y la penitencia" establishes the explicit opposition of the mother's pleasure and the child's pain within the title itself; the interludes occasioned by a child's punishment ("la peniten-cia") for bad behavior provide the necessary opportunity for the mother's affair ("el goce") with a painter hired to do the boy's portrait. The child is locked into an attic room while the pair dally in the studio. The story is complicated by the fact that the child enjoys the arrangement quite as much as the illicit couple, and that once the portrait is finished they seem unable to con-tinue their affair without the ritualized "punishment" meted out to the boy. Like a sacrificial victim, he atones for their guilty deeds. The father refuses to pay for the finished portrait because he and everyone else agree that it in no way resembles the boy. However, years later, the portrait is discovered to bear a perfect likeness of the child born of the extramarital affair. This humor-ous story and its ironic ending make an earlier argument be-tween husband and wife particularly significant. They discuss, in quite meta-artistic terms, important issues of mimesis:

> Mi marido sostenía que los retratos tenían que parecerse al modelo: si la nariz original era aguileña y horrible, o si era respingada y atroz, la copia tenía que serlo. Había que dejar de lado la belleza. En una palabra, le gustaban los mamarrachos. Yo sostenía que la expresión de una cara no dependía, en modo alguno, de sus líneas ni de sus proporciones, y que el parecido no se manifestaba en meros detalles. (*F* 161)

> [My husband argued that portraits should look like the model: if the original nose was aquiline and horrible, or if it was snubbed and atrocious, the copy had to be the same. One had to leave beauty aside. In a word, he liked ridiculous things. I argued that the expression of a face did not depend at all on its lines and proportions, and that a likeness was not based on mere details.]

The gender difference in the argument is corroborated in the story itself. The "rules," of mimesis, of representation, and by extension, of social conduct generally, are far more significant to the male, while a loosening of these provides a space for female desire.[40] The husband's acceptance of the painting's new signi-fied (the second son, actually the painter's son) points out the hollowness of (pictorial) representation and its relation to the fiction of fatherhood. These elements come together around a transgressive mother. Doane suggests that the love story in gen-eral is risky for patriarchy since it attributes, even if in a minor key, desire to the female. Adultery by the woman is an especially traumatic idea for, as Steven Heath explains: "what guarantees identity is the woman who is then equally the weak point in its system: if she gives, everything gives; moving from *her* right place, the adulterous woman leaves *no* place intact. . . . As mother the woman is sure, as wife always potentially unsure."[41] The story contains two fathers. It is unclear whether either of them is ever aware of the true identity of the second son. Both boys have the same mother, who manages to get away with breaking patriarchy's sacred laws. The story slyly suggests that the father's identity itself may be one of those "mere details" that are better left unclear.

The issues of adultery and motherhood are explored from the child's point of view in "Voz en el teléfono." It returns, in part, to the mother-child-servant dynamic explored in "El retrato mal hecho." In this case, however, the child manages to avenge himself on the adults who ignore or fail to understand him. Not surprisingly, his rebellious act cannot save him from becoming a victim of what Ocampo reveals to be an unhealthy arrangement for all. The narrative framing of the story, a telephone conversation in which the reader is positioned to "hear" only one side, produces the trivializing commentary which transforms this tragedy into a grotesque comedy. It also situates the narrative voice in flux between the adult and the child's point of view.

The narrator, a young man speaking to his girlfriend on the telephone, relates events of the day he celebrated his fourth birthday. In a lengthy digression, he describes in some detail the large, luxurious house and a prior episode which compelled his mother to fire their cook. Both of these seemingly unrelated elements are crucial to my understanding of the story. The boy clearly adores the cook, who teases him, significantly, with a long (phallic) carving knife; he gives him good things to eat, and, we deduce, the fatherly attention he does not receive from his biological father, who is mentioned briefly only once. The narrator says that the servants in the house had been divided in their loyalties between the arrogant cook and the equally arrogant mother. Without stating that he himself had been caught in the tension or that this episode relates in any way to what follows, the juxtaposition of events may allow readers to conclude that the mother's removal of an important father figure provides a motive for the revenge this little boy exacts. I read this story as an exaggeration of Jessica Benjamin's description of the origins of gender differences surrounding desire. She argues, with Irene

Fast, that both boys and girls go through an identificatory stage with the parent of the opposite sex which allows the child to feel heterosexual love. If renunciation takes place too soon, without full identification, it is compromised by repudiation or idealization.[42] This story illustrates a particularly brutal premature abjection of the mother.

The long description of the house with its many rooms and its objects both valuable and trivial, illustrates the child's acute powers of observation and his fascination with those objects representative of the mother's interests beyond and apart from her child: "Las alfombras, las arañas y las vitrinas de la casa me gustaban más que los juguetes" (F 134) [I liked the pillows, chandeliers and china cabinets of the house better than the toys]. The first thing this narrator remembers about the day of the birthday party itself is that his mother has removed all the valuable objects of the house and replaced them with things she thinks will be more appropriate for children. But this child's reactions do not match his mother's expectations. He not only prefers the household objects to toys, but also is more interested in the mothers, aunts, and grandmothers who accompany his party guests than he is in the children. His dismay at the marionette theater production, "donde Caperucita Roja me aterró como el lobo o la abuela, donde la Bella me pareció horrorosa como la Bestia" (135) [where Red Riding Hood terrified me as much as the wolf or the grandmother, where Beauty seemed more horrifying than the Beast], indicates the level of misunderstanding between mother and son. Once the party is well under way, the mother retreats with the adults to a separate room where the valuable objects have not been removed. The boy follows the women and hides behind a chair where his fascination with the adult world and his assiduous effort to enter its forbidden territory are now amply rewarded as he overhears their indiscreet conversation, worth quoting at length:

Las señoras reían tanto que apenas comprendía yo las palabras que pronunciaban. Hablaban de corpiños, y una de ellas se desabotonó la blusa hasta la cintura para mostrar el que llevaba puesto: era transparente como una media de Navidad, pensé que tendría algún juguete y sentí deseos de meter la mano adentro. Hablaron de medidas: resultó que se trataba de un juego. Por turno se pusieron de pie . . .
   Se midieron la cintura, el pecho y las caderas.
   —Te apuesto a que tengo cincuenta y ocho de cintura.
   —Y yo te apuesto a que tengo menos.

Las voces resonaban como en un teatro.

—Quisiera ganar con las caderas—decía una

—Yo me contento con la pechera—dijo otra—. A los hombres les interesa más el pecho, ¿no ves dónde miran?

—Si no me miran en los ojos no siento nada—dijo otra, con un suntuoso collar de perlas.

—No se trata de lo que sentís, sino de lo que ellos sienten—dijo la voz agresiva de una que no era madre de nadie. . . .

Sonó el teléfono que estaba colocado junto a uno de los sillones; Chinche y Elvira, repartiéndoselo, lo atendieron; luego, tapando el teléfono con un almohadón, dijeron a mi madre:

—Es para vos, che.

Las otras se codearon y Rosca tomó el teléfono para oír la voz.

—Apuesto a que es el barbudo—dijo una de las señoras.

—Apuesto a que es el duende—dijo otra, mordiendo sus collares.

Entonces comenzó un diálogo telefónico en que todas intervinieron pasándose el teléfono por turno. Olvidé que estaba escondido y me puse de pie para ver mejor el entusiasmo, con tintineo de pulseras y collares, de las señoras. Mi madre al verme cambió de voz y de rostro; como frente al espejo se alisó el pelo y se acomodó las medias; apagó con ahinco el cigarrillo en el cenicero, retorciéndolo dos o tres veces. Me tomó de la mano y yo, aprovechando su turbación, robé los fósforos largos y lujosos que estaban sobre la mesa, junto a los vasos de whisky. Salimos del cuarto. (*F* 136)

[The women were laughing so much I could scarcely understand the words they were saying. They were talking about bras and one of them unbuttoned her blouse to the waist to show the one she had on: it was transparent like a Christmas stocking, I thought it would have a toy inside and I felt a desire to put my hand in. They talked about measurements and it turned out to be a game. They took turns standing up. . . . They measured waist, breast and hips. "I bet I have fifty-eight for the waist." "I bet I have less." The voices resounded as in a theater. "I want to win with hips," said one. "I will be happy with breast," said another. "Men are more interested in the breast, don't you see where they look? "If they don't look me in the eyes I don't feel a thing," said another with a sumptuous pearl necklace. "It's not what you feel, its what they feel," said the aggressive voice of one who was no one's mother.

The telephone, next to one of the easy chairs, rang; Chinche and Elvira, sharing it, answered; then, covering the phone with a pillow, they said to my mother, "It's for you." The others nudged each other and Rosca took the phone to hear the voice. "I bet its the one with the beard," said one of the women. "I bet its the prankster," said another, biting her necklaces.

Then a phone conversation began in which everyone participated passing the phone by turn. I forgot that I was hidden and stood up

in order to see better the excitement of tinkling bracelets and necklaces of the women. My mother on seeing me, changed her voice
and face; as before a mirror she smoothed her hair and straightened
her stockings; she put out her cigarrette in the ashtray intently,
twisting it two or three times. She took me by the hand, and I, taking
advantage of her turmoil, stole the long, luxurious matches which
were on the table next to the glasses of whiskey. We left the room.]

I have cited this passage almost in its entirety because it demonstrates several important elements, not the least of which is its
deliciously wicked humor. The undisguised sexuality of all these
"mothers" is revealed in their giggling conversation with each
other and then with the male caller. The revelation of the "self-
pleasuring body behind the Mother" destroys her status as an
image of power for the child.[43] Their narcissistic display of bodies
and measurements is countered with desire in the male child/
observer as he fantasizes reaching into the woman's brassiere.
The mother's reaction on the discovery of the interloper into the
female world of exposed desire is immediate. She, like Rosaura
Pringles of "La gallina de membrillo," fixes her clothing and hair
"como frente al espejo" [as if before a mirror] and marches the
child out of the room. In other words, her instinctive reaction
is to replace herself in the legitimate scheme of things as object
of the male gaze, even a four-year-old's male gaze. Benjamin
states that the four-year-old boy, an oedipal boy, responds to
sexual difference with "triumphant contempt" for his mother
now revealed as "at best a desired object one may not possess."[44]
In this sanctum sanctorum Ocampo's child/narrator has discovered the desire of the mother; hers is a transgressive desire
which directs itself not toward him, the child, or to the father,
but to the caller, a male outside the oedipal triangle. In the boy's
eyes she now falls into the category of valuable object removed
or denied him, and he takes his revenge by stealing the long,
luxurious, phallic, fireplace matches. This little boy's efforts to
possess the mother's valuable objects, substitutes for the mother
herself, now succeed.

Once expelled from the Eden/Imaginary of the forbidden
room, the boy gathers his guests together for a new game; they
decide to use the stolen matches to burn the house. One of the
women realizes that the children have locked the door, but the
response from another is, "Mejor, así nos dejan tranquilas"
[Good, now they will leave us in peace]. The roomful of mothers
is punished for their indifference (at least momentary) to their

children and for their open display of transgressive desire. The narrator concludes his tale by returning to an object described earlier:

> La última visión que tengo de mi madre es de su cara inclinada hacia abajo, apoyada sobre un balaustre del balcón. ¿Y el mueble chino? El mueble chino se salvó del incendio, felizmente. Algunas figuritas se estropearon: una de una señora que llevaba un niño en los brazos y que se asemejaba un poco a mi madre y a mí. (138)

> [The last vision I have of my mother is of her face leaning down, resting on the banister of the balcony. And the Chinese cabinet? It was saved from the fire, fortunately. Some of the figures were ruined: one of a woman carryng a child in her arms and which looked a little like my mother and me.]

The elaborately carved Chinese cabinet is saved from the blaze, its idealized image of mother and child ruined, but its false connection in the narrator's mind between himself and his own mother intact. The boy kills off his real, desiring mother in order to maintain the image of the desexed, idealized mother as valuable object. Benjamin points out that the stronger the rejection of the mother, the more her ideal is tied into the unconscious because it is never countered by the real. "Voz en el teléfono" depicts a child who manages to avenge himself of the perceived misunderstanding and betrayal of his desirous mother. But as an adult he is unable to escape the false notion of the idealized mother, and his phobias—he starts his narrative to excuse himself from a children's party, claiming to be afraid of children's parties and fire—suggest that he has hardly escaped victimization.

All of these stories defend the child's point of view in relation to the abuse or neglect of "la madre terrible"; in all of Ocampo's stories the inner life, the unsuspected complexity of childhood, is one of her points. But here, as elsewhere, Ocampo further reveals the destructive characteristics of traditional family arrangements for both mother and child. Even her most exaggerated tales present the mother as another victim of a patriarchal system that serves no one well. Sara Ruddick, in detailing the thought processes dictated by mothering, explains that one of her obligations is to produce children acceptable to society.[45] In this sense, the upper-class mother is necessarily complicitous with the oligarchy. Within Ocampo's texts, however, the reader views the mother's unstated subordination. The mother of two stories is equated, not to the father, but to one of the servants in the house. The embrace between mistress and servant at the conclusion of "El retrato mal hecho" and the warfare between mother and cook in "Voz en el teléfono" situates the mother as comparable to them within the hierarchy. If anything, these stories demonstrate that Matamoro is overly optimistic when he suggests that the dangerous beings of these stories threaten the oligarchy. From these stories, it is clear that all the members of the subordinate group—mothers, children and servants—attack only each other. Whether the mother kills her child or the child kills her, the oligarchy itself, represented by the father, stays safely out of the frame. What Ocampo's stories offer is a vision of society viewed from below in which the suppressed elements of an impersonal system wear masks of innocence, frivolity, or complicity. The violence of their rebellion, when it occurs, falls on the beings closest to them. Only the silences of Ocampo's texts offer an accusation to the absent "padres terribles."

"El diario de Porfiria Bernal" is a story that has already been seen in chapter 1 to break out of patterns of imaginary and symbolic, refusing to return to a comfortable insertion in law. It breaks the pattern of the "madre terrible" as well: the figure of Porfiria's mother offers a vision of a desiring female character who manages to pursue her own pleasure and still protect her child. In this story the positive consequences of the transgressive mother, create the possibility of her daughter's subjectivity. Ana María Bernal is one of Ocampo's most fully delineated and fascinating maternal figures. She is viewed as menacing, but only by Miss Fielding. In Porfiria's account the constant refrain of "se lo dije a mi madre" [I told my mother] indicates a protective, benign presence from the perspective of the daughter. In chapter 1, I read the story itself as an image of subjectivity in that it is constituted by way of a split between Miss Fielding's letter and Porfiria's diary in which Miss Fielding's version performed as the conscious and Porfiria's the unconscious of the text. On that structural level, Porfiria and Miss Fielding represent the split of a single subject. In terms of the story's plot as it unfolds in Porfiria's (much longer) version, Miss Fielding and Porfiria's mother form another mad double, this time in competition not for the male, but for Porfiria.

As another pair of mad doubles, Ana María Bernal and Miss Fielding act out of a set of parameters not very different from

standard fairy tales in which the maternal figure is divided between good mother (fairy godmother) and bad mother (the
wicked stepmother).[46] In keeping with a reading of this story as
modern fairy tale, Miss Fielding's transformation at the end can
be construed as the mother's rescue of her daughter. Early in
the story, Ana María Bernal had warned Miss Fielding never to
give Porfiria chocolate. Her instructions are punctuated oddly
in the text: "En una hoja de block Ana María Bernal anotó con
un lápiz el régimen alimenticio de Porfiria y luego me lo entregó,
con un ademán grosero, mascando las sílabas de su última
frase:—No le dé chocolate, aunque se lo pida" (*I* 158) [On a sheet
of tablet paper Ana María Bernal noted in pencil Porfiria's diet
and then handed it to me with a crude gesture, chewing the
syllables of the last phrase: "Don't give her chocolate, even if
she asks for it"]. Significantly, it is as Miss Fielding is preparing
chocolate for Porfiria, against the express wishes of the mother,
that the governess turns into a cat.[47] If we assume that the dutiful, mild-mannered Miss Fielding represents the angelic cultural
ideal, her destruction at the end represents another case in
which the "ideal" half of the doubled figure is killed. However, as
in "El lazo" or "Las vestiduras peligrosas," the division between
"monstrous author" and angelic figure are held in balance because neither of the protagonists is presented as all good or all
bad; neither holds a monopoly on creative power or on domestic
passivity, and both are portrayed by Porfiria as transgressively
sexual. Miss Fielding presents herself as a dutiful domestic angel
figure in her own version, but in Porfiria's she becomes the
menacing and sexualized character. The mother of both their
texts is a creative and powerful presence.

The mother's transgressive sexual behavior, like Miss Fielding's, appears only in Porfiria's version. Porfiria describes with
an understandably intense curiosity what appears to be an adulterous liaison between her mother and a man eventually identified as Roberto Cárdenas, but she never suggests that their
behavior results in her neglect. Porfiria first sees them together
during their beach vacation. The arrival of this same man as a
visitor to their Buenos Aires house, where he is introduced to
the family, is the episode in Porfiria's diary which confirms for
Miss Fielding that Porfiria is predicting the future, not recording
the past. Porfiria's careful observations of her mother and Roberto Cárdenas in subsequent passages reinforce for the reader
the probability that they are lovers. The level of Porfiria's understanding of the situation is less clear, but she narrates episodes

involving them with a certain sympathy. Reading this story with Benjamin and Silverman allows us to see that the subjectivity (desire) of the mother opens the possibility for the subjectivity of the daughter. In addition to everything else, Ana María Bernal provides Porfiria a fascinating subplot for her diary's narrative. Porfiria's mother, unlike our culture's ideal, does have a story of her own.

"El diario de Porfiria Bernal" creates a triangle in which all principle points are female. Porfiria, rather than any of the males, motivates the actions of the female doubles. Miss Fielding, in turn, provides a third term for the break up of the mother-child duo. The mother, Ana María Bernal, is the pivot around which all else turns. It is a testament to the richness of Ocampo's story that it can be read as a fantasy of subversion of the symbolic, as I have shown in chapter 1, and in terms of several feminist revisions of the psychoanalytic model. For instance, its female trio duplicates one strategy described by Silverman's *Acoustic Mirror,* in which the negative Oedipus provides a liberating solution for female subjectivity.[48] In Silverman's argument as well as in Ocampo's story, the child's desire is complexly divided between the parent of the same sex, in this case the mother, and the law's representative, Miss Fielding. And as Silverman suggests, the absence of the male does not impede the subject's entrance into the symbolic, as Kristeva would insist, or threaten her access to meaning—Porfiria, after all, is author of the diary—but it does pose a serious challenge to patriarchy. Silverman urges a theoretical repositioning of desire for the mother to a place within the symbolic, as opposed to the imaginary, and therefore fully within the realm of representation. Viewing it this way, she suggests, allows for the possibility "to speak ... about a genuinely oppositional desire ... [whose] homosexual component ... poses a powerful threat to the father, the phallus, and the operations of dominant meaning, but not ... to meaning per se" (124). The closure of Porfiria's diary which presses toward an undisclosed future and the playful transformation of Miss Fielding into a cat provides an uncanny gloss of Silverman's proposed expansion of Kristeva's concept: "In order for the *choric* fantasy to function as an effective political implement, it must point forward as well as backward—accommodate transformation as well as return" (125).[49] In this way, I believe, Ocampo produces a complex image of subjectivity which corroborates Benjamin's assertion that "the 'real' solution to the dilemma of woman's desire must include a mother who is articulated as a sexual *subject,* one who expresses her own desire" (114). Benjamin suggests that in an ideal world both mother and father should be figures of both attachment and differentiation, but in the world without fathers (her chapter is entitled "The Missing Father"), Porfiria Bernal is lucky, it would seem, to have two such "madres terribles."[50] Ocampo's stories of transgressive motherhood create female subjects desirous of something beyond the child, and frequently beyond the marital/familial setting, doubly breaking the father's law. These are hardly the mute mothers of Kristeva's choric fantasy, but women of pleasure, actively pursuing the direction of their own desire. Both "Keif" and "El diario de Porfiria Bernal" create female doubles engaged with a female third term. These stories introduce the daughter, whose potential for disruption exceeds even the powers of the transgressive mother.

LA NENA TERRIBLE

Kaja Silverman has pointed out that the desire of the mother and child is what holds patriarchal culture together. She notes that the mother is the original object of desire both because of her direct role as nurturer/source of pleasure and because she is a source of *objects a* even before she is perceived as a discrete object.[51] But the subject's entry into the symbolic quickly changes the direction of desire from mother to father. The child wishes to be desired by the mother, desires the mother's desire. But the mother desires what she lacks, that is, the phallus, which both she and child associate with the father. Therefore, the son will wish to supply her with the missing phallus and the daughter will repudiate her and turn to the father as erotic love object. In either case, the father or "the paternal signifier emerges as the definitive one in the history of the subject." Silverman continues:

> this signifying transaction, whereby the child makes the mother's meaning and desires its own, is not just one among many. It is of crucial importance in the constitution of the Lacanian subject, and when it does not occur (*either because of the failure of the mother's desire, as in Hamlet, or because of the failure of the child's*), psychosis occurs. In other words, the subject's desires fail to conform to the larger symbolic order, *a deviance which threatens the perpetuation of that order.* (190, emphasis mine)

For those whose interest lies precisely in the disruption of that order, the deviation of desire in mother and child is of great importance. The mother's desire which perpetuates this system is predicated on her own definition as lack in opposition to the potency of the father. Silvina Ocampo's stories demonstrate the damage to the subject created by this social scheme, and, in several cases, dare to imagine a world with different directions for desire.

If "El diario de Porfiria Bernal" provides the figure of the transgressive but still good mother, it also, in the character of Porfiria herself, marks out the female subject. It is no accident that Porfiria's mother should act as a transgressive force within the family, for her subjectivity, clearly discernible in her agency as her daughter's protector and her sexual desire, opens a space for the subjectivity of the daughter. Both characters are "bad" or evil in traditional terms, the mother as adulteress (not to mention witch, if the chocolate can be considered her "brew") and Porfiria as sorceress who "murders" her governess, symbol and conveyor of the law. Porfiria and her mother in exhibiting desire transgress the positions fixed for them by the law. In placing all the male characters at the margins of plot, the story imagines an impossible escape from patriarchy. Miss Fielding becomes a father substitute on two different levels: As a structural element, her version becomes a metaphorical representation of the symbolic; and on the level of the plot, her character serves as the third term that interrupts the mother-child duo. The radical moves to kill the father of law are displaced and disguised by depicting the father figure as female. In this way Ocampo's story is all the more effective for having escaped the trap of which modern feminism is sometimes accused, of confusing the Father of Law with the biological male.

Far from a gentle story of female utopia, however, this is a violent tale of jealousy and cruelty. Porfiria's fury at Miss Fielding arises primarily from jealousy of her brother Miguel. Porfiria desires the love or recognition by the law's representatiave, Miss Fielding, and is furious when this adoration and approval are lavished on her brother instead. She writes, bluntly: "Miss Fielding está enamorada de Miguel. Así tienen que ser las institutrices con los discípulos y no tratarlos con la rudeza con que me trata a mí" (*I* 170) [Miss Fielding is in love with Miguel. That is the way governesses should be with their pupils and not treat them with the roughness with which she treats me]. Miss Fielding, in her own version, presents herself as loving and identifying with

Porfiria, and never mentions Miguel. Porfiria describes Miss Fielding as loving her only as the nondesiring Boticelli "angel," the mirror image of Miss Fielding's own idealized self. The desiring, plotting Porfiria, author of the diary, fills Miss Fielding only with horror and fear, and for good reason, for Porfiria's version reveals the governess's transgressive desire for a young boy as well as Porfiria's own violent reaction. One of Porfiria's diary entries sounds much like the horrifying Valentina Schleider of "El lazo" or the narrator of "Carta perdida en un cajón," both of whom seek a self-destructive revenge:

> Fui a misa con Miguel y Miss Fielding.
> Trataré de alejarlos. No me importa que me odien. Cuando uno no consigue el afecto que reclama, el odio es un alivio. El odio es lo único que puede reemplazar al amor.
> Conseguí que me pegara, que me clavara las uñas de nuevo. He triunfado, exasperándola. (*I* 170)

> [I went to mass with Miguel and Miss Fielding. I will try to separate them. I don't care if they hate me. When one fails to receive the affection one demands, hate is a relief. Hatred is the only thing which can replace love. I got her to hit me, to gouge me with her fingernails again. I have triumphed, exasperating her.]

Porfiria behaves in ways endemic to the angel figures of Ocampo's fiction, that is, with unsuspected passive-aggressive power. The subjectivity of this child unsettles the association developed in Western culture between seeing and knowing, eroticism and power. Still not fully assumed into law, she nevertheless sees and desires; she is a child deserving of protection, but powerful in unsuspected ways. She is angel and devil, master and slave, subject and object held perpetually in a series of contradictions without closure. As such, Porfiria is the best of Ocampo's "nenas terribles," made possible, as we have seen earlier, by her powerful, eroticized mother. Not all of Ocampo's children triumph as thoroughly as Porfiria does, however.

Silvina Ocampo selected for the volume *Mi mejor cuento* [My best story] her "Tales eran sus rostros," a tale whose main character is a collective of children, the entire group of students at a school for the deaf. Ocampo's introductory remarks for her selection, some of the very few nonfiction comments she published, reemphasize her interest in children. Her statement admits that this is not her favorite story, but she selects it deliberately: "Lo elijo tal vez porque es un cuento en que el protagonista es un secreto místico, un milagro colectivo, un multiplicado e inflnito niño, al cual dediqué mi atención con tanto amor" [I choose it perhaps because it is a story in which the protagonist is a mystical secret, a multiplied and inflnite child, to whom I dedicated my attention with so much love].[52] Though she suggests that her creative attention to childhood has been motivated by love, readers of her stories have more frequently stressed the many supposedly evil child characters that populate her works. It is possible, however, to reach a different conclusion about Ocampo's child characters, to view their transgressive violence with sympathy, and to agree with the author that she writes about them with love.

Matamoro argues that the children in Ocampo's stories rebel against bad parents. In the case of multiple child characters, groups of children who act as a single character, his statement is true. Several stories, like "Tales eran sus rostros," utilize a group of children in contrast to a group of adults to make the point that the former have access to superior knowledge, hidden from their elders. The deaf children of Ocampo's "best" story fly out the doors of an airplane, transformed into angels with wings. The most subversive aspect of the tale is not the conclusion, but the suggestion that they *knew* about the coming miracle in advance, had planned for it somehow as a shared secret, much to the amazement and consternation of the teachers who are left to explain the children's disappearance to their parents. Ocampo's stories of multiple child characters depict them as more intuitive than the adults who invariably underestimate them. Certainly they are not the "blank slates" so often assumed by the adults of her stories. "La raza inextinguible," "Exodo," "Ana Valerga" and "La cabeza de piedra" utilize a group of children similarly, as a kind of single protagonist. The group of school girls in the latter encounter a hostile woman and seem to speak for all of Ocampo's children when they say: "no sabíamos que vivíamos en un mundo raro y gracias a usted lo hemos descubierto" (*Y así* 114) [we didn't know that we were living in a strange world but thanks to you we have discovered it]. Ocampo's children occasionally act as one in a powerful disruption of the usual categories of individual identity, and can only wonder at the insanity that passes for normal in the world of adults.

These stories flt the description of Matamoro's undifferentiated "nenes terribles." Just as I have separated the figure of the mother from Matamoro's ungendered "padres terribles," I now want to distinguish Ocampo's child characters by gender. All of them, male and female, frequently possess special powers of extrasensory perception or the ability to foresee and/or cause events, but the girls' powers are more hidden, at least to the characters of their fictional world. Generally one can say that the boys are younger and more public with their sadistic violence or magical powers. Seven-year-old Tirso of "El vendedor de estatuas" is remembered for his heartless eyes: "Tenía unos ojos que nunca debían haber llorado, y solamente matándolo se le podía quizás lastimar un poco" (*Vo* 129) [He had eyes that must never have cried and only killing him could perhaps hurt him a little]. The awesome Cornelio ("Los amigos"), whose powers create mayhem on a massive scale including floods and epidemics, is identified by his entire family for his "inclinación mística" [mystical inclinations]; the only doubt about him lies with the narrator who sees a witch ("brujo") where others find a saint. Magush's "genio divinatorio" [genius for prediction] seems gentler and more private than those two, but does bring him clients who seek his expertise. Valentín Brumana of "La revelación," in spite of his retardation, is recognized as "una suerte de mago" [a kind of magician], Toñito ("La soga") magically transforms one of his toys into a live snake, fondly observed by members of his family. The special powers of the boy children are at least acknowledged, even if mistakenly, in all these narratives. They also retain a sense of innocence about them in spite of the real damage done. Violence, even cruelty, for these children is carried out, like play, with an air of innocent abandon. Where are Matamoro's horrible parents here? These stories indicate that childish male violence is absurd and meaningless, not necessarily predicated on revolt. Male violence for Ocampo, like male sexuality, does not *mean*.

Each of the stories cited above is narrated by a witness or friend of the main character. The boys ironically are nearly always the objects of narration and rarely the subjects of their own discourse. Little girls are more frequently the first-person narrators of their own stories, their magical deeds known, thereby, only to the "reader" of a first-person account—such as Porfiria's diary—and not to other characters in the story. At least Porfiria is read and believed by Miss Fielding; Irene, of "Autobiografía de Irene," tries but never succeeds in convincing anyone of her powers of divination; the same is true of the narrator of "La muñeca." The female children of Ocampo's fiction do not at first seem quiet to the readers for we are privy to their secret thoughts. But looked at closely, it is clear that most of the female narrators, like the little girl of "El vestido de terciopelo," never attempt to explain their perceptions to anyone within their fictional world. The secretive nature of childish narrative, imposed structurally for Ocampo's little girls, permits an entrance into the forbidden territory of female knowledge. What is uncovered, almost tangentially at times, is female sexuality. In contrast to the boys, the girls depict themselves as sexually precocious. Little boys, thanks to Freud, are assumed to be sexual from the very beginning, but the sexuality of the little girl is the well-known blind spot of his theory.[53] Ocampo's relentless exploration of prepubescent female sexuality is still one of the more shocking aspects of her work.

"Viaje olvidado" is the first story to present the outrage of a little girl on learning the truth about the forgotten journey of birth. At first the child believes the story traditionally told in Argentina, that babies come in a box from a warehouse in Paris. She hears a different version from a slightly older child, though this one is not accurate either, because it suggests that babies emerge from the mother's navel. This idea fills the child with shame, and she is relieved to be assured by her nanny that babies do come from Paris. When her mother finally tells her some part of the truth—though all we know is that "le habló de flores, le habló de pájaros"—the child insists stubbornly (the narrative says "desesperadamente," desperately) on the original story. The mother's talk of birds and flowers—in English we would say birds and bees—is perceived as a profound betrayal. This child's embarrassment and confusion are understandable given the outright deception to which she has been subjected. "Viaje olvidado" suggests that adults routinely underestimate a child's ability to understand and their basic need for truth. Other stories indicate that there is something outrageous to them about the truth itself.

The little girl's rage at learning of her place in the sexual scheme of things is carried to its most violent conclusion in "La hija del toro." The rich physical sensations and curious mixture of humans and animals charge its language from the beginning with sexual connotations. The slaughterhouse of an estate is situated among fig trees, and the smells of the raw meat and ripe fruit are evoked along with a mixture of animal-like humans and human-like animals: the butcher, Nieves Montovia, "llamado Pata de Perro porque tenía las uñas de los pies enruladas, duras y negras, como las de un perro" (*I* 13) [called Dog's Paw because he had curled toenails, hard and black, like those of a dog], is a man with feet of a dog; while the "escribano López" [Lopez the scribe] we learn only at the end of the story, is a cat:

> Antes de tomar el desayuno, el olor a carne cruda y a higos me daba náuseas; pero yo acudía junto a Pata de Perro a cualquier hora. Sobre el terreno de polvo de ladrillo apisonado, no se veían las manchas de sangre. Todo era rojo: los higos entreabiertos, la carne, el polvo de ladrillo, mis alpargatas, los arañazos del escribano López. (*I* 13)

> [Before breakfast the smell of raw meat and figs made me feel sick; but I turned up around Pata de Perro at all hours. Over the trodden ground of brick dust the spots of blood were not visible. Everything was red: the open figs, the meat, the brick dust, my sandals, the scratches of Lopez the scribe.]

The intense smells, especially of blood, define a sexualized female space which blurs not only the distinction between animal and human but also that of gender. Pato de Perro's slaughter yard is remembered as the imaginary from which the young narrator must emerge as subject in the symbolic field.

The first-person narrator describes herself in terms of connection to the other characters. Her description attempts to deny the difference it inadvertently names: "Con la cabeza rapada y el pantalón azul, me parecía a mis hermanos varones" (13) [With my closely cropped hair and blue pants I looked like my male siblings]. The children of the ranch enjoy great personal freedom to play together on a hillside or follow Pata de Perro as if he were the Pied Piper. He, in turn, teaches them the illicit skills coveted by childhood, winking, saying bad words and smoking. This last provides the moment in which the child narrator inadvertently poses the issue of gender. She asks Pato de Perro to explain the name of his brand of cigarettes, "la Hija del Toro" [Daugter of the Bull]:

> El papel que envolvía el atado llevaba la figura de una mujer, con una corona de flores, abrazando el toro (especie de calcomanía, que me fascinaba).
>   —¿Cómo puede un toro tener una hija?—yo preguntaba.
>   —Usted debe de saberlo mejor que nadie.
>   —¿Por qué he de saberlo?
>   —Porque usted también es hija del toro—decía Pata de Perro—. Ya le mostraré, curiosa, cómo hacen los toros para tener una hija. (*I* 13)

> [The paper which covered the pack carried the figure of a woman with a crown of flowers embracing a bull (a kind of transfer drawing

which fascinated me). "How can a bull have a daughter," I asked. "You should know better than anyone." "Why should I know?" "Because you are also the daughter of the bull," said Pata de Perro. "I will show you, nosey, what bulls do to have a daughter."]

The child's unspoken response to this exchange—"Yo no era curiosa. Tenía otros defectos, tal vez peores" [I was not nosey. I had other defects, perhaps worse]—is a statement which introduces a kind of parenthesis in the story's action while she explains a most unusual childhood game. With the help of Pata de Perro, the children make stick figures that are then named for family members and thrown into the boiling oil used to make soap. While it is clear that all participate, she states unequivocally that it was her own idea. Even though one of their uncles dies they keep on playing this game which she describes as "demonic" and which her brothers are said to remember as a crime.

In the story's conclusion the child escapes from the house during a siesta time and with Pata de Perro watches a bull mounting a cow. Pata de Perro asks: "—¿No está contenta? Ya vio lo que quería ver" (14) [Aren't you happy? Now you saw what you wanted to see]. The furious child vows to take her revenge. She labors with some difficulty to make a figure for the fire in the shape of Pata de Perro and his beloved horse Remigia. At the moment in which she names him along with others to be tossed into the vat, the man laughs, but on hearing his horse included he says, "Que me quemen a mí pero no a Remigia" [You can burn me but not Remigia]. So children and adult try to rescue the figures from the boiling oil, but succeed only in burning their fingers finding partial remains: "No hay salvación para Pata de Perro, ni para Remigia—dijo Nieves Montovia—. Enterrémoslos, niños" (15) ["There is no salvation for Pata de Perro nor for Remigia," said Nieves Montovia. "Let's bury them, kids"]. Nieves Montovia attends his own funeral in miniature as they bury the stick figures. The following day, he and his horse have disappeared forever.

Female innovation in this story destroys the one person for whom the character shows any affection. The immediate motive is the rage elicited by the episode of the story's title. The question, "How can a bull have a daughter?" is answered by Pata de Perro in the first sentence that definitively identifies the narrator as female ("Usted también es hija del toro"). She had indicated earlier her physical similarity to her brothers, a statement that simultaneously reveals her essential difference from them.

Pata de Perro's singling her out as female creates difference, as does the little song he invented for the occasion: "Conozco una niña/ que es hija del toro./ La llaman Amalia" (14) [I know a girl/ who is daughter of the bull./ They call her Amalia]. The recognition and naming of her as female is only later put into biological and cultural perspective by the sight of the animals copulating.

This retrospective understanding reflects Freud's description of the castration complex in the male wherein the little boy views female genitalia and only understands its importance to him when he later faces the father's threat of castration. Freud argues that the girl, in contrast to the boy, reacts in an immediate, unmediated way to the "discovery" of her own "castration." Kaja Silverman argues for the little girl's similar retrospective understanding of sexual difference in which genitals have no meaning in themselves but only as symbols of cultural inscription: "What is at issue here is not the female subject's biological inferiority, but her symbolic exclusion or lack—her isolation, that is, from those cultural privileges which define the male subject as potent and sufficient."[54] That process is clearly delineated in Ocampo's sequencing. Amalia sees—and the sighting is emphasized by verbs of vision—a familiar scene with new understanding: "Lo *miré*. ¡Tantas veces había *visto* los animales en esa postura! —Ya *vio* lo que quería *ver*" [I *looked*. So may times I had *seen* animals in that pose! Now you *saw* what you wanted to *see* (emphasis mine)]. She has understood in a flash of insight her positioning in the law. However, her comprehension is one remove from the scene of copulation itself. Only in combination with Pata de Perro's allusions does she comprehend her own relationship to the act. The name of the cigarettes, her original fascination, indicates that the woman of the image is the bull's daughter. What Amalia finds unacceptable is that she also be placed as daughter: "give up her wish for a penis . . . and take her father as love object" (Freud, quoted in Silverman, 143). Amalia refuses to accept her condition as lack, give up her desire for the phallus (freedom, power), and embrace the obvious symbol of male sexuality and potency: the bull/father. I have made the assumption, based on Pata de Perro's use of *usted,* formal address, in speaking to her, that Amalia and her brothers are children of the estate's owner, and therefore truly children of the oligarch, the most phallic man around. The girl's outrage at this vision of the law to which she must inevitably submit inspires her creative rebellion. However, her rage vents itself on the unfortunate messenger, the bearer of bad tidings, her friend

Pata de Perro and his beloved horse. She makes the mistake of confusing a real, biological man for the father of law. Her story ends with sadness and regret. But not without having shown us a female subject in full flower, subject of her own discourse, engaged in acts of invention and creativity, whose desire for knowledge, freedom, and power is the story's motivating force.

If this young character resists the absolute boundaries of male and female upon which the subject is constructed, other components of the story contest an even more radical split, that between human and animal. The key image, repeated in the title, consists of a sexually charged human/animal couple, a woman embracing a bull. Pata de Perro, on the other hand, is a nickname for a man (whose given name, Nieves [snow] Montovia, also indicates his connection with nature) with animal characteristics who in the conclusion is metaphorically tied to his horse: "Bauticé a uno de los muñecos con el nombre de Pata de Perro. Era una suerte de centauro, pues para simbolizar al carnicero quise que estuviese a horcajadas en la yegua Remigia, a la cual el hombre quería tanto" (*I* 14) [I baptized one of the stick figures with the name of Pata de Perro. It was a kind of centaur, since to symbolize the butcher I wanted him to be astride his mare Remigia, which the man loved so much]. The word "centauro" is thereafter used to describe the created image of Pata de Perro and his horse. We have then a female human with male animal (la hija del toro) versus a male human with female animal (Pata de Perro and Remigia). These two couples represent, quite ironically, "normal" sexuality in our society: The young woman embracing the father (bull), and the man attached to, taking as object of desire the sacrificing mother/horse, named Remigia. The mythological origin of both images reinforces their normative quality.[55] Amalia at age seven lashes out at a system of sexual/social arrangements based on ancient Mediterranean tradition by inventing her own cult. The children's ritual game borrows from African or New World voodoo traditions. That it always takes place on a Sunday offers a perfect sacrilegious counter to the Christian and pre-Christian world she attempts to overthrow. No wonder the boys later deny having participated in such a game: In Amalia's cult religion all the family members named and tossed into the boiling vat are men, something her brothers only later recognize as a crime. In resisting the law, Amalia resists all the dichotomies on which subjectivity and language are based: male/female, human/ animal, subject/object. The characters mix human and animal, male and female, and in the burial scene, Nieves Montovia "becomes" the doll. Ocampo's fantastic themes of metamorphosis and magical objects enact a serious female rebellion. If we cannot identify a revolt against the system by male children, the little girls such as Amalia, Porfiria, and Fedora do pose a challenge to both symbolic and patriarchal systems. Matamoro's title accurately names, with the convenient gender difference available in Spanish, "la nena terrible" as the only true challenger to what Jane Austen calls "the world's law."[56]

Amalia, like Porfiria and Fedora, express desire in the broad sense suggested by Lacan, as the motor for subjectivity itself, as desire for power, freedom, creativity. The more colloquial, sexualized sense of the word is never far from either Lacan or Ocampo, and several of her stories of very young girls deal overtly with their sexual desire. "Anillo de humo," for instance, details the fascination of a young child, eleven years old, for a fifteen-year-old mechanic. The narrator makes it clear that the poverty and brutality of the boy are precisely what attracts the protected girl of the upper classes. The first paragraph of the story recalls her first sight of him in which he kills a dog wounded by a passing car. Though the adults who accompany the child decry his act as cruel, another interpretation suggests that the boy's act was one of mercy to the suffering animal. In any case, the narrative voice declares unambiguously, "Desdeñaste el dolor del perro para admirar la belleza de Gabriel. . . . Amaste su perfil y su pobreza" (*I* 54) [You disdained the dog's pain in order to admire Gabriel's beauty. . . . You loved his profile and his poverty].[57]

The story captures the innocence and the intensity of childhood passion and lavishes a respect on childhood emotion that it rarely receives in other writers. One of Ocampo's phrases poetically defines desire as being itself: "Eras la mera prolongación de tu sentimiento: el cirio que sostiene la llama" (55) [You were the mere extension of your emotion: the votive candle that sustains the flame]. The title's reference to "smoke rings" becomes a related sexual image but initially refers to the pretext used by the young characters for their secret meetings; she asks him to buy cigarettes for her, which they smoke together in an erotic simulation of the sex act. The first erotic experiences lead a child to many of the elements of adult romance: her sense of betrayal when she realizes that Gabriel is bragging to his friends about their secret meetings, her elaborate lie to lure him to the train tracks, and her melodramatic suggestion that they commit suicide together. Although, as always, Ocampo demonstrates what is false or dangerous in romantic thralldom, her acknowledgment of desire in certain very young girls gives them the ability to desire a true Other, a capacity no other type of character possesses. This particular little girl's desire crosses impossible oceans of social class, as she suggests in the conclusion: "Lo miraste dentro del aire con incienso de la iglesia, como un pez en el agua mira un pez cuando hace el amor" (56) [You looked at him in the air of the church filled with incense, like a fish in water looks at another fish when it makes love]. Other child characters cross even more impossible boundaries.

One of the youngest characters to portray herself as explicitly sexual is the first-person narrator of "Albino Orma." Her childhood sexual initiation at the age of six with another child is complexly narrated in relation to an adult romance with the title character. Here is how she remembers her experience with a little boy named Juan:

> Mientras las niñeras conversaban con íntima animación, nosotros, Juan y yo, escondidos detrás de los arbustos, jugábamos a juegos inocentemente obscenos. . . . Fornicar era una de las palabras más atrayentes en el libro de catecismo. Queríamos en la práctica descubrir su significado. Lo descubrimos. (*Ldn* 94)

> [While the babysitters conversed with intimate animation, we, Juan and I, hidden behind the shrubs, played innocently obscene games. . . . Fornicate was one of the most attractive words in the catechism. We wanted to discover in practice what it meant. We discovered it.]

To this point, the mutuality is complete, emphasized by the first-person plural of the key verbs. This character remembers her six-year old self as the female desiring subject par excellence. But things change abruptly as she continues: "Juan era tan precoz como yo y me cubrió de oprobio cuando blandió su sexo como un palo contra mí. Soporté aquello con heroísmo, pero juré vengarme y lo hice en la primera oportunidad" (95) [Juan was as precocious as I and covered me with shame as he blandished his sex organ like a club against me. I bore up with heroism, but I vowed to take vengeance and did so at the first opportunity]. Her vengeance consists in befriending a little girl and heaping scorn upon her "lascivo amiguito" [lascivious little friend]. Nevertheless, she continues to speak of the early experience as the intensely passionate one of her life, forming a sym-

metry, she now supposes, with those of the title character, Albino
Orma.[58] The narrator plans to abandon the latter by befriending
a woman just as she had earlier abandoned Juan. The insistence
on parallelism and repetition forces the reader to conclude that
the motivation is the same, that she defends herself against male
superiority, even when it brings pleasure, by seeking refuge in
female companionship.[59]

The overt sexual desire displayed by small girls in Ocampo's
fiction functions as a subversive element in that often they triumph over forces usually considered more powerful than they
and rearrange the laws of the symbolic. However, as "Albino
Orma" suggests, the freely expressed sexuality of the female has
its dark side. The stories discussed in the concluding section
delve into the consequences of the more normative silencing of
female desire. The desire of the child, especially of the female
child, is a hidden element of our culture, usually denied, unnamed, and therefore, invisible. Several of Ocampo's works explore the darker side of childish impotence and victimization to
discover the dangers for freely displayed female desire,[60] and
one or two include the child in what can only be considered
perversion, a scenario that, by definition, places the child's desire out of the frame. My arguments in this chapter follow
Ocampo's stories in a roughly chronological manner; generally
the stories of playful subversion are followed by more pessimis-
tic tales of female silencing and resignation.

CONCLUSION: BLESS THE BEASTS AND THE CHILDREN

I have read in "Keif" the clearest reconciliation of Ocampo's
fictional preoccupations; the menacing forces of magical objects,
mad doubles, "madres terribles," "nenas terribles" and sexualized animals are all figured as positive images in a world of female pleasure and creativity. The trajectory I have traced closely
mimics Gallop's proposal for female subjectivity: "It may be historically necessary to be momentarily blind to father-love; it may
be politically effective to defend—tightly, unlucidly—against its
inducements, in order . . . to rediscover some feminine desire,
some desire for a masculine body that does not respect the Father's Law."[61] Amalia of "La hija del toro" and Porfiria defend
themselves against father-love, while Fedora ("Keif") and a few of
Ocampo's later female characters take the next step in directing
desire in a way counter to the law. These positive images of

female rebellion undeniably suggest that sexual impulses occasionally cross species. The vaguely eroticized ambiance of "Mimoso," "La gallina de membrillo," and "Keif" attribute human qualities to intensely beloved pets, while "La hija del toro," "El diario de Porfiria Bernal," "Malva," and many others describe humans as animal-like. Starting with "Paisaje de trapecios," in which the close association of a woman and her pet monkey causes jealousy in her boyfriend, stories involving animals and humans become ever more overtly sexualized. Ocampo gives a positive and playful spin to a few of these stories as we have seen; others explore much more disturbing possibilities in the breakdown between human and animal.

A few of Ocampo's stories depict the most transgressive of sexual behaviors, perversion, an act that Louise J. Kaplan defines as one which, among other things, uses a substitute for a consenting partner. Ocampo's stories of perversion demonstrate Kaplan's primary argument, that sexual perversion itself is no liberating way out of conservative social arrangements, for it is enacted by a person "who has no other choices": "what distinguishes perversion is its quality of desperation and fixity."[62] Kaplan further suggests that perversion, as a performance, reinscribes the most conventional and stereotyped images of male and female offered by culture. Ocampo's works identify little girls and animals, the lowest forms of life on the social/political hierarchy, as the beings most often used as the unconsenting partners of perversion, their desire most easily silenced or denied.

While the narration contains only a diffuse sexual fantasy, "El Destino" portrays quite literally the invisibility of female desire. The narrator, probably an adolescent, begins her story at the bakery called El Destino whose clerk, Roque, is the object of her long-term crush. The attraction seems to be almost completely one-sided and carried out in unspoken flirtation. When Roque's friend Silvio enters the girl is forgotten. She fades into the shadows of the store and listens in horrified fascination as they arrange an assignation for later in the evening with two prostitutes. From this point, the girl never emerges from the shadows and by story's end has become invisible, not just metaphorically, but literally. At one point she overhears Roque describe her as "más aburrida que un vaso de agua tibia" (Y así 161). Though insulted, she seems powerless to overcome the timidity and reticence which convert her to a glass of warm water, essential yet tasteless. Her desire is the unseen for the other characters of her world, a situation to which she reacts, like other Ocampo characters, with an acute sense of injustice.

"El incesto" and "Atinganos" leave the expression of injustice to the reader, for the children have no voice. Both stories seem to promise a focus on the child's sexuality, but both place the child at the margins, rather than at the center of the plot. The interplay of title with plot invites a careful consideration in both cases of what is marginal and what is central, how the stories' plot direction leads first away and then back to the desire of the child. "El incesto" is set in a dressmaker's shop where the family business creates an extended family of its own.[63] In this sense, the narrator's positioning as worker in the shop, favorite "daughter" of the mother/owner, creates an ambiguity surrounding the word *incest*. The betrayal implicit in the word is transferred by story's end from the biological to the spiritual daughter. The narrator's self-serving version of events puts every aspect of the story in question. The narrator invites speculation regarding the sexualized relationship between father and daughter—the narrator blames the twelve-year-old girl for the couple's marital problems and at one point describes her as "coqueta"—at the same time she attempts to absolve him of improper interest in his daughter. In absolving him, however, she accuses herself. She describes in detail one episode in which he kisses his daughter with what the narrator takes to be double meaning: "Horacio la besaba mirándome como diciendo: 'Estoy besando a Livia, pero en mi imaginación te beso a ti'" (*I* 87) [Horacio was kissing her while looking at me as if saying, "I am kissing Livia, but in my imagination I am kissing you"].[64] The narrator effectively accuses the child of incestual desires at the same time she attempts to prove the father innocent of everything but adulterous ones. In other passages, the narrator's double-speak demonstrates her flirtatious behavior toward Horacio at the same time it overtly attempts to prove the opposite.

The narrator's repeated expressions of devotion to her boss, her identity as the owner's spiritual daughter in response to the woman's maternal affection and confidence, attempt to reinforce her own innocence. In fact, they alert the reader to the narrator's emotional positioning. By her own account, she places herself in sibling rivalry with the child Livia and in Oedipal conflict with the mother/owner, named, of all things, Dionisia.[65] The familial dynamics of the whole sexually charged situation make Horacio, the father, a contested prize among three embattled females. The narrator makes it clear that she has no doubt of

Horacio's innocence in terms of Dionisia's growing suspicions. Unwilling to lose the love of the "mother," she decides not to tell her what she considers to be the truth, that Horacio is interested in her and not in his daughter. Dionisia, convinced that her husband is sexually pursuing their daughter, escapes with her on a ship to Spain, presumably without confronting him. The conclusion rewards this adopted daughter with everything she desired, the love of both "mother" and "father," and leaves open the possibility that all members of the "family" are innocent except for the hypocritical narrator.

Though the child Livia is named by insinuation in the story's title and the reader would expect her to be its focus, she remains a marginal figure within the plot. Similarly, the story "Atinganos" carries the name of a child character, also a twelve-year-old girl, but the plot directs attention elsewhere. The story focuses on political corruption and greed. Atinganos, the daughter of a gypsy chief, makes her appearance only in the last paragraphs of the story, where she is used as a bargaining point over rent to be paid for a vacant lot where a gypsy tribe has set up camp. The third-person narrator briefly describes the child's situation through the main character Rómulo Pancras, who watches as one of the city inspectors seats Atinganos in his lap: "Él, Rómulo, . . . nunca se había atrevido a sentarla sobre sus rodillas en público, aunque hubiera sido natural que lo hiciera, ya que tantas cosas había hecho con ella en la oscuridad, por más que ella le dijera 'No me toques, no me toques' siempre inútilmente" (*Ldn* 58) [He, Romulo, never would have dared to seat her on his knees in public, although it would have been natural for him to do so, since he had done so many things to her in the dark, no matter how much she said, "Don't touch me, don't touch me," always to no avail]. The story concludes with Atinganos's father awarding Rómulo her hand in marriage in exchange for a good deal on the rent. In "El incesto" and in "Atinganos" the child's sexuality is the issue, but the child herself remains unheard.

The silence and passivity of the child is also painfully related in "Clavel," a story which suggests that a retarded girl is the sexual target of the family's pet dog. The narrator in this case is a second child, a guest in the house, and also the recipient of attentions from the dog that she describes in remarkably human terms: "Sus modales eran extraños e incómodos; se abrazaba a mis piernas, o a mi espalda, arqueándose como un galgo, cuando yo estaba sentada en el suelo" (*Ldn* 91 [His manners were strange and uncomfortable; he embraced my legs or my back, arching himself like a greyhound when I was seated on the floor]. The retarded daughter of the household, called "La boba" [The idiot], is the same age as the narrator, and remains confined to one isolated room of the house. The young narrator's account allows the reader to assume by extension that the dog's behavior is similar in both cases but that "La boba" would be even less able to defend herself: "A ella también Clavel la quería; era natural porque hacía mucho tiempo que se conocían. ¡Pobre Clavel!, su vida de perro consistía en visitarla y en visitarme, por turno" (92) [Clavel also loved her; it was natural because they had known each other a long time. Poor Clavel, his dog's life consisted of visiting her and visiting me in turn]. When the father kills Clavel with a gunshot, the narrator does not need to specify the reason. In case Ocampo's reader doubts what may be implied here, the story is situated in the original collection between "Albino Orma," discussed above as an overt portrayal of the sexual potential of six-year-old girl, and "Livio Roca," a narrative that makes veiled suggestions regarding the bestiality of a man with his mule, Clemencia.[66]

Of the stories just described, "Atinganos" comes closest to suggesting perversion due to the unequal power relations between sexual partners. Rómulo Pancras uses an unwilling partner, a child. "Livio Roca" and "Clavel" describe relationships of bestiality that leave open the question of consent. Ocampo seems to suggest in both of the latter that the human world which kills the animal in both cases, may have been too quick to judge a sexual liaison of innocent mutuality. Of interest to me here is the observation, regardless of the value of good/evil imposed on the stories, of the passivity of the female. Atinganos a twelve-year-old girl, La Boba a retarded six-year-old, and Clemencia the mule are situated as romantic love objects. The dog, Clavel, inverts the usual definition of bestiality since he is positioned as the aggressor and the children the passive recipients of his attentions. The female, whether animal or human, is frighteningly, even disgustingly passive in all three stories.

"El rival" combines themes of metamorphosis and the double within an unambiguously sexual scenario that repeats similar dynamics. The male narrator proclaims his love for a woman, but significantly describes in detail only his male rival for her affection. The contrast between the two men is the one often attributed to women in Ocampo's fiction: The narrator prides himself on his good looks, while his rival is, in his opinion, ugly because of his triangular pupils. But he could speak for many another Ocampo character when he moans, "De nada sirve la hermosura. Nuestra vida es un pandemonium si no atrae al ser amado" (*Y así* 92) [Beauty is useless. Life is in pandemonium if it does not attract the beloved]. The sexual "menage a trois" is openly affirmed in this story, which takes its trio off to the wilderness of Misiones on an extended camping trip where, isolated from civilization, their unusual relationship will not be noticed. There the rival disappears into the forest. A jaguar with the same triangular pupils repeatedly described as characteristic of the man, enters the camp early the morning following his disappearance, and walks into the tent "como si la conociera" [as if he were familiar with it/as if he knew her]. The sexual activities associated with the tent make the pronoun deliberately ambiguous, as "la" refers here to "la carpa," but by extension, to the woman sleeping inside. Ocampo's version of a classic horror tale (of metamorphosis) makes explicit what lies just below the surface of the genre, a deviant sexuality. Although this one is not, as far as the reader knows, an instance of perversion since all parties are presented as consenting, if silent.

Cornelia frente al espejo contains the story, entitled "El mi, el si, o el la," of an otherwise typical love triangle but among a woman with the suggestively comic name, Alma Bestiglia, and two of her pets. The cat, named Terco, runs off one day because of Alma's singing, hence the story's title, a humorous reference to musical notation. Upon his return the cat attacks the woman, tearing at her vocal chords, and narrowly misses killing her; instead, he is killed by the dog who saves his owner's life. Though the story seems to suggest that the cat's motivation for the attack was jealousy of the dog who had supplanted him in Alma's bed during his absence, it is worth noting that his departure was motivated in the first place by the woman's voice and that on his return the cat attacks her throat rendering her dumb. What are we to make of a story that depicts male desire as emanating from an animal and that seeks to silence the human female? This story's almost raucous humor presents a grim image of male and female sexuality.

"Miren como se aman" (*Cornelia*) not only repeats the suggestion of sexual alliance between a woman and her pet, but deliberately gestures to a much earlier story, "Paisaje de trapecios" (*Vo*), as an intertext for the new one. Both explore the relationship between Adriana and her monkey, and just to make sure we notice the connection between the two stories, the later one uses the original title phase, "paisaje de trapecios" [scenery with trapezes], in one of the descriptions of the circus where it is set. While the earlier narrative employs veiled language to suggest that the monkey, eventually killed by the owner's jealous boyfriend, represents a sexual object for her, the new story dramatizes this notion more extravagantly. In "Miren como se aman" the monkey talks at one point, asking her to marry him. After the monkey has been killed, she kisses him, and with a radical switch in narrative code, he turns into a prince. Since it is time for their circus act, Adriana and the monkey-*cum*-prince appear on stage where the crowd greets them with ambivalent cries, as at a soccer game:

> —Señoras y señores, verán un espectáculo nuevo: el príncipe vuelve a ser mono en los brazos de su amada. Miren cómo se aman.
> Los aplausos fueron atronadores. El público gritó:
> —Mono no, príncipe sí. Mono no, príncipe sí. Mono sí, príncipe no. Mono sí, príncipe no (*Cornelia* 63).
>
> ["Ladies and gentlemen, you will see a new show: the prince turns back into a monkey in the arms of his beloved. Look how they love each other." The applause was thunderous. The audience shouted: "Monkey no, prince yes. Monkey no, prince yes. Monkey yes, prince no. Monkey yes, prince no."]

The structural and verbal disjunctures notable throughout this last collection are obvious here. One idea that emerges from this absurd ending is that the public has no idea what it wants, is both embarrassed by and addicted to romance.

"Pier" takes the denial of difference one more level in depicting the romantic devotion between a small dog and a dust rag. They and their "history" are described in unmistakably human terms. They meet, fall in love, are inseparable, then she "dies" giving birth to "trapitos" [baby rags], and he is left to mourn: "Ningún trapo, ningún otro es el que busca, pero el que busca ya no es el mismo. Perdió su virginidad, su integridad, su belleza, su olor atroz" (*Y así* 138) [No rag, no other is the one he searches for, but the one he looks for is no longer the same. She lost her virginity, her integrity, her beauty and her atrocious odor]. The sentimentalized depiction of human emotion contrasts with the blunt details of excrement and filth. Despite the obvious irony, the story examines the dynamics of human romance, and returns to favorite themes, especially the irrational nature of love's object and the surprisingly complex issues of power: "Nunca nadie prevé el peligro que existe en esclavizar al prójimo. Esclavizar implica la esclavitud, a la larga, del que esclaviza" (134) [No one ever foresees the danger that exists in enslaving another. To enslave implies the slavery, in the end, of the one who enslaves]. The mutual dependence of both parties in conventional arrangements ultimately damages both.

Ocampo's animal stories break down the rigidly held difference between animal and human, and between animate and inanimate. Aside from their obvious relation to fantastic and grotesque elements, they are also utilized to draw parallels to conventions of romance. I have argued that in many kinds of narratives Ocampo creates female subjects; but several of her animal stories reinscribe the male and female in their positions of subject and object. The female animals, Remigia ("La hija del toro") and Clemencia ("Livio Roca"), function eerily like the silenced, compliant little girls of stories like "Atinganos," while the male animals, Terco ("El mi, el si, o el la") and Clavel take up the position of subject whose desire creates pain and madness. Kaplan relates all sexual perversions to the need to deny difference, and defines the fetish as a senseless substitute for a live human. Animals and children do serve the function of fetish in a few of Ocampo's stories: "Atinganos," for instance, seems the example of a child's desire ignored by the male. However, the story allows the child's protest to be heard by the reader, if not by the characters of her world. Ocampo creates no senseless beings. The author's insistence on the subjectivity of both children and animals makes their stories of abuse particularly tragic. At the same time, it is not their status as child or as animal that constitutes abuse, but rather the issue of consent. Both children and animals are presented as desirous and capable of sexual pleasure; they are also easy victims.

Gallop has suggested that one way of undoing the law of the father is to flaunt its abusive power.[67] I want to make a careful distinction in closing between what I have called transgressive sexuality and perversion. The former is, in my opinion, held by Ocampo's stories as a positive mode of female "breaking out" into pleasurable, non(re)productive sexual activities, and can be liberating to the female subject, as Gallop suggests. The latter, however, with its implication of coercion and obsession, is found rarely in Ocampo's stories and is always negatively connoted. The difference will be crucial to the stories discussed in chapter 4. Ocampo's works enact a lengthy and complex examination of the conventions of romance. Her stories effectively exaggerate male power by placing desire in unexpected male subjects: dogs, cats, tigers and monkeys! By exaggerating its "normal" operations she makes them ridiculous indeed; by inverting their terms of subject/object, passive/aggressive, male/female she asks us to re-examine many fondly held assumptions; and finally, by imaginatively, fantastically forcing a subjectivity on the most abject of objects (a dishrag, a mule), she has uncovered a most original way to "write beyond the ending" of the woman's plot and calls for the more humane treatment of all the creatures of our world.

Ocampo's application of the subversive powers of the fantastic and grotesque to conventions of romance and of gender is one of her most original contributions to twentieth-century literature. This study has been at pains to show that Ocampo portrays both male and female positions as constructs in language and in culture in which both male and female are structured by an absence that has nothing to do with anatomy. The connection between the feminine and the fantastic is summarized by Kaja Silverman's remarks regarding Freud's use of the word *uncanny* in yet another instance, in his essay on "Feminine Sexuality." Freud, of course, argues that the first sight of the genitals of the opposite sex provokes a crisis in both male and female children. The male responds with a horror that motivates him to renounce his desire of the mother and identify with the father, while both sexes agree that "the female subject is established as being both different and inferior."[68] Silverman suggests that when Freud describes the revelation of woman's perceived lack as "uncanny and traumatic," however, he unwittingly admits that the implications of castration involve the boy as much as the little girl, that he views something horrifying because familiar:

> According to the terms of Freud's own argument, if the spectacle of female castration strikes the male viewer as "uncanny," he himself must already have experienced castration; far from functioning merely as an "innocent" (albeit horrified) onlooker, he too inhabits the frame of the unpleasurable image. In other words, the recurrence of the word *uncanny* in the essay on fetishism reminds us that even before the so-called castration crisis, the male subject has an intimate knowledge of loss—that he undergoes numerous divisions or splittings prior to the moment at which he is made to fear the loss of his sexual organ. Thus, what seems to confront him from without, in the guise of the "mutilated" female body, actually threatens him from within, in the form of his own history. (17)

Silverman argues that woman is designated by our culture to cover over the unacceptable knowledge of male castration. But what culture is so careful to construct—sexual difference based on female lack—is always having to be reconfigured, is continually on the verge of breaking down: "what is now associated with the female subject has been transferred to her from the male subject, and that the transfer is by no means irreversible" (18). Ocampo's works demonstrate the various ways in which woman is forced to pose in order to cover over that unacceptable knowledge. If nineteenth-century fantastic spoke of sexuality itself as the "unseen" of culture, twentieth-century works, especially those of Silvina Ocampo, uncover what our culture still strives to keep hidden, male castration and female desire. This, I would argue, is the "dark area" (Jackson's term) of absence toward which her fantasies move.

Part II
Writing the Feminine

Introduction

When virginia woolf speculated about the consequences of women writers taking up the pen she observed famously that they would "break the sequence" and the "sentence" of inherited tradition.[1] Part 1 of this study has looked primarily at the former, the ways in which positing a female subject transforms the sweep of plot, the accustomed sequence of story. Part 2 attempts an approach to the "sentence," a word Woolf uses to encompass the set of assumptions about the world and about literature that reader and writer must share in order to communicate. Male writers have available to them a long tradition which Woolf describes as "common property," common to past writers, to new authors who will "take their own tint" at it, and to readers who in approaching their writing know what to expect.[2] The common sentence of masculine tradition can not situate the woman writer adequately into discourse. The different "sentence" she develops for herself, because unfamiliar, inevitably makes its reception slower and more difficult.[3] Woolf's essay was published in 1929, less than ten years before Ocampo's first published collection of short stories (1937). Though there are differences in English and Spanish literary traditions, a similar if not identical set of problems existed for Silvina Ocampo as she set out to write fiction. Woolf's word *break* suggests the subversive intent that is emphasized in Part 1. In turning to the "sentence" I modify my focus on subversion to emphasize more active elements of the creative process. Nevertheless, the difference between subversion and creation is not meant to be absolute, as all works of art entail both processes at once.

Part 2 wades into the "dark continent" (Schor's term) of the

157

feminine with several questions in mind. Specifically, I began with a paraphrase of a set of questions posed by Gilbert and Gubar's *No Man's Land:* how did Silvina Ocampo imagine her own relation to language? In taking up the pen, did she empower her own voice with "dreams of an archaic language which predates the patronymics of culture" or does she prefer to invent a "new 'maiden' language which postdates the inscriptions and descriptions of patriarchy"?[4] Does she try to adopt (perhaps appropriate?) the "father speech" in order to play with the boys or does she seek out the "mother tongue"? My conclusions, perhaps frustrating to any reader, reveal that Ocampo has tried most if not all these strategies.

Chapter 3 attempts to deduce from the works themselves some idea of Ocampo's aesthetic vision first by way of an exploration of metafictional commentary revealed in works dealing with artists and writers and then by an exploration of her use of details. To my surprise, I found a preoccupation with the maternal as font of creativity. Therefore, the previous chapter's struggle with the bad mother reappears here in images of the creative process. Now Ocampo's critique of motherhood as it is commonly imagined redefines the maternal as creative, not merely biological, and envisions artistic creativity itself as essentially maternal. In both arenas of creative activity, writing and painting, Ocampo imagines the artist "herself" as androgynous, in the words of one of her poems, "un espíritu bizco," a cross-eyed spirit who cannot be identified by gender. Whatever we may think in the late twentieth century about Woolf's call for androgyny, I believe that ideal underlies and helps to explain much about Ocampo's artistry.[5] The strategies for depicting "feminine contingency," the focus of the chapter's second half, rests on literary elements often associated with a negative assessment of female creativity. My debt to Naomi Schor's *Reading in Detail* is evident throughout this section. Woolf's breaking the sentence describes what I take to be Ocampo's literary practice, while Schor's reading in detail describes my own. My reading in detail will, I hope, elucidate Ocampo's aesthetic orientation and also demonstrate more exactly the revolutionary character of her breaking the sentence. Indeed, Ocampo's works exemplify what Virginia Woolf staked out as ideal for the woman writer: a subject matter which "lighted on small things and showed that perhaps they were not small after all . . . ;" which "brought buried things to light and made one wonder what need there had been to bury them;" and a point of view which cannot be identified as "a man or woman pure and simple," but one that is "woman-manly or man-womanly."[6]

Ocampo's use of literary elements associated with a traditional feminine, already observed in her taste for everyday or ornamental details, is the focus of chapter 4. Here the letter, a mode of writing most often associated with ordinary women, a supposed obsession with the self in mirrors, a mode of communication based on ambiguity and silence—often denigrated as part of an inferior feminine aesthetic—become powerful tools in the process to transform inherited notions about gender and art. My categories should not be mistaken for a belief by Ocampo (or myself) in anything like an "essential feminine"; her works are rather a systematic denial of such a belief. I have viewed Ocampo's task as one of writing from what Rosario Castellanos called "the feminine situation."[7] These stories display the constructedness of femininity, the hard work, in fact, of maintaining the fiction of the feminine.

The female body under analysis here is necessarily a discursive, not a biological, one.[8] The confusion of the two is most at risk in the last section of chapter 4, the discussion of rape, but is everywhere an issue in the final chapter. Though I have quoted Kaja Silverman's *Acoustic Mirror* throughout, no series of footnotes can convey my debt to this book. The way in which issues are approached, the choice of questions to ask, all are influenced by her brilliant reconsideration of current feminist theory in which she maintains a rigorously theoretical attentiveness to "the ways in which authorship is both deployed and limited" within a text, while "developing hermeneutic strategies capable of foregrounding rather than neutralizing female authorship."[9] In the words of Teresa de Lauretis, the French feminists have asked the wrong question. Instead of asking, what is the nature of Woman (and arriving at all-too-familiar conclusions: the obverse of man, i.e., irrational, closer to the body, unable to speak for herself, oriented toward pleasure), we need to ask how do women keep turning into Woman.[10] Silverman elaborates the need to seek strategies to maintain the power of the French theorists' deconstruction of phallic economy without falling into its negative mode, of returning Woman to mute, irrational nature all over again.[11] Silvina Ocampo in my readings offers concrete fictional examples of both impulses: she explores the "dark continent" of femininity as it is currently lived while holding this up to the reader as constructed, not essential. I hope to demonstrate that Ocampo's works "know" the secret of the feminine, that this creature, woman, who appears to embody lack is revealing what men are allowed, nay required, to hide: "what passes for femininity is actually an inevitable part of all subjectivity."[12]

3

Aesthetic Fantasies

(RE)IMAGINING THE CREATOR

Algunos dicen con palabras prestigiosas que el sujeto de la escritura es andrógino: yo creo que es así, pero prefiero imaginar ese andrógino como alguien cuyos caracteres femeninos permanentemente lo traicionan; como andrógino quiere vendar sus pechos pero éstos delatan su volumen a través de la ropa, se sujeta los cabellos pero éstos se le sueltan irredentos. En otras palabras, ese andrógino que escribe es una mujer.

—Tunuma Mercado[13]

[Some say with prestigious phrases that the subject of writing is androgynous: I believe this is true, but I prefer to imagine that androgynous being as someone whose feminine characteristics constantly betray it; as androgyn it wants to bind its breasts, but their volume under clothing gives them away, it ties up its hair but it comes loose, unredeemed. In other words, that androgyn who writes is a woman.]

In reading for an aesthetics contained within Ocampo's works, I have divided the material between images of writing and depictions of the other arts. In both categories I look at stories that contain overtly metafictional representations of professional writers and artists and broaden the arena of investigation to include the "amateurs." If Ocampo rarely depicts intellectuals or artists of any kind, she frequently presents characters engaged in more broadly conceived creative activities, and these provide the best clues to her approach to the creative enterprise generally. The two sections are organized in opposite directions. The first section on artists begins with creative outlets by ordinary women characters and only then takes up the professional woman artist; the section on authors takes the reverse course. The difference is generated by the historic relationship of women to artistic medium. Ocampo's fictional world, unlike that

161

of her own life, includes no intellectuals, but common people occupied with family rather than professional life. In such a milieu it is easier to situate ordinary women as writers than as artists, for the composition of letters and journals has long been an accepted activity. Women have been more systematically excluded from the fine arts, however, and a depiction of female characters as professional artists sets them apart from the outset as exceptional, not ordinary. Ocampo's interest in her characters' creative investment in everyday activities occasions a reconception of the notion of art. Ocampo does portray female artists and performers in her fiction, but without an expanded definition, they remain hidden from view. A feminist (re)definition opens her works to reveal a wide-ranging exploration of the issues of artistic expression and the feminine.

ARTISTS

In reading Ocampo's stories in light of a specifically feminine aesthetic, I have been influenced by Josephine Donovan's elaboration of six "structural conditions" that shape women's worldviews and, hence, their poetics.[14] Several of her points, acknowledging women's oppression, bodily processes, and psychology of difference have been incorporated indirectly elsewhere in this study. However, her points that women's work is repetitive and static, essentially cyclical and interruptible and that it is done for use rather than exchange, have proved valuable to my approach to Ocampo's works. In her elaboration of these points Donovan relies on Kathryn Allen Rabuzzi's study of women's work and art which makes a convincing argument for traditional women's path to transcendental experience via the routine work of the home. Rabuzzi describes the efforts of feminist artists to expand the definition of art to include womanly activities traditionally designated as "crafts" or even "chores," specifically fine embroidery, sewing, quilting, gardening, cooking, and even cleaning. Ocampo's short stories implicitly recognize the creativity invested in these tasks and draw upon them as part of a uniquely female artistic aesthetic. All of these thinkers coincide with Kristeva's definition of art itself as a process rather than as an object.[15]

In a process that Rabuzzi calls cosmization, the act of placing oneself in a world context, "the creation of world out of chaos," women use household objects or monotonous tasks as paths to a more transcendental state.[16] Ocampo's story, "La escalera," serves as an example of the contemplative, meditative mental realm that Rabuzzi suggests is possible by means of the disengagement of mind that a vulgar, routine task affords. The old char woman, Isaura, relives her life envisioned in each of the marble stairs she cleans. As she climbs the stairway, each numbered stair evokes a specific event in her long life of violence, sex, birth, and death. An ordinary object is transformed by this old woman into something sacred, the simple tasks of her days into a kind of meditation. Just as many of Ocampo's fantastic stories evoke what Rabuzzi calls the demonic realm of housework, this story illustrates what she means by the sacred realm, the creative act which connects object, self, and universe.

In spite of the "seriousness" of Ocampo's own education, both artistic and literary, she incorporates into her work a validation of artistic creativity specific to a woman's culture. Her obsession with the power of ordinary objects, to which, in the realm of the fantastic and the grotesque, she attributes magical properties, also creates the world of female contingency decried by traditional proponents of fine art.[17] Taking this debased world as unexplored territory, Ocampo has spent a lifetime elaborating its aesthetic possibilities. The importance of details, household and otherwise, is such that I return to them later. For our purposes here, many aspects of homemaking, including selecting and cleaning household objects, are validated in Ocampo's works as artistic in and of themselves. "La escalera" and other stories turn to artistic advantage the assumptions commonplace in our culture regarding a woman's special connection to the material world. Since women buy and clean household objects, they are more aware of them as such and of their larger significance as elements of self-expression.

Ocampo's first story collection, *Viaje olvidado,* was published following her decision to concentrate on fiction instead of painting. Not surprisingly it contains several plotlines and characters which utilize artists or art to make more general aesthetic statements. The narrator of "Los pies desnudos" describes the main (male) character as a person buried in paper, papers that he is afraid to lose and that in the story come to symbolize arguments and resentments between himself and his lover. The title refers to an embedded memory in which a former love tells him of losing all her possessions and of her decision therefore to become a dancer:

> Se hizo bailarina y bailaba con los pies desnudos para no tener que depender de los zapatos de baile que se pierden en los viajes debajo de las camas de los hoteles. Ethel tenía razón.
>
> Pero él, Cristián ¡necesitaba tal equipaje! ¡Tal regimiento de libros, de cuadernos y papeles para hacer cualquier cosa, tal regimiento de zapatos para usar al fin y al cabo siempre los mismos y no bailar con ellos!
>
> ¡Oh! la felicidad de los bailarines contorsionistas y pruebistas que no necesitan llevar sino su cuerpo! (*Vo* 179)

[She became a dancer and danced with bare feet so as not to depend on dance shoes which are lost on trips under hotel beds. Ethel was right. But he, Cristián, needed such baggage! Such a mass of books, notebooks and papers in order to do anything, such a mass of shoes to end up using the same ones all the time and never to dance in them! Oh! the joy of ballerinas, contortionists and acrobats who need to wear nothing but the body.]

The pervasive fear of losing things is attributed obliquely to the female character who has solved the problem here by paring artistic expression to the bare essentials. We will return below to the frequent connection made between losing things and female creativity. In the present instance, the female artist frees herself to utilize only the body itself. The implied aesthetic ideal, the elimination of excess and the validation of an unencumbered female artist, proclaims a vision of beauty which underlies Ocampo's further production, but which will be expressed hereafter in more oblique, less optimistic form. The various characters in dance, acrobatics, ice skating, or other bodily feats can be taken as a veiled image of the ideal artist in her stories.[18]

Ocampo's other important image of the artist is the seamstress. The poor old woman of "Esperanza en Flores" punctuates her thoughts by counting the stitches of her knitting; and the young pregnant woman of "El cuaderno" sits mending in the first scene of that story. The repetitive, mechanical nature of these tasks, knitting and mending, are intimately associated with a specifically female culture. Their professional equivalent appears in the guise of the many seamstresses, milliners, florists, and other skilled craftswomen who populate Ocampo's fiction. The various characters engaged in fine handwork all have a sense of vocation, absent from the characters busy with more routine tasks. The difference between the routine and the professional, and the tension that Ocampo brings to that difference, is illustrated in "El cuaderno." The young pregnant woman seen mending at the window of her dark apartment, once was a hat-maker whose astounding artistic ability with her materials made her the best worker in her shop. Paula, the shop's owner, has given this most valuable employee a brass bed as a wedding present. In the first scene Ermelina muses that: "Esa cama era el testimonio de su felicidad" [That bed was the evidence of her happiness]. Since marrying, however, she has lost her abilities as a hatmaker; she reflects on a scene in which the same owner had recently complained of her work:

—Ya te dije Ermelina, ya te dije que no te casaras. Ahora estás triste. Has perdido hasta la habilidad que tenías para adornar sombreros— y sacudiendo un sombrero adornado con cintas, añadía con una pequeñísima risa, que parecía una carraspera—: ¿Qué significa este moño? ¿Qué significa esta costura?
Ermelina sabía que el sombrero era un cachivache, pero quedaba en silencio (era su manera de contestar). No estaba triste. Hasta entonces había tratado los sombreros como a recién nacidos, frágiles e importantes. Ahora le inspiraban un gran cansancio, que se tra-ducía en moños mal hechos y pegados con grandes puntadas, que martirizaban la frescura de las cintas. (*F* 48)

[I told you, Ermelina, not to get married. Now you are sad. You have lost the ability you had for decorating hats—and shaking a hat adorned with ribbons, she added with a small laugh, that seemed like a cough—"What does this knot mean? What about this stitching?" Ermelia knew that the hat was a mess but she remained silent (it was her way of replying). She was not sad. Until then she had treated the hats as newborns, fragile and important. Now they inspired fatigue, which translated itself into badly made bows stuck on with large stitches which tortured the freshness of the ribbon.]

In the past Ermelina had dealt with the hats as if they were newborns ("recién nacidos"). The comparison of hats to new-borns is repeated in another phrase, in which Ermelina reflects that Paula, the owner, "no la quería a ella, sino a su habilidad, no la quería a ella, sino a los sombreros que salían de sus manos como pájaros recién nacidos" (47) [did not love her, but rather her skill, she did not love her, but the hats that escaped from her hands like new born birds]. Now that she has enjoyed the happiness of the brass bed, and is about to have her own new-born, the interest Ermelina once took in her work has disappeared.

As Ermelina awaits the birth of her child, she reflects on past events as she sits at the window mending, an activity that evokes a contemplative state through which we as readers have learned about her past. Her hat-making skill—done for exchange in a "male" economy—has been put to everyday household use. The story develops a fantastic plot in which Ermelina predicts the physical appearance of her child by means of an illustration in a friend's album. As she pages through the album or scrapbook of the story's title, Ermelina tells her friend that one of the images presents the way she would like her child to look. She then adds that an aunt has told her that if one looks at an image during pregnancy the baby will be born looking just like it. Ermelina's first sentence regarding her baby's appearance, expressed in Spanish with multiple subjunctive verbs, is understood as pure wish: "Así quisiera que fuese mi hijo" [This is how I would like my child to look]. When the neighbor objects to the image, Ermelina is more forceful: "Es un niño precioso. . . . Así quiero que sea mi hijo" [It is a beautiful baby. . . . This is the way I want my child to be]. Finally when she leaves a note for her husband to tell him that she is off to the hospital, she writes, "la figura que está en la hoja abierta de este cuaderno es igual a nuestro hijo" [The figure on the open page of this album is exactly like our child]. The final paragraph of the story confirms Ermelina's wish/prediction:

> Entre envoltorios de llantos y pañales Ermelina reconoció la cara rosada pegada contra las lilas del cuaderno. La cara era quizá demasiado colorada, pero ella pensó que tenía el mismo color chillón que tienen los juguetes nuevos, para que no se decoloren de mano en mano. (*F* 51)

> [From within the folds of crying and diapers, Ermelina recongnized the pink face stuck among lilacs of the album. The face was perhaps too red, but she thought that it had the same bright color that new toys have so that they won't fade from being handled.]

The images of child as greeting card print and then painted toy evoke humorous responses in the reader, of course. They also suggest either that Ermelina's perceptions are a form of wish fulfillment or that she possesses fantastic creative powers as a mother.

My reading of the story places Ermelina's role as professional artist (milliner) in tension with the traditional woman's more meditative course viewed during her moments mending at the window. A straight, unironic reading of this tension suggests an unlikely conclusion in view of Ocampo's lifelong devotion to art: that a woman's priorities and happiness lie in the business of life, and not in devotion to art or a profession. Silvia Molloy reads this story as one of many of Ocampo's *cursi* [affected] narrators to be viewed with irony, and as a kind of joke on the reader, whose "truculenta imaginación" [extravagant imagination] no doubt expected a comfortingly horrifying ending: "El cuento era más 'normal' de lo que suponíamos y en esa normalidad—en esa coherencia—reside su básica extrañeza" [The story was more "normal" than we had supposed and in this normalcy—in this coherence—resides its basic strangeness].[19] The birth of a perfect, beautiful baby is no less miraculous than whatever the reader may have been expecting. What remains of a supernatural reading of this story validates the creative aspects of what is more usually considered a biological rather than artistic process, the creation of a human child. When we recall that the works produced for exchange—the hats—were also depicted, at least in Ermelina's mind, as newborns, it is clear that this character's activities, both as traditional and as paid worker, are each viewed simultaneously as artistic, consciously controlled and maternal. Ocampo's story provides an impossible fusion of seemingly contradictory impulses.

The underlying tension/connection between the artistic and the maternal becomes a subtheme in more than one story, not always so cheerfully resolved as in "El cuaderno." "El goce y la penitencia" repeats one element of "El cuaderno," the fantastic connection between an image, in this case a painted portrait, and the appearance of an unborn child. A wonderfully funny story, it nevertheless seems less positive in terms of female creativity. The professional artist, who predicts or "creates" the child, and the mother are no longer one and the same character. The conscious power of creativity is here reserved for the male painter. Furthermore, the presence of a child victim in this story is an uncomfortable image of the dangers of female pleasure, especially of the mother. The mother's pleasure is the source of suffering by more than one child victim of Ocampo's world. In several of these the figure of rescue for the child is a seamstress, that is, a creative artist in disguise.[20]

Three stories present the creative professional seamstress as ideal mother. Clotilde Ifrán is a character in two different stories, in both cases already dead when the stories begin. "La sibila" introduces the reader to one of Ocampo's most engaging "nenas terribles," Aurora. Though she is not the primary narrator of the story, her description of her relationship to a "corsetera" [lingerie specialist] dominates the narrative:

> Hacía fajas y corpiños para señoras y tenía los cajones de su cuarto llenos de cintas celestes y rosadas, elásticos y broches, botones y encajes por todas partes. Cuando yo iba a su casa con mamá y la esperaba, me dejaba jugar con todo y a veces, cuando yo no iba al colegio, y que mamá iba al teatro o Dios sabe dónde, me dejaba en la casa de Clotilde Ifrán, para que ella me cuidara. Y entonces sí que me divertía. (F 57)

> [She made girdles and bodices for ladies and had drawers of her room filled with blue and pink ribbon, elastic and hooks, buttons and lace all over. When I would go to her house with my mother and had to wait, she would let me play with everything and sometimes when I didn't have school and my mother would go to the theater or God knows where, she would leave me at Clotilde Ifran's house so that she could watch me. And then I would really have fun.]

The elements of just this brief description hint at this child's loneliness and neglect at the hands of her upper-class *madre terrible*. Aurora's relationship with Clotilde Ifrán is that of substitute mother. The substitute father is known as "El Señor" [The Lord] who according to Aurora's understanding, had taken Clotilde Ifrán away and would eventually come for Aurora as well. This accounts, then, for the tiny child's fearless reaction to the main narrator, a common thug who has broken into the great house to steal. "Usted es el Señor, porque tiene barba crecida" [You are the Lord because you have a beard], she says.[21] As Aurora chats happily with this man, she also mentions that Clotilde Ifrán taught her to read the future in cards. She then proceeds to lay them out for him and predict his imminent death.

A later story, "Clotilde Ifrán," uses the same name to tell a different story. In this case a nine-year-old girl is told by her busy mother to find herself a seamstress to make a devil costume for Carnival, which this particular year also coincides with her birthday. She finds a phone number in an old address book, which clearly marks the name with the word "deceased" ("la finada"), but when she dials the number, Clotilde Ifrán answers. The fitting for the costume takes place when no one else is at home. Several phrases hint at the conclusion: "se sentía envejecida," "se hubiera dicho que los relojes se habían detenido" (104) [she felt older, one might have said that the clocks had stopped]. Clotilde Ifrán's kindness stands in marked contrast to the brusqueness of the mother, and in the conclusion, the child decides to leave with her. The good mother here is the dead artist, and the child, it seems, goes off with this kindly agent of death, in an act clearly posited as revenge ("pequeña venganza") against the neglectful mother.

The costume itself is described in terms that echo another earlier story, "El árbol grabado." The earlier devil costume, which like this one also "olía a aceite de ricino" [smelled of castor oil], is thought, at least in the mind of the child narrator, to cause the story's violence. Here, to the detail of its smell the story adds another of more obvious sexual connotation, the "cuernos del gorro" [the horns of its cap]. Clemencia, the girl's name, is also the name used in yet another story, "Livio Roca," of same collection (*Ldn*) about a mule with a sexualized relationship with the owner. The vague sensuality of these stories recalls "El vestido de terciopelo," which also implies that the seamstress serves as substitute mother for the young narrator (though she refers to her as "amiga"). The sumptuous descriptions of the black velvet of the dress and the glistening sequined dragon on its front are erotically charged. The stories have in common the seamstress as mother substitute, and all contain the hint of an untimely death directly associated with or indirectly attributable to her. The demonic or sinister elements which belie the kindness of these seamstresses, their status as creative artists, and their vaguely erotic quality is most fully developed in the bizarre story, "Las vestiduras peligrosas," where the sexual energy latent in previous stories becomes explicit.

In this puzzling narrative Ocampo presents characters which were identified in chapter 2 as mad doubles of a modified sort. The "angel" figure is the seamstress and narrator, while the "monster," Artemia, is Ocampo's most complex take on the female artist and the nature of female desire. The multiple mythological associations implied by the protagonist's name, Artemia/Artemis, reinforce the fantastic interpretation, that Artemia is causing other women's deaths, and further associates her with hatred of men and cruelty to women. Piluca makes some fanfare of her own name, declaring Piluca to be only a nickname; her real name, Régula, underlines her dominating personality.[22] Through naming the story confers powers on both its protagonists.

Several of Artemia's painted canvases are described in the first paragraph by Piluca, the narrator:

> hacía cada dibujo que lo dejaba a uno bizco. Caras que parecía que hablaban, sin contar cualquier perfil del lado derecho que es tan difícil; paisajes con fogatas que daba miedo que incendiaran la casa cuando uno los miraba. Pero lo que hacía mejor era dibujar vestidos. (*Ldn* 45)

> [she made drawings that would make you cross-eyed. Faces that seemed to talk, not to mention the right profile which is so difficult; scenes with bonfires that made you think the house would burn down as you looked at them. But what she did best was sketch dresses.]

This passage associates the design of clothing on the same artistic level as painting, at least from the perspective of an uneducated speaker who uses crudely colloquial language throughout. Indeed the remainder of the story concerns Artemia as dress designer, making one forget perhaps that she had been first described as a painter. Piluca, from whose point of view the story is told, is hired by Artemia to adapt designs from drawing board to fabric. But first she explains her own prehistory, the incident that precipitated the loss of her original job as "pantalonera" [specialist in pants] in a shop. The sexual prudery that underlies her character is revealed in her version of the episode, especially in her use of the words "asqueroso" [nauseating] and "puerco" [filthy] to describe the male client. As Piluca struggles to adjust the fabric of the crotch, the man urges her to take in more and more of the cloth: "Mientras hablaba, se le formó una protuberancia que estorbaba el manejo de los alfileres" (46) [While he talked a protuberance formed which impeded the placement of the pins]. She is fired from her job when she hits the man in the face with her pincushion. The episode ends with Piluca's concluding self assessment: "Soy una mujer seria y siempre lo fui" [I am an honest woman and I always was].

Piluca's narrating language is highly colloquial, replete with religious overtones, and filled with hypocritical contradictions. Though her stated interest in telling the story is to praise her mistress, the language she chooses obviously undercuts her declared purpose. In referring to herself as "mujer seria" and elsewhere as "mujer honrada," by punctuating sentences with expressions such as "¡Dios mío! ¡Virgen Santísima!" and by having Artemia herself agree at one point, "Usted es una santulona, pero no hay derecho de imponerle sus ideas a los demás" (49) [You may be a big saint, but you have no right to impose your ideas on others], Piluca sets up a contrast between herself, the virtuous woman, and Artemia, the evil artist. The reader may intuit Piluca's desire to free herself from any undo complicity with what occurs in the story, though her actions belie her words. For instance, Piluca makes each of the "dangerous vestments" of the story's title. She claims to have acted only unwillingly, yet the repeated descriptions of the real work involved (staying up all night, working many hours at a stretch) contradict this stated unwillingness. Piluca gives the advice and makes the outfit that eventually kills Artemia, but by her own account Piluca is the good woman, cautious, religious and obedient, while Artemia, in contrast, is associated with vice, danger, and creative power.

Piluca describes three indecent dresses that she sews according to Artemia's designs. One is a velvet jumper with a scandalously low neckline, "que con pezón y todo se veían [los pechos] como en una compotera, dentro del escote" (48) [which with nipple and all the breasts were visible like in a jam jar in the low neckline]. The next is a net dress covered with designs of hands and feet, which seem to caress her body as she moves. The last also is a transparent dress through which Artemia's body may be seen, this time covered with flesh-colored male and female nudes: "Al moverse todos esos cuerpos, representaban una orgía" (51) [when she moved all those bodies pictured an orgy]. Each time she wears one of these costumes into the street, she returns the next morning to read in the newspaper that in another part of the world (in Budapest, in Tokyo, and in Oklahoma), a woman had been raped and murdered the night before, in an outfit of exactly the description of Artemia's dress. The dresses and their destructive power associate Artemia with two different traditions of the ancient goddess. The Greek Artemis, known as the virgin huntress, is notable for cruel and vengeful acts to women,[23] while the Artemis of Ephesus, the goddess of the Amazons, is best known for her horror of men.[24] The garment ascribed to the latter by the *Larousse Encyclopedia of Mythology* closely resembles the costumes invented by Ocampo's Artemia: "the crowned Artemis of Ephesus ... is tightly sheathed in a robe covered with animal heads which leaves her bosom with its multiple breasts exposed." Artemia's dresses leave the breasts exposed but depict human, rather than animal, bodies on the sheer fabric. The description of such a costume in a modern newspaper makes the possibility of coincidence between Artemia's dresses and those of the distant women who die in them most unlikely and reveals the garment's, or its designer's, magical power.

Ocampo's modern goddess appears disappointed in her powers, for Artemia's reaction to reading of other women's tragedies in dresses of her own design is always tears of rage, "Debió de sucederme a mí" [It shoud have happened to me], she says at one point, and at another, "No puedo hacer nada en el mundo sin que otras mujeres me copien.... Son unas copionas. Y las copionas son las que tienen éxito" (*Ldn* 50) [I can't do anything without other women copying me.... They are copycats. And the copycats are the ones who succeed]. In the conclusion, the cautious Piluca advises her mistress to wear a simple outfit of dark pants and a man's shirt. Since everyone wears such clothing, she could not complain that others were copying her. The next morning the police inform Piluca that her mistress was found raped and murdered in a dark street. This strange story, which appears to treat with irony the sexualized murder of women, also seems to offer a dismal interpretation of women's creativity. While Artemia created outrageous, original, and aggressively sexual garments, her efforts proved destructive to other women; when she compromised her energies in accordance with custom and convention, they proved destructive to herself. The garb in which she is killed, significantly, is described as masculine or at least as sexually neutral: "Aconsejé a la Artemia que se vistiera con pantalón oscuro y camisa de hombre. Una vestimenta sobria, que nadie podía copiarle, porque todas la jóvenes la llevaban.... Verla así, vestida de muchachito, me encantó, porque con esa figurita ¿a quién no le queda bien el pantalón?" (52) [I advised Artemia to wear dark pants and a man's shirt. A dignified outfit which no one could copy because all the young women wore it. I loved seeing her that way, dressed like a boy, because with that figure who would't look good in pants?]. Hiding the female element of art proves at first glance even more dangerous than openly flaunting it.

On the other hand, if we take seriously the notion that Artemia wanted to be raped and killed, then this final garment is her most "successful." In this case, the garb that Piluca recommends to her may represent, not a compromise with convention, but an artistic creation most authentically true to herself. Instead of outrageously exotic creations, she has produced one that expresses the artist's most genuine self, the ordinary, the everyday. Furthermore, the narrator finds this last outfit truly attractive: "verla así me encantó," Piluca writes. Somehow when dressed as a boy ("muchachito") Artemia's figure is all the more pleasing. In a curious sliding of sexual identities, the seamstress gazes with pleasure on her mistress who is dressed as a boy. If Artemia's idea of success is rape and murder, the story offers a serious deconstruction of the term. Corporal violence may be Ocampo's metaphor for what happens to any successful artist. An author instinctively wants to be read, yet success for Ocampo, as for her creation, Artemia, is a double-edged sword, a trampling, an invasion, a destruction, as it has been viewed by many women.[25] Ocampo in a rare autobiographical moment confirms this assessment: "But I did not hope to be known: that seemed the most horrible thing in the world to me. I will never know what I was hoping for. A beggar who sleeps under a tree without anything in the world to shelter him is happier than a famous man."[26] Artemia as artist illustrates not just the dangers of female masochism, but the perversity of seeking worldly success.

Chapter 2 uses "Las vestiduras peligrosas" as one example of Ocampo's destabilizing of the angel/monster dichotomy. Piluca as servant necessarily plays the role of "angel" but, in fact, acts here as author and backstage manager of the entire plot.[27] Piluca also provides a new take on the maternal element revealed in other stories of the seamstress/artist. Jane Gallop, in an analysis of class differences in women's artistic expression, says: "The women of another class who serve us recall the mother, recall her attentions to our material needs. . . . The will to write, to write what the maid, the mother, the lover knows but keeps to herself, keeps secret, distinguishes the writer from the other woman."[28] On the level of the fiction, Ocampo's story makes impossible the distinction that Gallop articulates in this passage. Here the lower-class woman, who does serve as assistant/mother to the upper-class creative artist, Artemia, is also the narrator, the woman who speaks, tells the secrets. Ocampo's story, by giving voice to the lower-class woman, does not, paraphrasing Gallop's conclusion, "forget the other woman." Unlike either Gallop or Annie Leclerc (or Vermeer, for that matter), Ocampo offers no idealization of the other woman; instead of radiating silently a "plenitude [of] erotic self-sufficiency,"[29] Ocampo's character voices her desire and her disapproval. She is mother-servant, mother-dictator, Régula, the petty tyrant who attempts to restrain both the sexuality and the creativity of the daughter-artist, who kills her with well-meaning advice, and pronounces the final judgment on her: Piluca's last word on Artemia, the last word of the story, is "tramposa" [shifty swindler]. Ocampo allows the reader no answers, no ease from the tensions produced by this story: The domestic angel is also crafty narrator, the wickedly creative monster/victim, inevitably associated with the fraudulent artifice of art, is at the same time a likeable version of the virgin goddess.

Artemia is one of several flagrantly bizarre characters who break the rules of feminine behavior in what Nancy K. Miller has called an act of "crucial barbarism": "To build a narrative around a character whose behavior is deliberately idiopathic, however, is not merely to create a puzzling fiction but to fly in the face of a certain ideology (of the text and its context), to violate a grammar of motives that describes while prescribing . . . what women should or should not do."[30] While she appears to transgress rules of behavior and of logic, all Artemia's artistic creations and even her sad fate are scripted in accordance with mythic tradition and inherited notions of the feminine. The mythic story which has no direct reference but which palpitates behind the name of Artemis is the episode in which the goddess transforms the hunter Acteon into a stag to be killed by his own dogs in punishment for having gazed upon her nakedness.[31] Ocampo's revision of the story makes several reversals: The chaste goddess of the hunt becomes a desiring woman who actively seeks the male gaze and also, apparently, the disturbingly masochistic punishment presented as the inevitable result. Whereas the mythic version depicts the goddess as surprised by the male intrusion and punishes the hapless interloper, Artemia, "la tramposa," appears to plot consciously her own demise. Jessica Benjamin helps in understanding the temptations, even the inevitability, of masochism for women. The desire to be "found," to be really "seen," in a patriarchal culture results in female masochism.[32] Ocampo's story, disturbing as it may be, no longer seems outrageous, but hauntingly true to what we know of female desire.

"Las vestiduras peligrosas" provides the most complete fantasy of the artist as extension of women's traditional creative enterprises. The evolution of Artemia's garments confirms what has already been noted elsewhere regarding Ocampo's validation of the ordinary. It anticipates conclusions drawn below regarding the gender neutrality of the author. A gender ambiguity seems important to Ocampo's notion of the true creative spirit. If the dresses are the work of art, there is a definite progression in the aesthetics they reveal. The first dress, of solid fabric (velvet), reveals the feminine self by exposing the breasts blatantly. The subsequent dresses are both transparent, revealing the feminine form beneath but veiling it slightly with sheer fabric and superimposed designs. These are first of hands and feet and then of whole bodies; the first seems to caress the body, the second, as an orgy, to possess it (multiply). This play of revelation and disguise gives way to the stark simplicity of the everyday shirt and pants, which, nevertheless, shows to advantage the "figurita" contained within. Could this not serve as metaphor for the representation of the feminine in Ocampo's fiction? Ocampo's own works experiment with the possibilities depicted here, at times boldly flaunting the feminine body, at others, coyly veiling it with verbal complexity and feminine masquerade, at yet others opting for a stark simplicity which reveals difference as part of the same, in which the fantastic and the real, the male and the female, are impossible to distinguish.

AUTHORS

"La continuación" contains Ocampo's most extended depiction of a fictional author; the only other story to deal with a professional writer is "La pluma mágica." The two stories have several important elements in common: Both present issues of the writing process in tandem with the theme of betrayal, both play consciously with notions of gender, and both stage the fiction as a form of monolog spoken directly to an absent "you."

"La continuación" is about the process involved in writing an autobiographical work of fiction. The fictional character's story creates an inner plot, a story-within-a story that Genette calls a metadiegesis, whose intimate connections to the outer plot, the diegeses, demonstrate the ways in which the writer modifies reality for the sake of fiction.[33] The "author" of the diegesis utilizes elements of lived experience to create the inner plot, eventually finding it difficult to separate from "reality": "Que tú no te llames Ursula, que yo no me llame Leonardo Morán, aún hoy me parece increíble"(F 18) [That your name is not Ursula and mine is not Leonardo Morán, even now seems incredible to me]. When reading this story as part of the mad double I assumed the narrator of the outer plot to be female even though "her" double in the inner plot is male. After reading the story with a different lens, so to speak, I realize that neither the "I" nor the "you" of the diegesis can be definitively identified by gender. That Ocampo accomplishes this feat without ever seeming forced is, in Spanish, a kind of *tour de force*. It is especially interesting to note that "La pluma mágica" creates the same ambiguity: It is written in direct address from an "I" to a "you" in which neither is identified by gender. Cristina Ferreira-Pinto discusses the sexual indeterminacy of the first-person narrator of "La continuación," but finds a hint of feminine identity in the following passage in which the narrator of the diegesis confesses to having fallen in love with "her" own creation, the character of the metadiegesis:

> Cuando caminaba por las calles pensaba encontrarme en cualquier esquina con Leonardo, no contigo. Su pelo, sus ojos, su modo de andar me enamoraban. Al besarte imaginé sus labios y olvidé los tuyos.[34]

> [When I walked along the streets I imagined encountering Leonardo, not you, around the next corner. His hair, his eyes, his walk enthralled me. On kissing you I imagined his lips and forgot yours.]

My analysis in the mirror section of the following chapter will identify another passage of this story—where the narrator glances in a mirror, giving the act existential significance—as a feminine gesture: "Volví a mirarme en tu espejo, para asegurar mi presencia" (15) [I looked at myself again in your mirror in order to prove my presence]. Despite the fact that the narrator "gives herself away" as a woman, however, it is clear that Ocampo meant to obscure gender identity. Instead of laying claim to write "like a woman," Ocampo evidently wishes to erase gender as a category for the author. "La continuación" can be read, as I have done, as a story of uniquely female struggles with creativity, but apparently Ocampo would rather that we view it as a problem of creativity per se.

Likewise, "La pluma mágica" is, at the very least, far more interesting as a woman's plot but neither of its characters, either the "author" or the "friend," are identified by name or by gender. The only two words of the story that could have been used in the feminine are "escritor" [writer] and "discípulo" [follower], two terms which even a female speaker might choose to use in their masculine forms. The narrator suspects that a friend has taken advantage of a careless moment to steal his/her most prized possession. Read as male characters, the story becomes a Bloomian anxiety of influence question in which a younger man steals the powers (the magic pen) from an older and more experienced male.[35] If female, the interest shifts to the narrator's attitude toward owning the magic pen in the first place. Louise Kaplan's *Female Perversion* argues that many women (unconsciously) view any personal power they may possess as having been stolen from its rightful owner and secretly fear its repossession. Ocampo, like Kaplan, attributes this fear to both male and female characters, marking phallic power as illusory for both sexes. In any case, the dynamics described by Kaplan certainly operate for the narrator of "La pluma mágica" who guards her/his discovery of the magic pen as a surprising secret, its creative power wholly separate from her/himself; it also explains her/his resignation regarding the friend's treachery.[36] Nevertheless, Ocampo has gone to a great deal of trouble to eliminate any gender identity, so that the imposition of it comes from the reader. Is it possible to read without imagining a gender? Apparently Silvina Ocampo would like us to learn how.

Ocampo's narrator of "La pluma mágica" finds an intense fear of plagiarism the biggest impediment to the creative process. The story can be read as a humorous gloss of psychoanalytic theories of writing, which bring Gilbert and Gubar's "anxiety of authorship," especially as it recalls Bloom's earlier "anxiety of influence," immediately to mind. The narrator explains: "Sufrí durante años este espantoso horror que consiste en repetir involuntariamente el cuento, la novela, el poema que otros habían escrito. ... De ese modo escribí algunos de los libros más célebres, que quedaron guardados en mi cajón, sin esperanza de ser reconocidos ni apreciados por nadie" (*I* 152) [I suffered for years a horror which consisted in unwittingly repeating the story, the novel or the poem which others had written. ... So I wrote some of the most famous books which stayed hidden in my drawer, with no hope of being recongnized nor appreciated by anyone]. If we remember that Borges's Pierre Menard faced the same issue, it is all the more interesting to compare Ocampo's modification of the problem. Instead of accepting plagiarism and laboriously attempting to reproduce the undisputed master, Cervantes, and rejoicing in this perfect repetition as does Pierre Menard, Ocampo's fictional author finds a more externalized solution. The magic pen makes originality possible for its owner, by, in effect, giving her (him?) "permission" to repeat what others have already done. If we remember that Pierre Menard needed no such permission, Ocampo's narrator becomes all the more feminized in Gilbert and Gubar's terms. Finally, and even more tragically, the "author" is convinced that the magic pen, not the human writer, is responsible for the works produced. In this short short (two-page) story the narrator/author confides the secret of literary success to a friend who then steals the magic pen and writes a book of the same title as the short story, *La pluma mágica*. There are, then, two authors, the narrator and the friend, both subsumed under the magic of the originary pen.

Once the fears and insecurities of authorship are vanquished, what exactly does the pen write? The titles listed in the story, *La verdad es muda, La esperanza se infiltra,* and *La fuente del Asilo,* are suggestive of what can be recognized as Ocampo's own concerns: the silence of truth, the sneaky quality of hope and literature itself as a sanctuary, a source of refuge.[37] Finally, of course, the narrator comes across a new title displayed in a book store, *La pluma mágica,* presumably written by the treacherous "friend." The magical, fantastic quality of fiction, Ocampo's theme of themes, is mirrored in an unusual play of inside/outside the text, more typical of Borges.

The friend who steals the pen is repeating one of Ocampo's favorite plotlines. The coincidence of the theme of betrayal in the two stories of authorship, "La pluma mágica" and "La continuación," suggests that writing itself is a kind of treachery. The final word of "Las vestiduras peligrosas" comes to mind in this context; Artemia, like all artists, is "tramposa." The narrator of "La pluma mágica" becomes the victim of an ambitious friend, whereas the self-absorbed writer of "La continuación" commits acts of cruelty, makes victims of others, which here are deemed essential to the creative process itself. The relationship between betrayal and creativity is thoroughly explored in this latter story, which I would now like to examine in more detail.

The narrator of "La continuación" deliberately orchestrates the alienation of all intimate connections: a friend, Elena; a young boy, Hernán; and finally the story's "you" whom we suppose to be her/his lover. In addition to the major acts of treachery are smaller ones in which the narrator transforms the everyday events of life into parts of the fiction:

> Cuando me hablaste de tus problemas, yo apenas te escuchaba. Mentalmente componía mis frases. . . . Me fascinaba el abstracto placer de construir personajes, situaciones, lugares en mi mente, de acuerdo a los cánones efímeros que me había propuesto. . . . Siempre me costó inventar paisajes y por ese motivo el que estaba viendo me sirvió de modelo. A esa misma hora, en un lugar parecido, Leonardo

Morán comienza a escribir su despedida y refiere cómo concibió el proyecto de suicidarse. (*F* 12)

[When you spoke of your problems I barely listened. Mentally I was composing my phrases. . . . I was fascinated by the abstract pleasure of contructing characters, situations, places in my mind in accordance with the ephemeral laws I had set for myself. . . . It had always been difficult for me to invent settings and therefore the one I was seeing served as model. At that same hour, in a similar place, Leonardo Morán starts to write his good-bye and speaks of how he conceived the idea of suicide.]

The act of writing is perceived as a kind of theft from the lived moment. The writer steals from nature and also from the emotional charge of the affective scene. In contrast to the poignancy produced by the beloved's absence, which initiates the writing of works of art according to a topos of ancient lineage, this story brutally assesses the problems for art if the beloved is present. In order for a serious artist to create, the beloved—all the beloveds—must be ruthlessly eliminated: "From the fictional point of view, oddly enough, life that is lived, rather than deferred, is of no interest."[38] Ocampo's story comes to the problem of absence and writing from the opposite direction to the topos, that is, instead of utilizing the longing produced by the beloved's absence to create art, Ocampo explores the threat to artistic production that bodily presence and emotional fulfillment present.

The narrator becomes submerged in the invented plot, but after some time suddenly abandons the work in progress, and comes back to "reality," emerging from the world of creation "como si saliera de un sótano húmedo y oscuro" (14) [as if coming out of a dark, moist basement]. This metaphor for an author's absorption may perhaps shed light on one of Ocampo's strangest stories, "El sótano," from the same collection. The first-person narrator lives in a basement with mice she has named for Hollywood actors and actresses of the 1940s and 1950s. The story's enigmatic ending suggest that she will allow the house to be razed while she remains inside, an original notion of suicide. From the perspective of the previous story, it may be clear that the dark basement and the companionable mice are another image of the creative process which has isolated the artist from the rest of the world but which she refuses to abandon. "El sótano" stresses the isolation required of artistic creation. "La continuación" suggests that the demands of ordinary life are both a major source of and the biggest obstacle to creativity. The narrator of "La continuación" climbs out of her/his creative basement for several reasons: the exigencies of everyday life, fear that what s/he is creating is actually plagiarized somehow and disgust at "el tono falsamente sublime de mis frases" [the falsely sublime tone of my phrases]. Each of these preoccupations, the world of female domesticity, the falsely sublime, and the fear of unintentional plagiarism, all are identifiable issues in Ocampo's works.

The precise moment in which the narrator returns to the completion of the inner story of Leonardo Morán's suicide is never indicated, and thereby produces the story's central ambiguity. In the last lines of "La continuación," the narrator explains that when the creative effort was abandoned earlier, the return to "reality" was not to the world s/he had left behind, but to the "continuation" of her/his own plot, a plot which s/he now modifies in life instead of in words. The inner and outer stories end the same way, both characters having plotted a suicide, but neither confirming that it will in fact take place. The "inner" narrator, Leonardo Morán, in the conclusion seems to speak for both when he says: "Vi un mundo claro, nuevo, un mundo donde no tenía que perder nada, salvo el deseo del suicidio que ya me había abandonado . . . el mundo ha llegado a ser para mí lo que nunca fue ni pensé que sería: algo infinitamente precioso" (17) [I saw a clear, new world, a world where I had nothing to lose except the desire for suicide that had now abandoned me . . . the world had become what it never was for me and I thought would never be: something infintely precious]. Normal life is incompatible with creation. Both narrators are planning an escape, whether through suicide or simply as departure from the scene is uncertain. Both endings imply death of the story, however, for if the plot is "lived" in the body it will not be written and will therefore be impossible to read.

"La continuación" presents urgent issues for artistic creativity: the association of writing with cold calculation, with plotting, and with death make it a most dangerous undertaking. The writer here is prepared to sacrifice love and domestic happiness for art; the story suggests that the stakes of that sacrifice for writers whether male or female are equally high. Ocampo has dramatized the problem by playing with readerly assumptions about gender. One of the story's images reinforces the gender confusion. So intertwined with the fictional story is this narrator that s/he says at one point: "Yo vivía dentro de mi personaje como un niño dentro de su madre: me alimentaba de él" (13) [I lived within my character as a child lives inside its mother: I nourished myself from him]. The work of art as an author's child is a familiar metaphor, but here the elements are reversed: The character invents, gives birth, to the author. The "me" cannot be identified by gender but the character who acts as womb, mother, is definitively male (Leonardo Morán). In "La continuación," the male writer of the metadiegesis holds a position traditionally reserved for the female, the writer of a suicide letter. He writes as feminized subject to a female object of desire (Ursula).[39] This creation is imaged by its "author" as male "mother" who nurtures the developing (ungendered) artist/ narrator of the diegesis.

The genderless author of the outer story, like Leonardo Morán of the inner story, also seems to write a suicide letter. Though there is no address and no signature, its opening and closing suggest the form of a last will and testament. The first sentence lists unrelated objects too trivial to mention under the circumstances: "En los estantes del dormitorio encontrarás el libro de medicina, el pañuelo de seda y el dinero que me prestaste" (*F* 10) [On the bookshelves of the bedroom you will find the medical book, the silk handkerchief and the money that you loaned me]. The concluding line provides the enigmatic farewell: "Si no he muerto, no me busques y si muero tampoco: nunca me gustó que miraras mi cara mientras dormía" (18) [If I have not died, don't look for me and if I do die, likewise: I never liked for you to look at my face while I was sleeping]. But in the story's conclusion one of those "impossible" events occurs. The narrator concludes the conversation with the boy Hernán, and leaves the house to sit on a park bench. From that spot s/he never seems to move. So how does the *tú* ever receive the letter? During musings on the park bench the narrator speaks of copying parts of the story, selections of which appear in italics on the printed page; the italics presume to distinguish the words of the fictional narrator from her/his own, but since they refer to identical situations and since s/he quotes them in order to explain her/his own motivation the distinction becomes meaningless. In the last paragraph s/he tears up some of the pages just copied: "No sé si al romperlas, rompí un maleficio" (18) [I am not sure if on tearing them I broke a spell]. This narrator plans either to leave forever or to kill her/himself, but in any case, to disappear. But isn't that what any writer has to do, to absent herself? Writing is by definition the absence of the body, the letter (and by extension, all literature) stands in for the absent body. "La continuación" suggests that the writer must exile herself, be absent, for those for whom she writes; simultaneously, she must subtract all beloved people and objects so that their loss can be recovered in words. The last words of the metadiegesis, the farewell of Leonardo Morán to Ursula, refer to several specific objects just as the main narrator had done in the opening sentences: "Encontrarás mi anillo en el fondo de este sobre y esa maldita medallita con un trébol que ya no tiene ningún significado para mí" (17) [You will find my ring at the bottom of this envelope and that damned medal with the clover which no longer has any meaning for me]. The precious objects and people have been dispensed with and both narrators are ready for departure. The two levels of narration have closed and the laws of narrative dictate a return to the original moment of the story's opening. The "impossible" gap here—the story begins by describing objects in the narrator's own room, but ends on a park bench—forces the reader to project into the "future" beyond the story. Logic dictates that the narrator must walk from the park bench, return home, and leave the letter for the *tú* before leaving forever. And that gap marks the letter as story, as fiction, and as endlessly open.

"La pluma mágica," like "La continuación," addresses a *tú*; but while it begins with the word "Sabes" [You know] in direct address, it is clear that the *tú* will never actually read it, that it is intended solely as internal monolog or as letter to the self. There are no traces of the writing as there are in "La continuación" in which the narrator overtly refers to copying, quoting, writing, and reading. Neither are there specific instructions to the *tú* that more overtly dramatize a character as reader. The consequences of these differences between modes of address is the first of Ocampo's feminine strategies undertaken in chapter 4.

Our readings of the metafictional implications of Ocampo's "art" reveal a struggle with the feminine. Her aesthetic practice validates the everyday as worthy of artistic representation and as a legitimate source of creative expression for many female characters. The struggle with the conflicting demands of human love and artistic creativity are not unique to professional artists, but are viewed as part of the human condition. The creative spirit is imagined as androgynous, while the creative impulse has its source in the maternal. The maternal itself undergoes a thorough revision in the stories to be redefined as a creative and conscious undertaking, in short, as an artistic endeavor.

Finally, the various authorial inscriptions of Ocampo's stories reveal a systematic questioning of the relationship between artistic expression and reality, not in terms of the fantastic exclusively, but in terms of language's ability to convey meaning. Ocampo's story, "La creación," framed as autobiographical in its subtitle "Un cuento autobiográfico," confirms the notion that music is her originary image of creativity. This highly metaphorical story imagines a parade whose magnificent music is later transformed into tinny whistling by people on the streets. Two stories from her most recent collections express what is surely some autobiographical frustration with painting. The narrator of "Lección de dibujo" describes her renunciation of drawing in the painful terms of physical deprivation. She gives it up because she cannot reproduce on paper an adequate imitation of real objects. Sadly she concludes, "Tardé en darme cuenta de que la realidad no tiene nada que ver con la pintura" (*Y así* 67) [I was slow to realize that reality has nothing to do with painting]. Similarly, "Del color de los vidrios" creates a fantastic work of art, a house made of glass bottles. Many bystanders on the street watch the family's movements inside: "Las rajaduras de los vidrios deformaban los cuerpos, las posturas, los movimientos. . . . inventaban posturas, las multiplicaban, pero nunca reflejaban la verdad" (*Cornelia* 73)[The cracks in the glass deformed bodies, postures, movements. . . . (they) invented postures, multiplied them, but never reflected the truth]. Music, art, and language can only deform and misrepresent reality. Language, especially, with its inevitable falsifications, conceived as a thief of lived reality, as a betrayal, appears in Ocampo's world as a particularly mediated mode of creativity. To language, however, she has devoted her energies. Silvina Ocampo came to literature in her mid-thirties after having studied art in Paris with masters of the grotesque, Chirico and Léger. If she took "too long," as her character suggests, to learn in the plastic arts that the imagination, not reality, are the subjects of creativity, she had learned the lesson by the time she started writing stories. The female body in naked freedom, dancing to music, is an early image of Ocampo's ideal of art.[40] The concluding chapter studies this ideal body as it is deformed and transformed in fictional representation. Each of the feminine strategies described in chapter 4 deals in some way with bodies, with the body in the "voice" of the text, in mirrors, and finally with its abuse. Each suggests ways in which Ocampo reimagines the feminine in literary representation. The many details that characterize her fiction, while consciously creating a feminized fictional world, never completely lose their negative connotation in Ocampo's works. The following section's positive reading of them is not meant to deny the ambivalence of Ocampo's fascination.

DETAILS AND TRANSCENDENCE

> D'autre part, les objets ne sont pas moins importants que les êtres dans ces nouvelles: ils définissent une société, composent un language, indiquent aux vivants les chemins de la mort. . . . Autour de la minutieuse réalité des objets, s'ordonne la métaphysique de Silvina.
> —Italo Calvino[41]

> [On the other hand, objects are no less important in these stories than beings: they define a society, compose a language, indicate to the living the road of death. . . . Around the minute reality of objects, Silvina orders her metaphysics.]

The association of the female body and literary details has, according to Naomi Schor, a long history.[42] While a wide range of feminist approaches to literature have centered on the female body as locus of creativity, Schor's study concentrates on ways in which male-authored texts have negatively gendered artistic and literary details as feminine. Schor demonstrates the ways in which the detail is gradually disassociated from the feminine as it is increasingly validated in twentieth-century art and literature, and argues against that defeminization. My discussion here of Ocampo's use of details relates directly to earlier arguments regarding her creation of grotesque and fantastic subversions by the object world. A concept of the feminine as marked by attention to details is already implicated especially in the argument regarding a grotesque vision which seeks to subvert the grandiose or tragic with what has been considered trivial. Schor describes details as "restless," "anxiety-producing," and "anarchic," words reminiscent of those used to describe the grotesque. Furthermore, Schor, like Bakhtin, makes an overtly political as well as aesthetic argument. One of her citations of Baudelaire, for instance, compares "a riot of details" with "the fury of a mob." Schor observes: "Baudelaire's troping of the detail as revolutionary mob overtly politicizes the aesthetic; the peril posed by succumbing to the invasion of the barbaric or feminine upstart detail—the crowd and the female are on the same continuum in the nineteenth-century male imaginary—is nothing less than the end of civilization itself."[43] My return to this aspect of Ocampo's work may reveal a certain obsession of my own, but rather than conflate the two arguments, I think it is worth returning to object/details as a category of feminine creation, not just of grotesque subversion. Naomi Schor's history of the detail helps to suggest ways in which Ocampo performs a subversion of inherited aesthetic categories and simultaneously creates a new object language of her own. Ocampo's details will be investigated both in terms of their subversive power and in terms of their projection of a feminine world of "contingency" historically un(der)represented in fiction.

A so-called feminine impulse to represent the everyday, on the one hand, or the ornamental, on the other, validates "what is most threatening about the detail: its tendency to subvert an internal hierarchic ordering of the work of art which clearly subordinates the periphery to the center, the accessory to the principal, the foreground to the background."[44] Schor points out that the valorization of this subversive potential is the project of postmodernism itself, "an essential aspect of that dismantling of Idealist metaphysics which looms so large on the agenda of modernity" (ibid., 4), and argues for a resistance to the degendering of details just at the point of their artistic legitimation. The origin of the detail's importance to the contemporary period lies, as one might suspect, with Freud: "Freud's radical . . . formulation of the principle by which libidinal energy can be transferred from the significant to the insignificant (that is, displacement) . . . makes intelligible and, more important, legitimate the multiple modes of investment in the trivial everywhere at work in modern society" (ibid., 6). Schor first presents the Idealist aesthetic against which the modern period can be said to react. Sir Joshua Reynolds's influential objections to the detail are stated in terms of his distinction between the Ideal and the Sublime:[45]

> Reynold's strictures against detailism fall into two distinct groups which must be clearly distinguished if the subsequent destiny of the detail as aesthetic category is to become intelligible: on the one hand there are the qualitative arguments (those according to the Ideal), on the other the quantitative (those according to the Sublime). In the first instance, Reynolds argues that because of their material contingency details are incompatible with the Ideal; in the second he argues that because of their tendency to proliferation, details subvert the Sublime. (ibid., 15)

Details subvert the Ideal because of their narrow and prosaic particularity while they undercut the Sublime with their messy numbers. The prosaic and the prolific, of course, suggest the realm of the feminine, an association made more explicit in Reynold's repudiation of "brute Nature." As Schor points out, the association of the feminine with nature and the particular spans not only cultures but centuries. If details are incompatible with the Ideal and the Sublime because of their inconvenient materiality and distracting numbers, however, even Reynolds (according to Schor) admits that the details of realism do "produce a truth effect." The triumph of realism demonstrates the validity of his point; Schor concludes, however, by insisting that "the association of details, femininity, and decadence is perhaps the most persistent legacy left to us by Classicism" (ibid., 22).

Later Hegel extols the vitality produced in art forms by a certain level of particularity. His evident approval of the Dutch genre paintings (of Vermeer and Van Eyk, et al.) and their careful elaboration of ordinary moments of frequently flawed and banal bourgeois life, contrast with his stated disdain elsewhere for the "prose of the world." Schor suggests that the *Aesthetics*'s missing theory of the novel can actually be found in Hegel's discussion of painting. Hegel theorizes the flowering of painting over sculpture in the Christian era as due to painting's potential for greater subjectivity. The humanization of the divine which occurs in Christianity results in the divinization of the human available in Renaissance and Baroque art. In tracing the secularization of art, Hegel, in Schor's account, also describes its relation to the detail:

> There is then according to Hegel a sort of *transference* onto profane subjects of the love initially lavished exclusively on sacred subjects. If we admit that the detail is, as it were, sponsored by the religious, it follows that whatever the degree of secularization attained by a given civilization, the detail will never completely liquidate its debt to the sacred. . . . Even camouflaged by the fetishism peculiar to our dechristianized consumer society, the detail entertains a relationship—however degraded—to the sacred. God, as Mies van der Rohe, Aby Warburg and others are credited with saying, dwells in the details (ibid., 35).

I would like to take a rather exaggerated view of this latter point, that the modern age has transferred the sacred onto secular details, in order to articulate what I propose as Ocampo's creative use of the detail as both religious and feminine in her fiction.

Ocampo's stories not only reveal a "passion for detail," but also produce an insistent hostility toward all notions of perfection and beauty and a quite postmodern regard for the "dispersed detail." I believe Ocampo has consciously sought to create a version of the sacred by way of ordinary details.

I am aware that my choice of direction in this argument stresses an archaic quality of Ocampo's work. While what follows emphasizes the more positive aspects of Hegel's "prose of the world," there is no question that Ocampo's works amply demonstrate the demonic and perverse aspects of the detail. It would be possible to follow a different path and relate to Ocampo's stories Schor's later observations regarding desublimation, the insistence on the detail's meaninglessness. Schor describes Flaubert's denial of the detail's potential for grandiosity in a manner equally appropriate to many of Ocampo's works: "His [Flaubert's] descriptions are notable for their juxtaposition of heterogeneous details which, in extreme cases, work to reduce the objects of referential reality to inert and stupid matter" (ibid., 41). My argument in chapter 1 should give readers some idea of the negative and degraded possibilities of Ocampo's details. The general anxiety over objects in Ocampo's fiction beyond their magical or grotesque properties is expressed elsewhere in this study, the repeated worries over losing things, forgetting things, and cleaning things, for instance. All of this might lead to observations regarding Ocampo's impulse to decry commercialization and materialism, her evident disapproval of mass-produced objects. The undeniable fragmentation of Ocampo's later works in which the narrative is completely taken over by details could also be studied as a related aspect of desublimation. My arguments, however, take a completely different turn at this point toward sublimation, the elevation of certain otherwise random objects to metaphysical importance. If Ocampo's works provide a mixed view of the detail, it only confirms Schor's conclusion about the lure of the detail and its dangers: "To read in detail is, however tacitly, to invest the detail with a truth-bearing function, and yet . . . the truth value of the detail is anything but assured" (ibid., 7). I wade into the dangers, lured by what I perceive to be the elusive moral center of Ocampo's works.

Schor's definition of the detail is broad and not limited to objects, nor even to literary forms. The useful connections she is able to draw between painting, sculpture, architecture, music, and literary representation is particularly helpful with regard to a writer like Ocampo who herself is both poet and painter as well as writer of fiction. For the purpose of this discussion, I use the term *detail* to refer to objects mentioned in the text, minor characters, events that seem out of proportion, names, words, and allusions to mythical, historical, or intertextual fictional sources. Many of Ocampo's stories describe objects without overtly magical power which nevertheless linger in the reader's memory, attaining an importance within the narrative some- what out of proportion to their overt significance. Among my favorites is the door knocker from "El diario de Porfiria Bernal," which foreshadows the strange events that will occur inside the house (whose description is quoted in chapter 1). A short list of other arresting objects might include the stuffed tiger over which the narrator of "Esclavas de las criadas" stumbles, the incredible pastries in "La propiedad," the purring cat of "La hija del toro," or the dahlia-covered wallpaper of "La inauguración del monumento." None of these are precisely magical, but all hold the reader's interest in ways which exceed their usefulness as elements of characterization or creation of setting. They de- center the "internal hierarchy" (Schor's phrase) of a work. Silvia Molloy suggests that the dual effect of this accumulation of de- tails is a trivialization of events and an accentuation of literary artifice: "la función principal de estos detalles—a la vez que crean una circunstancia real la acusan de tal modo que la trans- forman en parodia, en escenario teatral" [the principle function of these details—at the same time that they create a real situ- ation they reveal it in such a way as to transform it into parody, into theatrical staging].[46]

If single elements attract/distract the reader's attention with an excess of particularity, Ocampo's lists of things are excess itself. Several stories are devoted almost entirely to creating col- lections of various kinds: "Los objetos" describes a group of lost objects, while "Informe del cielo y del infierno" uses unrelated items to account for the arbitrariness of fate, relayed in terms, as the title indicates, of heavenly judgment. But other stories include more minor accumulations of details: the carefully enumerated refreshments for the party in "Las fotografías," the descriptive features of the main character in "Esclavas de las criadas," flirtatious men in "La oración." Implements from a beauty parlor in "La boda" are described as playthings: "Mientras que le teñían el pelo de rubio con agua oxigenada y amoníaco, yo jugaba con los guantes del peluquero, con el vaporizador, con las peinetas, con las horquillas, con el secador que parecía el yelmo de un guerrero y con una peluca vieja, que el peluquero me cedía con mucha amabilidad" (*F* 121) [While they were dying her hair blond with peroxide and ammonia, I played with the hairdresser's gloves, with the vaporizor, the combs, the hairpins, with the drier that looked like a warrior's helmet and with an old wig which the hairdresser handed over to me with great kindness]. Schor relates Hegel's discussion of the pleasure derived from such details to his discussion of Dutch genre painting. Hegel's concern was to describe how "natural" or ordinary objects become aesthetic ones in these paintings through a double process of distancing and defamiliarization. Schor demonstrates the ways in which the same process operates in fiction: Ordinary details become "art" when seen in a new way. In the case of Ocampo they are seen from heaven ("Informe del cielo y del infierno"), for instance, or from a child's vantage.

In the context of her entire work Silvina Ocampo establishes a sort of object code in which certain recurring elements, while unassimilable in individual stories, seem to acquire a meaning by virtue of their repetition. One of the items to which I refer is the velvet dress. Read in isolation, the several stories that mention this particular element ("El vestido verde aceituna," "El vestido de terciopelo," "La casa de azúcar", "Las vestiduras peligrosas") hardly present the velvet dress in any obvious symbolic way. Read together, however, the stories gradually give the impression that the velvet dress is always associated with female sexuality. The longest description of the fabric's fascination comes from the *señora* of "El vestido de terciopelo":

> El terciopelo hace rechinar mis dientes, me eriza, como me erizaban los guantes de hilo en la infancia y, sin embargo, para mí no hay en el mundo otro género comparable. Sentir su suavidad en mi mano, me atrae aunque a veces me repugne. ¡Qué mujer está mejor vestida que aquella que se viste de terciopelo negro! Ni un cuello de puntilla le hace falta, ni un collar de perlas; todo estaría de más. El terciopelo se basta a sí mismo. Es suntuoso y es sobrio. (*F* 108)

> [Velvet makes me grind my teeth, it sets my hair on end, just like linen gloves did in my childhood, and yet for me there is in the world no other fabric comparable. To feel its softness in my hand attracts me and yet revolts me. What woman is better dressed than the one in black velvet! Not even a lace collar is needed, nor a pearl necklace; everything else is too much. The velvet is enough by itself. It is sumptuous and dignified.]

From the story's conclusion, we may add to this sensuous plenitude a sense of danger. It is no surprise after this to read later in *Las invitadas* that the moment of sexual initiation for the protagonist of "La expiación" takes place on a velvet bedspread: "Antonio me arrastró temblando a la cama nupcial, cuya colcha, entre los regalos, había sido para él fuente de felicidad y para mí terror durante las vísperas de nuestro casamiento. La colcha de terciopelo granate llevaba bordado un viaje en diligencia" (103) [Antonio pulled me trembling to the nuptial bed, whose bedspread among the gifts had been for him a source of happiness and for me terror during the days before our wedding. The red velvet spread was embroidered with a journey by coach (also the name of an embroidery stitch)]. Here also the velvet bedspread both repels and attracts. Such a discovery adds to the pleasure of reading both earlier and later works in which the use of the element may not be so obvious.

It is not possible to analyze every such detail in a body of stories numbering more than two hundred, but one object, the ubiquitous "Virgen de Luján," merits special attention. So many of Ocampo's stories make reference to this virgin that by the time she is mentioned in "Del color de los vidrios" of *Cornelia frente al espejo* she has become an intertextual joke by Ocampo on herself. Most of the stories that mention the Virgin of Luján give no further commentary about her; they are usually one-line references, as in "La revelación" and "La boda" in which the focus of the comment is elsewhere: In the former, the virgin's image is stamped on a small medal attached to a valuable silver watch; in the latter she appears as a candleholder among a list of wedding presents. The image in general is associated with gifts, with children and with divination. Though Irene ("Autobiografía de Irene") is the first of Ocampo's characters to receive of a statue of the virgin, Porfiria ("El diario de Porfiria Bernal") perhaps best expresses the typical childhood reaction to such a gift, resignation: "Me regalaron una virgen que sirve de velador. Son las más prácticas" (*I* 104) They gave me as a gift a virgin which serves as candleholder. They are the most practical]. Irene's longer comments describe key features which are repeated elsewhere:

[E]l sol iluminó un manto y una cara colorada, diminuta y redonda, informe, que al principio me pareció sacrílega. La belleza y la santidad eran dos virtudes, para mí, inseparables. Deploré que su rostro no fuera hermoso. . . . [Mi madre] Quiso regalarme un San Antonio y una Santa Rosa, reliquias que habían pertenecido a su madre. No las acepté; dije que mi virgen estaba toda vestida de celeste y de oro. Indicándole con mis manos el tamaño de la virgen, le expliqué tímidamente que su cara era roja y pequeña, tostada por el sol, sin dulzura, como la cara de una muñeca, pero expresiva como la de un ángel. (*AI* 154)

[The sun illuminated a cloak and a red face, small, round, and shapeless, which at first seemed sacriligious. Beauty and holiness were two virtues, for me, inseparable. I regretted that the face was not beautiful. . . . [My mother] Wanted to give me a Saint Anthony and a Saint Rosa, relics which had belonged to her mother. I did not accept them; I said that my virgin was dressed all in sky blue and gold. Showing her with my hands the virgin's size, I explained timidly that her face was red and small, browned by the sun, without sweetness, like the face of a doll but with the expressiveness of an angel.]

The unbeautiful face of this virgin is red, according to Irene, because of exposure to the sun, suggesting that like Mexico's Virgin of Guadalupe, this is a native American image.

Indeed, the *Enciclopedia Universal Ilustrada* relates the origins of this icon in terms, if not quite as dramatic as those of Guadalupe, as thoroughly emblematic of the New World. Constructed in Brazil, the image was part of a pair sent overland for a chapel near Córdoba in 1630.[47] After crossing the Luján River on its third day out, the wagon carrying the boxed virgins became stuck in the mud. Noticing that it remained stuck only when loaded with one specific box, the drivers took this as a sign that the particular statue was destined to stay. They therefore proceeded on their journey with one image, leaving the other behind where it remained in an estate's private chapel for some forty years. After the death of the owner the property fell into ruin, and the statue of the virgin was exposed to Indian raids until it was moved to a neighboring ranch, closer to the Luján River. About 1680 a separate chapel was constructed around which a small village has grown.[48]

The description of the physical image given by the encyclopedia matches that of Irene very well; Irene fails to mention, however, that the Virgin is depicted emerging from a cloud and surrounded by cherubim, a factor no doubt important to one of Ocampo's stories involving her, "Tales eran sus rostros." The children of this story, forty deaf mutes, eventually grow wings and fly out of an airplane on their return flight to Buenos Aires following a vacation at the beach. The Virgin of Luján is used here to describe the children as a single character: "En efecto, sus caras eran tan parecidas entre sí, tan inexpresivas como las caras de las escarapelas o de las vírgenes de Luján en las medallas que lucían sobre sus pechos" (*F* 8) [In fact, their faces were as similar to each other, as inexpressive as the faces of a badge or of the medals of the Virgin of Luján that they wore around their necks].[49] This description is hardly flattering either to the children or to the virgin to whom they are compared because of her inexpressivity. This description partially contradicts the words of Irene who earlier had specifically declared that her face is "expresiva como la de un angel."

The image of the Virgin of Luján in "Los objetos" adorns the only object mourned by Camila Ersky: "lloró por la desaparición de una cadenita de plata, con una medalla de la virgen de Luján, enchapada en oro, que uno de sus novios le había regalado" (*F* 75) [she cried at the disappearance of the little silver chain, with the medal of the Virgin of Luján, plated in gold, which one of her boyfriends had given her]. This, from a character who loses many objects, including her house, without regret. The object is appreciated for its association with a beloved person, perhaps, and not for itself alone. Then again, this character goes mad by the end of the story, haunted by lost possessions of her past. Generally the Virgin of Luján is associated with people, like Camila Ersky, who have special powers, such as predicting the future. The statue of the virgin described by Irene proves her gift of divination (to the reader if not to the characters of the story), because shortly after the conversation reported above in which she describes so precisely the statue she wants, Irene and her mother find a perfect replica in a shop window. The image matches the one described earlier with one exception, the one she buys has been damaged ("averiada"). The features assigned to this statue, then, include the words "informe" [shapeless], "sacrílega" [sacrilegious] "sin dulzura" [without sweetness] and now "averiada" [damaged]. A much later story entitled "Livio Roca" contains a family altar with a damaged virgin. In this case, the defect is specified, the statue has a broken foot. Though the virgin of this story is not named as the Virgin of Luján, its situation in an abandoned, rural private chapel matches the condition of the original statue. This unnamed virgin is also associated with a supposedly mad character, in this case for love of his mule, Clemencia.

The *Enciclopedia Universal* provides another set of associations with the town of Luján. The expression "Has ido a Luján?"

[Have you gone to Luján?] is used as a substitute for a common phrase in Buenos Aires, "pasar por Merlo" [go through Merlo]: "Para ir de Buenos Aires al pueblo de Luján hay que pasar por Merlo; se usa, pues, esta frase para dar a entender a uno enfáticamente y de un modo gracioso que *ha pasado por Merlo*" (681) [In order to go from Buenos Aires to the town of Luján one must go through Merlo; this phrase is used, therefore, to mean emphatically and humorously that one has "gone through Merlo"]. Furthermore, "Pasar por Merlo" is a figurative way to say "zonzo, simple, tonto; pasar por tonto o simple, o hacer papel de tal" [silly, simple, stupid; to pass for stupid or simple or pretend to be]. This set of associations also coincides with the characters of nearly all the stories in which the Virgin de Luján appears. For Ocampo she is the patron saint of misunderstood, handicapped, or retarded children with special powers ("Irene," "Tales eran sus rostros," "La revelación") and of adults gone mad ("Los objetos," "La boda," "Livio Roca," "Del color de los vidrios").

Ocampo's Virgin of Luján breaks all of Reynold's rules about the work of art: She is a small object, particularized (and therefore the opposite of divine according to his standards) by her flaws, and serves as a detail unassimilable by most of the narratives she inhabits. Often she is mentioned in one of Ocampo's lists of other objects. By her imperfect extraneousness she fails to perform either as Ideal or as Sublime. This virgin performs a postmodernist rebellion against particularly Hegel's insistence on the equation of Truth and Beauty when Beauty is defined as the perfection of form and content. She represents, in fact, what Hegel has called "kitsch," in other words, "All the things Hegel rejects [in a work of art]: arbitrariness, the loss of substance, the erosion of individuality by repetition, and the inappropriateness of form and content."[50] But I argue that, while Ocampo presents the statue as thoroughly modernist, inert, stupid matter (Schor's terms), the very antithesis of what Ocampo herself would call true religious conviction, through repetition and association, the image becomes more than a joke at popularized religion. Occupying a position within Hegel's concept of Dutch genre painting, the Virgin becomes one of those details that Hegel suggests has become a remnant of the sacred within the modern secular world. It is a remnant that poignantly marks, however, the absence of a perfect all-powerful divine. More than anything else, these damaged, unbeautiful virgins become an icon in Ocampo's opus which removes female beauty as avenue to the sacred, a secret, almost subliminal message that the ugly, the humble, and the flawed are holy, too. Beyond that, it is clear that this figure encapsulates many of Ocampo's concerns: children, female doubles, and, what has not been visible in discussion to this point, the natively Argentine.

The overtly religious content of the Virgin of Luján represents a double irony because, if anything, Ocampo's works perform a consistent devaluation of institutionalized religion. One of Ocampo's impulses throughout her work is to mark the difference between institutional religious practice and authentic religious experience, to transform traditional modes of perceiving transcendence. Ocampo presents an exaggerated version of the secularization of the detail because in her work truth lies in the details, the often inexplicable small objects that mark her fiction. She consistently desublimates the traditional religious objects, subverts their standard mechanism of meaning, making them into inert matter while elevating other, surprising elements. "Los sueños de Leopoldina" illustrates this process. A series of details, primarily names, situates the story in Argentina's northwest region near the border with Bolivia and suggests, without actually declaring outright, that the characters are indigenous people rather than of European descent. Place names, especially Tafí del Valle, locate the story in the region of Tucumán. The first sentences contain family names, the surnames Yapurra and Mamanís and the nickname of the narrator, Changuito. The first two sound like native American names, and the second is a diminutive of a widely used native word *chango,* meaning young boy. In the opening paragraphs two young girls carry *damajuanas* [jugs] to fill with water and later consult a *curandera.* The possibility that Leopoldina, the title character, may be an old Indian woman makes the lack of understanding between her and her young nieces a matter of culture as well as of generation. The description of Leopoldina reinforces her situation in an impoverished rural setting and further associates her with the natural world, with the "brute nature" of Reynold's dismissive phrase:

> Era tan vieja que parecía un garabato; no se le veían los ojos, ni la boca. Olía a tierra, a hierba, a hoja seca; no a persona.... A pesar de que hacía treinta años que no salía de la casa, sabía, como los pájaros, en qué valle, junto a qué arroyo estaban las nueces, los higos, los duraznos maduros, y hasta el mismo crispín, con su canto desolado, que es arisco como el zorro, bajó un día a comer migas de

la galleta, mojadas en leche, de sus manos, creyendo seguramente
que era un arbusto. (*F* 111–12)

[She was so old that she looked like a hook; one could not see her
eyes or her mouth. She smelled of earth, of herb, of dry leaf; not
like a person. In spite of the fact that it had been thirty years since
she had left the house, she knew like the birds, in which valley, next
to which stream were the nuts, the figs, the ripe peaches, and even
the *crispín,* with its desolate song, shy like a fox, flew down one day
to eat crumbs soaked in milk from her hands, believing probably
that she was a shrub.]

Leopoldina's communion with nature, viewed positively, emphasises in contrast the negative value placed on the commercialized interests of her young relatives.

The young girls' opening conversation, reported by the ever-
present Changuito whose identity remains unclear until the final paragraph, indicates that they are seeking a "miracle." They
hope to witness a new appearance of the Virgin, not as means
to spiritual grace, but as a way to attract the attention of a man,
get their names in the papers, and receive presents. As in a fairy
tale, they meet an old man on the way home, who asks them:
"¿Para qué buscar milagros afuera de la casa, cuando la tiene a
Leopoldina, que hace milagros con los sueños?" (111) [Why
search for miracles outside your house when you have Leopoldina, who makes miracles with her dreams?]. The girls then
discover that the old woman has dreams which produce small
objects. The adolescents remain uninterested in the stones,
feathers, and twigs that Leopoldina finds in her lap after a nap,
and try to induce her to dream about valuable items—cars, jewels, and so forth—but to no avail. Leopoldina explains, "Tengo
como ciento veinte años y he sido muy pobre" (112) [I am about
one hundred and twenty years old and I have been very poor].
The girls then undertake a series of efforts to produce more
spectacular and lucrative dreams for Leopoldina. First, they try
several home remedies to produce dreams, then call on a *curandera* for special herbs, and eventually travel on horseback
for a day as far as the nearest hospital in Tafí del Valle for special
injections. In the process, they kill one of their mules which
gets stuck in the mud of the swamp, frighten the old woman
into insomnia, and threaten her with bodily harm. She, however,
escapes in the story's conclusion, swept up in a magical wind
reminiscent of the assumption of the Virgin.[51]

The first sentence identifies the narrator as male by stating that all the women of the family have names beginning with the letter *L* whereas he is called Changuito because he is so small. Shortly after he is warned to stay away from poisonous spiders and not to urinate in the creek water. We know he trembles even in warm water, but it is not until the final sentence that he is finally identified as Leopoldina's pet dog. Leopoldina dreams that a dog will write the story of her life and then finds several sheets of wrinkled paper in her lap at the dream's conclusion. She asks the girls to read them to her, but they throw the pages on the floor and take out a book with illustrations of cars, watches, and jewels, saying, "Con estas cosas tiene que soñar y no con basuritas" (114) [These are the things you must dream about and not little pieces of trash]. Among the "basuritas" to which the girls contrast their list of valuable objects are the twigs, stones, feathers, and presumably the story of Leopoldina's life contained on the wrinkled pages, which "is" the story we are reading.

Those wrinkled pages contain a list of objects from Leopoldina's past which the narrator (the dog) says are intimately associated with his own ancestors:

> ¿Te acuerdas de mis antepasados? Si los evocas panzones, ásperos, hirvientes y temblorosos como yo, recordarás los objetos más suntuosos que conociste: aquel medallón, con baño de oro, y en el interior un mechón de pelo, que te regalaron para el casamiento; las piedras del collar de tu madre, que tu nuera robó; aquel cofre lleno de medallitas con agua marinas; la máquina de coser, el reloj; el coche con caballos tan viejos que eran mansos. (*F* 114)

> [Do you remember my ancestors? If you evoke them, paunchy, rough, nervous and trembling like me, you will remember the most sumptuous objects you knew: that gold-plated medallion with a lock of hair inside, which they gave you for your wedding; the stones of your mother's necklace, which your daughter-in-law stole; that chest filled with medals with aquamarines; the sewing machine, the watch; the coach with horses so old they were gentle.]

Here is a list of things that do have intrinsic value for the modern world. Some of the items are recognizable as part of Ocampo's repertoire: the sewing machine, associated elsewhere with artistic creativity; an object stolen by a trusted person, a recurring tragedy. The objects of this list recall either a person, the mother, for instance, or her dog, or are useful, like the clock or the sewing machine. They contrast not only with the elements of nature always associated with Leopoldina, but also with the strictly ornamental, impersonal objects presented by the girls. The pair offer Leopoldina a book, which smells of cat pee according to the narrator, with an assortment of photographs. The objects represented, a car and luxurious articles of personal adornment, are all items of no use to Leopoldina, and contrast sharply to her list of practical or sentimental possessions.

There is, nevertheless, the matter of "aquel cofre lleno de medallitas con agua marinas," an object so out of place that it becomes one of those jolting details, luxurious, out of character, in short, unassimilable. Even the word "cofre" evokes a treasure chest from a pirate story or fairy tale, something wondrous, not just monetary. The old Indian woman, close to nature and to familial ties, leads a miraculous life in contrast with that of her modern young relatives whose sole interest was delineated in the story's first paragraphs and is emphasized in their cold-blooded pursuit, through religious means, of commercial ends. If only they were to take the trouble to read the pages abandoned on the floor, they would know exactly how to induce Leopoldina to dream of valuable possessions from her past. Her memory of them, according to the narrator, is triggered through her pets, Changuito's ancestors. He (and she) have given the girls the key to their own desires, but they are too blinded by their greed to see it. "El sueño de Leopoldina" makes obvious what is not so clear in later stories, the connections between religion—the younger girls' interest in "buscar un milagro," in the form of a new virgin—the fantastic, and the object world, especially the unspectacular everyday things that do not strike us as particularly valuable. It reveals a feminine aesthetic of the detail that not only values "brute nature," but also other characters and beings marked as inferior. Devalued characters, like Leopoldina and her dreams of "basuritas," inevitably have in Ocampo's world special access to transcendent meaning.

"La revelación" is a story whose close reading is helped by elements discovered in "El sueño de Leopoldina," which reveal that the sacred can be found "elsewhere" in the overlooked, unbeautiful beings and objects of our world. The title, as in English, is a pun on photographic and religious revelation. Valentín Brumana, the main character, is retarded, a suggestion by now to acute readers that, like Isis, Leopoldina, the young deaf mutes of "Tales eran sus rostros," and so many other marginalized characters of Ocampo's fiction, he can see better, truer, than the "normal" characters. One of the arresting details of this narrative is the gorgeous silver watch which one of his uncles gives to Valentín. The narrator describes it with evident envy:

> Era un verdadero reloj, no de chocolate, ni de lata, ni de celuloide, como lo hubiera merecido, según comentábamos; creo que era de plata, con una cadena que tenía una medallita de la Virgen de Luján. El sonido que hacía el reloj, al golpearse contra la medallita, cuando lo sacaba del bolsillo, infundía respeto, si no mirábamos al dueño del reloj, que hacía reír. (*I* 29)

> [It was a real watch, not made of chocolate, nor of tin, nor of plastic, as he would have deserved, according to ourselves; I think it was silver, with a chain which had a medal of the Virgin of Luján. The sound that the watch made as it hit the medal, when he would take it out of his pocket, inspired respect if we did not look at its owner, who made one laugh.]

The value of the impressive object contrasts here with the little regard that the other children attach to Valentín at this point. Its association with religious insight is stressed by the appearance of the Virgin of Luján, but also by another joke told on Valentín: When asked what he wants to be when he grows up, he always answers, priest or waiter. Why those two? Because he likes to polish silver. The precious silver of the watch is associated with both the profound (Virgin of Luján) and the superficial (polishing) aspects of religious observance.

The "normal" characters of this story are another of Ocampo's plural narrators, identified about midway as an unspecified number of cousins. Valentín's retardation makes him an easy victim of the cruelty heaped upon him by the as yet unidentified "nosotros" who say(s) simply, "Nos placía torturarlo" [We enjoyed torturing him] and then proceed to list with a certain glee a number of imaginative agonies they inflict on the child. But they eventually discover that Valentín's condition grants him unexpected telepathic powers. The plural verbs, so insistent at first, become a singularized (male) *yo* in the moment of identifying the group. The teasing and torturing of the retarded boy in the first half of the story is related in plural, while the growing revelation of his worth in the second half is made in the singular. The division between singular and plural comes with the knowledge of death:

> Un día Valentín Brumana amaneció enfermo. Los médicos dijeron con eufemismos que iba a morir y que para arrastrar semejante vida, tal vez fuera lo mejor; él estaba presente y oyó sin congoja aquellas

palabras que estremecieron la desolada casa, pues en ese instante la familia entera, aun nosotros, sus primos, pensamos que Valentín Brumana alegraba a las personas por ser tan distinto de ellas y que sería, en la ausencia, irreemplazable. (*I* 30)

[One day Valentín Brumana woke up sick. The doctors said with euphemisms that he was going to die and rather than to drag on with such a life, perhaps it was for the best; he was present and heard without distress those words which sent a shudder through the desolated house, since in that instant the entire family, even we, his cousins, thought that Valentin Brumana made people happy by being so different from them and that he would be, in his absence, irreplaceable.]

After this point the narration continues in first-person singular, stressing the private nature of religious or personal revelation.

The realization of imminent loss changes the narrator's attitude; the revelation contained in Valentín's dying moments challenges his, and the reader's, notion of the possible and the valuable. Valentín asks the narrator to take his picture with someone no one else can see, a beautiful lady, he says. To humor him, the narrator takes the photograph with the invisible woman seated supposedly beside Valentín on the bed. Later, after Valentín's death, the film is developed. At first, one of the six photos is rejected as a mistake, as belonging to someone else. Upon careful examination ("un detallado estudio"), however, the narrator recognizes Valentín in the photo and sees someone else seated beside him on the bed: "La figura . . . de una mujer cubierta de velos y de escapularios, un poco vieja ya y con grandes ojos hambrientos, que resultó ser Pola Negri" (31) [The figure . . . of a woman covered in veils and scapularies, a little old by now and with large hungry eyes, which turned out to be Pola Negri]. In his final moments, Valentín evokes as the image of death the profane, commercialized feminine, the silent screen star, Pola Negri. Suddenly the first words of the story make sense: "Valentín Brumana era idiota. Solía decir:—Voy a casarme con una estrella" (28) [Valentín Brumana was an idiot. He used to say, "I am going to marry a star]. Pola Negri, a genuine movie star of the 1920s and 1930s, was described in one obituary as a "vamp" and "a green-eyed madame" whose real talent was squandered in roles in which she portrayed the prototype of the dark-haired seductress. The same obituary indicates that Pola Negri was involved romantically on and off screen with Rudolph Valentino.[52] The pun on his name, Valentín, eroticizes this poignant moment. Death as seductress is not a new concept, but such an image is not usually associated with a child, much less a dying retarded child. The humorous blasphemy of the final image creates a profoundly satisfying subversion of standard religious belief and of our own readerly expectations. Its religious overtones provide a revelation to the young narrator, that each person is precious and special; and to the reader, that the sacred is available even in quite secular objects like photographs and aging movie stars. Its unexpected and purely secular redemption illustrates the peculiar access to transcendent meaning attributed to details in Ocampo's fiction.

Read in isolation, the story reveals nothing about the Virgin of Luján. Only in the context of other stories can its brief reference in "La revelación" be construed as something beyond the "kitsch" it appears to be here. Ocampo's attentive and systematic reader can deduce a kind of object code which creates a remnant of Hegel's sacred. It is a remnant that poignantly marks, however, the absence of a perfect all-powerful divine, which underscores our modern view of truth as partial and inadequate. "La revelación" works to unravel many traditional associations of the Other as embodiment of evil. Here, as elsewhere in Ocampo's works, the Other can be an unexpected source of the Divine. Evil, in turn, cannot be localized in any one enemy or evil creature, but is more likely part of the collective which itself seems to need a category of evil. Ocampo's plural narrators, like the cousins of "La revelación," are the evil ones, those who in their group need to exclude and torture others. Whatever is exclusionary or hierarchical becomes evil in her stories, including whatever defines humans as superior to animals, men as superior to women, adults as superior to children, the normal as superior to the abnormal.

The potential for transcendent meaning within purely secular objects explains the appeal of "El almacén negro," which uses no standard religious motifs but offers an unexpected redemption. The story's title refers to the business—a country general store—whose owner has just died as the story begins. The opening paragraph presents an example of what I mean by the proliferation of anarchic detail. The baroque phrases, with their deliberately inverted word order, emphasize the sensuous quality of the objects and smells: "Aquella noche de enero, por las persianas, junto al piano enfundado, donde me recliné a mirar el crucifijo, entraba del cielo luz de luna y de la planta baja, donde estaban las provisiones, olor a yerba y a vino derramado"

(*I* 30) [That January night, through the blinds, next to the un-
tuned piano where I reclined to look at the crucifix, moonlight
entered from the sky and from the ground floor where the provi-
sions were stored, the smell of herb and spilled wine]. Among
the several objects mentioned in this sentence, one should note
the crucifix at which the narrator is staring. This tiny detail
relates perhaps to the next sentence in which the dead man
is identified as Néstor Medina. The name Néstor provides two
connections that may be relevant to this story, one refers to a
heresy of the fifth century, which maintained the exclusively
human nature of Jesus; the other Nestor is a kindly, ineffectual
old man from both the *Iliad* and Ovid's *Metamorphosis,* who is
described as: "retaining some mental vigour and bodily strength
long after his youth was passed. The *Iliad* gives a humorous,
kindly portrait of an old and respected but rather ineffective
man, full of advice generally either platitudinous or unsuccess-
ful."[53] The name "Néstor" compresses two historical associations
important to the character: the kindly, deluded old man and the
founder of a cult or heresy. The evocation of a peaceful summer
night reflects the calm, secure, untroubled life of the owner who
is about to be buried, but also prepares the reader for his possible failure of judgment regarding his own family and hints ever
so imperceptibly at the adoration of him demonstrated later by
his neighbors.

According to the narrator's subsequent description of him,
Néstor was a kindly father who considered his children happy
and united. He left them a comfortable fortune, but they proceed to try to squeeze even more out of the old man by selling his
personal possessions. The family's disrespect for their father's
personal items contrasts vividly with the acute interest shown
in them by the townspeople. The narrator, Nestor Medina's son-
in-law, declares that the sale made money because the items had
belonged to a beloved person, as if they were relics. The list of
articles sold at auction is given at length and forms a set of
details which acts, I would say, in the way Schor suggests as a
subversion of the natural ordering of a work. What appears to
be excessive and accessory is, in fact, central to the story's meaning. Personal possessions here as elsewhere for Ocampo define
the person:

Reloj de oro, con cadena y medalla de bautismo, zapatos, botas y
sacabotas, escarbadientes de oro, tintero de bronce, con Mercurio
(que hubiera podido competir con el de cualquier médico de Buenos

Aires), ropero con espejo, salivadera de mayólica, juego de sombreros de verano y de invierno, calzador de hueso, peine y cepillo, gemelos de esmalte, alfiler de corbata con turquesa, anillo de compromiso doble, bufanda de seda, medias de lana, tiradores, cinturón, cincha, bozal, riendas y freno con virolas de plata, estribos, bastos de Casimiro Gómez, boquilla de madera negra, sobrepuesto de carpincho, mate con iniciales de plata, y bombilla ídem., par de pantúflas, poncho deteriorado, navaja, podadora, medalla de bronce y esmalte, par de lentes con estuche recubierto de nácar y forrado en felpa. (*I* 31)

[Gold watch with chain and baptismal medal, shoes, boots and bootjacks, gold toothpicks, bronze inkwell with Mercury (which would compete with that of any doctor in Buenos Aires), armoir with mirror, majolica spitoon, set of hats for summer and winter, bone shoehorn, brush and comb, enamel cufflinks, tie pin with turquoise, double wedding ring, silk scarf, wool hose, suspenders, belt, cinch, bridle, reins and bit with silver discs, stirrups, pack saddle by Casimiro Gómez, cigarette holder made of black wood, overcoat, *mate* with silver initials and *bombilla* idem., pair of slippers, worn poncho, knife, pruning shears, medal of bronze and enamel, pair of eyeglasses with case covered in mother of pearl and lined with felt.]

For a man described as having left his children a fortune, the set of his personal belongings presents a clear and even poignant portrait of a modest unpretentious man of simple tastes and an active country life. The narrator adds immediately following the above list: "Me entristece a veces la falta de juicio de la gente. El sobrepuesto de carpincho estaba apolillado, las riendas y el freno rotos, al peine le faltaba un diente, las medias tenían tremendos zurcidos y todo lo pagaron como nuevo" (31) [Sometimes people's lack of judgment makes me sad. The overcoat was motheaten, the reins and bit broken, the comb was missing a tooth, and the hose had tremendous runs and they paid for everything as if it were new]. These additional details indicate that all the objects were heavily used, not bought carelessly on a rich man's whim. If he left his children a fortune it was due to his own careful management and moderation.

It is, furthermore, a truly Argentine set of things, which not only evokes a particular person, but a specific geographic location and mode of life.[54] If his children could not be expected to react with the same nostalgia that the reader will no doubt bring, they might, nevertheless, be expected to value some of these items as intrinsically valuable or simply as reminders of a loved father. Several of the objects seem particularly scandalous to sell at an auction: his gold watch, wedding rings, tie pin, bronze ink well, silver *mate* and *bombilla,* for instance; others seem simply pathetic, how can one sell house slippers? The narrator views Nestor Medina's ungrateful heirs as greedy almost beyond belief, and asks himself, "¡Cómo, si amaban la memoria del padre, podían desprenderse de aquellos objetos con tanta satisfacción!" (32) [How, if they loved the memory of their father, could they get rid of those objects with such satisfaction!].

Of course one of the articles, the eyeglasses bought during the sale by a new shopkeeper, becomes important to the story. An inexplicable series of disasters causes the destruction of the store's reputation, and Néstor Medina's children begin to lose money. The narrator suggests that their bad luck and Roberto Spellman's good fortune may be due to the eyeglasses that he had purchased at the auction. The four children unite in a determination to retrieve them. At a banquet planned for the purpose of his murder, Spellman dies of a heart attack before they can poison him. Though the siblings did not actually murder Spellman, they do try to disinter the body looking for the glasses that they could not find in ransacking his house, and are accused of the murder anyway. In the story's conclusion the Medina children are imprisoned for a crime they were capable of committing and had planned to commit, but in fact did not carry out, while the narrator has taken over the store. He suggests that his in-laws would attribute his business success to the eyeglasses he has been prescribed by a doctor. The store is forgotten by the siblings in their mad pursuit of the glasses, but Nestor Medina's supposed magic eyeglasses are replaced by others at some point. All the coincidences, near misses, and misunderstandings involving a pair of glasses make ironic commentary on the destructive power of human envy and greed displaced onto a trivial object. But the story's title does not refer to magic eyeglasses but to the odd color of the building. The building's original black color which leaks through the repeated whitewashes, by story's end, symbolizes the family's flaws which cannot be disguised. While nothing in the story warrants a reading of it as fantastic, Ocampo's use of details prevents a reading in the manner of a realistic story as well. The subversion of the conventions of logic are carried out by way of a play with readers' notions of the possible.

If the eyeglasses are the most obvious of the anarchic details in this story, there are a few others. For instance, one relatively minor incident risks taking over the entire narrative. The episode, an engagement which happens by accident, is repeated at greater length in other Ocampo narratives, but nowhere is it more compactly or humorously told:

> Para ver a Amanda Rimbosa, de quien yo estaba enamorado, buscaba la compañía de Ema, que era su íntima amiga. Ema aprovechó la circunstancia para ennoviarse conmigo. Un domingo en que fue a comulgar quedó en ayunas hasta las once; volvió de la iglesia en *break* y, al bajar, se desmayó en mis brazos. Después de este episodio tuve que regalarle un anillo y olvidar a Amanda Rimbosa. ¡Yo sé lo que es la vida en un pueblo! (*I* 30)

> [In order to see Amanda Rimbosa, with whom I was in love, I sought the company of Ema, her close friend. Ema took advantage of the circumstance to become engaged to me. One Sunday in which she went to mass she fasted until eleven; she returned from the church in a carriage and, as she stepped down, fainted in my arms. After that episode I had to give her a ring and forget about Amanda Rimbosa. I know what life is in a small town!]

The narrator's engagement to Ema occurs before Nestor Medina's death, and they are married shortly afterward in mourning clothes. In the story's conclusion he claims to be miserable without his beloved Ema. However, the earlier episode and everything he has narrated regarding Ema and her brothers directly contradicts this supposed devotion. The narrator's sincerity is placed in doubt when one remembers that he was the first to suggest that magical powers attributable to the eyeglasses accounted for Spellman's success and their own failure; he also speculated aloud that Spellman may have been buried with the glasses in a pocket. But whether we believe that the narrator's motivation is completely above reproach, poetic justice is done in the end. The eyeglasses, just like other objects in Ocampo's stories, appear to carry out a sort of retribution in the name of their owner.[55]

"El almacén negro" uses what have long been supposed as feminine stratagems: the character names, the anarchic list of objects, the minor episodes which assume a larger role than expected, word order that disrupts the ordinary sentence structure, all contribute to a narrative which places disproportionate value on what might be considered minutiae. This story privileges the subversive potential of the detail at the same time that it demonstrates its creative power. The story's many ironies contribute to a comic reading of what, in effect, is a highly moral tale. The eyeglasses are a trivial object ordinarily devoid of religious significance which become invested here with a magical power which turns out to be purely imaginary; at the same time, that imaginary wields the power that "real" magic might be expected to have if we could believe in its existence. Within the fictional plot the eyeglasses become invested with the hopes and dreams of people, none of whom are entirely good or entirely evil, and serve effectively to reward and punish in a way acceptable to traditional religious practice *and* to skeptical moderns who would prefer to believe that the imagination of the involved humans, and not some supernatural being, is responsible. In "El almacén negro" the eyeglasses can be read both ways, as the inert matter of our modern world and also as the elevated, sublimated "remnant of the sacred" described by Hegel so long ago.

Ocampo's ironic use of standard religious motifs—statues of the virgin, crosses, and catechisms—marks the absence of religious belief. Her stories find transcendence in other ways, as we have seen. The Virgin of Luján is the only traditionally religious icon that seems to have any validity for Ocampo, and this by virtue of its deviance from the norm, heavily laden with ironic associations. As in "La revelación," evil is embodied in the siblings of "El almacén negro" who goad each other to ever greater extremes of wrongdoing and seek in Roberto Spellman a scapegoat for their own failures (his Jewish-sounding name cannot be accidental). That the sacred space marked out by the fantastic in Ocampo's work is further defined by the quotidian forms the basis for one of the first studies devoted to her fiction. I refer to Rosario Castellanos's pioneering collection of critical essays, *Mujer que sabe latín,* whose study of Ocampo is significantly titled "Silvina Ocampo y el más acá" [Silvina Ocampo and the here and now]. Castellanos quotes one of Ocampo's most frequently anthologized works, "Informe del cielo y del infierno:"

Las leyes del Cielo y del Infierno son versátiles. Que vayas a un lugar o a otro depende de un ínfimo detalle. Conozco personas que por una llave rota o una jaula de mimbre fueron al Infierno y otras que por un papel de diario o una taza de leche, al Cielo. (*F* 173)

[The laws of Heaven and Hell are whimsical. Whether you go to one place or another depends on a lowly detail. I know people who because of a broken key or a wicker birdcage went to Hell and others that because of a page of the newspaper or a cup of milk, went to Heaven.]

Castellanos notes that Ocampo's appreciation of religious or philosophical ideas for their aesthetic value is a sign of "un escepticismo esencial" [an essential skepticism]. She concludes: "Lo que Silvina Ocampo nos advierte, al fin de cuentas, es que el abismo no es un paréntesis abierto entre nuestros hábitos cotidianos, un hiato que rompe la continuidad de nuestros días y que nos exalta hasta la apoteosis o nos precipita a la catástrofe, sino que el abismo es el hábito cotidiano" [What Silvina Ocampo warns us, finally, is that the abyss is not an open parenthesis in our daily routine, a pause that breaks the continuity of our days and that exalts us toward apotheosis or plunges us to catastrophe, but that the abyss is our daily routine].[56] Ocampo's stories deny any transcendence apart from the ordinary objects and details of everyday life.

Ocampo's works deconstruct religious or mythological meaning in just the way described by Frederic Jameson's seminal article on the fantastic. For Jameson, any notion of Northrup Frye's epiphany must be abandoned for modern literature:

> the sense of a whole environment slowly gathering, organizing itself into a revelation of meaning, or better still, into some new and unimaginable language . . . [is] misleading, precisely to the degree to which it suggests that epiphany or revelation is conceivable *as an event* within the secularized world of modern capitalism. . . . However, the great realizations of the modern fantastic—the last unrecognizable avatars of romance as a mode—draw their magical power from their unsentimental loyalty to those henceforth abandoned clearings across which higher and lower worlds once passed.[57]

Ocampo's loyalty to the higher and lower realms of good and evil presents an unsentimental reassessment of both terms. Very Hegelian, I believe, in her belief that the work of art must engage and change us, that it should be somehow profoundly moral, Ocampo nevertheless works to shake up traditional terms of morality. Her works empower the weak, detach truth from beauty, especially from a narrowly defined female beauty, and lead her aesthetic practice to validate the ordinary or even the ugly. Furthermore, what appears to be violent, cruel, or perverse in terms of the plot structures becomes surprisingly humane by way of the details.

4

Feminine Strategies

THE SUBJECT OF LETTERS AND OTHER VOICES IN THE TEXT

IF FEW OF SILVINA OCAMPO'S CHARACTERS ARE PRESENTED AS PRO-
fessional literary authors, many are depicted writing other kinds
of documents, such as Irene's autobiography ("Autobiografía de
Irene"), a journal of recorded dreams ("El impostor"), a school
composition ("La casa de los relojes"), a diary and an "account" of
its reading ("El diario de Porfiria Bernal"), as well as numerous
letters.[1] All these documents stage the first-person narration in
concrete terms which allow the author to explore the issues
of gender within narrative structure. The letter has long been
associated with women in fiction undoubtedly because it provides a context that garners verisimilitude for a female speaking
subject absent from other forms of writing. However, the long
tradition of epistolary fiction from Ovid's *Heroides* to Richard-
son's *Clarissa* and beyond has been written by men, and produces a female letter writer who has been seduced and
abandoned by the male addressee. The heroine's lament while
supposedly giving expression to feminine thoughts and feelings
serves to put woman "in her place" with repeated declarations of
her self-definition as loss.[2] Shari Benstock, among others, views
epistolary fiction in both the French and English traditions as
a kind of appropriation of female creativity by males equivalent
to the rape so often depicted in the plot.[3] If a man writes "like
a woman" or as a woman, he can write about himself from the
position of what Kristeva calls the "pseudo-Other."[4] It is a contemplation of the self by the self. The traditional male-authored
texts portray the languishing heroine in order to contemplate
at length the desirability and power of the absent male.

This said, however, Benstock notices that despite the structural positioning of woman as repository of loss and lack, epistolary fiction contradicts itself by providing a space for the female

subject: "Letters are a vehicle for the expression of that which is, for whatever reasons, denied, repressed, silenced by the culture."[5] Linda Kauffman's book-length study likewise identifies a subversive thread in even male-authored epistolary works which do make a place for the female subject even in their obsessive and repetitive expressions of loss (lack). Kauffman traces the long tradition of love letters, beginning with Ovid's lyric letters of the *Heroides* which, she says, served to validate Ovid's emphasis on the personal and everyday over the heroic and grandiose; in presenting the case of his heroines he makes his own against Virgil's epic with its national and grandiose aesthetic.[6] Kauffman confirms the accusation of appropriation of female talent lodged against epistolary fiction, but she also shows convincingly that the form since Ovid's time has tended to be "antigeneric and anticanonical, ... a critique of ideologies and of language," which stages a sustained examination of desire, gender and genre.[7] In joining this ancient tradition, Ocampo gives herself ample scope for her own exploration of these issues.

Most of Ocampo's epistolary fictions have no address and no signature. They are identified as letters solely by their title. Many of them lack even this identifying feature and are recognizable as letters by virtue of the situation described in the text itself: A narrator addresses himself or herself directly to a "you," speaks of the writing process in the physical sense, i.e., looking for paper or pen, copying or correcting text. Of the stories discussed in detail in this book, several are identified as epistolary only with this broad definition in mind: "El diario de Porfiria Bernal," "La furia," "La continuación" and "La pluma mágica." Furthermore, many are framed within situations which suggest they were never sent or never received by their intended addressee ("Carta perdida en un cajón," "Carta bajo la cama"), thereby intensifying the usual tension between reader of the story and reader of the "letter." Ocampo's stories draw attention to a factor already recognized in this non-genre, that they are really letters to the self about the self. Her loosely defined epistolary structures have been seen in chapter 3 to situate authorial inscription within a gender-neutral setting. In delving further into the structures of her letter stories, it becomes clear that the autocontemplation highlighted within them addresses a tradition which has long allowed the female voice within the text to transform herself "from victim to artist" (Kauffman, 26).

Kauffman describes Ovid's work in terms I would like to claim for Ocampo:

> The Ovidian rhetorical ideal challenges the concepts of unity, fixity, and consistency; instead, it celebrates the fluid, the multiple, the capricious. Rather than seeing illusion as veiling a central reality or a fixed truth, Ovid values illusion for its own sake and recognizes how large a role artifice plays in arousing desire. His rhetoric, with its word play, masks, and poses, is both radically antimimetic and profoundly political. (ibid., 21)

In drawing on this tradition, Ocampo explores ways to allow the female to speak "for herself"; these strategies shed light on other narrative gestures regarding the voice in the text.

Ocampo's "La furia" is a discourse of (sexual) desire whose grotesque laughter can be understood by way of its epistolary structure. The narration's complex story-within-a-story involves a frame narration, in the form of a letter, by a male suitor of the mysterious Winifred whose childhood is the subject of the inner story. By way of direct quotation, Winifred appears to narrate her version in first-person. The bizarre "inner" tale of Winifred's obsession with and murder of her childhood friend, Lavinia, is what the reader most remembers about this story. Winifred, as a child of the inner story, certainly counts as one of Ocampo's most vicious "nenas terribles." Typical of Ocampo's disturbingly "innocent" narrators, Winifred reveals her sadistic nature in a recitation of what she claims are helpful deeds. She says, "Yo vivía dedicada como una verdadera madre a cuidarla, a educarla, a corregir sus defectos" (*F* 84) [I lived dedicated like a true mother to caring for her, educating her and correcting her defects]. This friendly help consists of cutting off a lock of Lavinia's hair, forcing her to have the rest of it cut to match, and spilling cologne on her face to correct supposed defects of vanity and pride. Lavinia's irrational fears are dealt with by putting live spiders, a dead rat, and a toad in her bed on different occassions. Sadly Winifred admits, "A pesar de todo no conseguí corregirla; su miedo, por lo contrario, durante un tiempo se agravó" (86) [In spite of everything I did not manage to correct her; her fears, on the contrary, for a while got worse]. It becomes apparent that Winifred intentionally burned her friend to death, but when the male narrator accuses her of having been cruel to Lavinia, Winifred responds, "¿Cruel, cruel? . . . Cruel soy con el resto del mundo. Cruel seré contigo"(88) [Cruel, cruel? . . . I am cruel to the rest of the world. I will be cruel to you]. The greater cruelty that she plans to inflict on the principal narrator is soon revealed.

Throughout Winifred's recounting of her childhood obsession with Lavinia, the male narrator and she are repeatedly interrupted by the child that Winifred always has in tow. The little boy's favorite activity, banging on a toy drum, drives the young man to distraction, but Winifred resolutely refuses to meet him without the boy. Winifred says that she is the child's baby-sitter, but at one point the narrator speculates that the child may in fact be Winifred's own since she is so indulgent with him. Finally the trio ends up in a *hotel por hora,* a hotel that charges by the hour, where the narrator and Winifred make love while the child wanders in the hallways. Winifred then disappears. In the story's enigmatic conclusion, the narrator finds himself in the compromising situation alone with the child in the hotel. He realizes that he knows nothing of the boy's or Winifred's surnames, where either lives or how to return the child to his family. In panic at the boy's insistent banging on the drum, he smothers him with a pillow. His rueful comment at the end is, "Siempre fui así: por no provocar un escándalo fui capaz de cometer un crimen" (89) [I was always like this: so as not to cause a scandal I was capable of committing a crime]. The male narrator's conclusion contends that Winifred has deliberately manipulated him into murdering the boy: "Ahora comprendo que Winifred sólo quería redimirse para Lavinia, cometiendo mayores crueldades con las demás personas. Redimirse a través de la maldad" [Now I understand that Winifred only wanted to redeem herself for Lavinia, committing greater cruelties on other people. To redeem herself through evil]. Meanwhile she escapes, presumably, to repeat her efforts elsewhere. This strange story derives its horror from the lighthearted irony with which it narrates bizarre violence.

"La furia" executes a grotesque parody of the traditional elements of epistolary fiction, transforming every expectation of the genre's gender.[8] Kauffman's introduction describes recurring strains of the heroines' lament for the absent lover: longing, reproach, sometimes anger and condemnation, and always reflection on the process of writing itself. The women characters of literary convention, according to Kauffman, write from convents or sick beds, their enclosure in society reflecting their enclosure within the text. The male lover of Ocampo's story writes from a hotel where he has just been abandoned by Winifred. In the final sentence he describes his room as a prison ("mi cárcel") thus situating himself within the enclosure of traditional female characters; however, it is clear that his prison is a metaphoric, not a literal one, for he has not moved from the place where he originally found himself trapped and began to write "para no volverme loco" [so as not to go crazy]. Instead of a passionate tale of love and loss, he relays the most sordid of brief encounters. He takes the position of the one who passively waits, while Winifred as the absent "beloved" looms like the vengeful goddess of the title, obsessed and cruel.

The ancient Furies of the story's title sought revenge for those who had committed crimes against family members. In this case, Winifred seems to be avenging her own crime. The title's association of Winifred with the Gods of antiquity helps to reinforce her connection to the two children in question, Lavinia and the boy with the drum. She is seen as a mother figure to both. In the passages quoted earlier she is devoted "como una verdadera madre" [like a true mother] to Lavinia and later the narrator speculates that Winifred may in fact be the mother of the child she cares for in the story's present.

Winifred subverts every normal representation of the feminine. She kills Lavinia, the angelic child, the angel in the house, as a perverse act of creativity "para perfeccionarla" [to perfect her]. She punishes the male narrator for his inability to hear her tale of female friendship betrayed, and in so doing she turns the tables on the traditional romance plot, because it is he who is seduced and abandoned. Finally, most terribly of all, she abandons her young charge, the boy with the drum, the future patriarch whom she is paid to tend. The story suggests that she knew somehow that the narrator would kill the child, that she planned, plotted, the story's and the child's terrible end. Of course, this is the interpretation presented by way of the male letter writer. Through his eyes Winifred dramatizes the consequences of forsaking roles of the innocent female child, the passive object of desire and the good mother. The story unwrites the conventions of female goodness, and structurally and thematically all our expectations about gender. The story's epistolary structure inverts the usual gender orientation of the form by having the abandoned male narrate the story, write the letter, thereby, occupying the space defined by tradition as feminine. "La furia," a female-authored text, uses a male voice to contemplate at length the power of the female, the author's "self," but it offers no comforting image of desirability. The absent female, placed structurally by the feminized male narrator in the position of narrative power, is awarded that role at the expense of every normal female virtue. The story's negative valuation of both male and female characters keeps it from falling into the trap of simply reversing the terms of cultural assumptions. Ocampo's story succeeds in holding up the problem of gender and genre as problem without falling into easy solutions.

A final observation regarding this story involves its addressee. In traditional epistolary fiction, the female character/letter writer directly addresses the absent male. Ocampo's story has no initial address, but it does have a dedication, "Para mi amigo Octavio" [For my friend Octavio]. Usually such messages, placed just under the story's title, are read as "outside" the fiction, as belonging to the author's extratextual voice in reference to a biological person. Nevertheless, within Ocampo's story, the male narrator addresses himself twice to "Octavio" as the addressee of his document. The first, early in the story, appears as part of his description of Winifred, "Era frágil y nerviosa, como suelen ser las mujeres que no te gustan, Octavio" [She was fragile and nervous, like the women you don't usually like, Octavio]; the second is an aside contained in parenthesis, again refering to Octavio's relations with women, "(Recordé tus consejos, Octavio, no hay que ser tímido para conquistar a una mujer)" [I remembered your advice, Octavio, one must not be timid in order to conquer a woman]. This blending of authorial and fictionalized narrative voice is an important element in Ocampo's deconstruction of textual conventions.[9]

Another male-narrated text, "El fantasma," reveals a complex reversal of subject/object positions. The letter is addressed to "Mi alma," a term of endearment that can refer to a beloved, or more literally (and infrequently), to the self, and describes the narrator's obsession with a mysterious perfume which he perceives wherever he goes and with which he describes himself as being in love. In the story's last sentence he discovers that the perfume is a fantastic revenge on the part of a woman, Claudia, whom he has never met. Claudia, the creator of the perfume, had been a friend of this man's girlfriend; at her sudden death in an accident Claudia had vowed to take revenge on her friend for an unnamed wrong. The narrator falls out of love with one woman and in love with a haunting (literally!) fragrance created by another. The absent beloved in this story has died, but her seduction and abandonment of the narrator can be perpetuated infinitely. Only in the last sentence does the narrator (and the reader) discover that the subject in thrall to a strange, feminized object of desire is himself the object of a desire for revenge. He learns of his role as pawn and victim, and we are left to admire the ingenuity of the dead Claudia who has engineered the "plot" from beyond the grave. Seducing her enemy's lover with a ghostly perfume certainly creates a sweet revenge. The male narrator describes female power from his perspective as victim, just as a traditional epistolary plot written by a man creates female narrator/victims as a display of male power. The male characters of "La furia" and "El fantasma" write ironic versions of what Nancy K. Miller has called "the possibility of a male voice of absence."[10]

The narrators of these stories duplicate for Ocampo a position analogous to normal male-authored positioning in epistolary fiction. The fantastic plots and wry humor parody traditional gender arrangements without allowing anyone to think seriously that such a simple reversal of power is somehow better. Once the gender consequences of these stories have been uncovered, a striking observation can be made: Ocampo's stories always put love letters in the voice of the male. In fact, all of Ocampo's male letter writers write of love (sexual desire) while none of the female-narrated letters do. Ironically, when Ocampo puts epistolary narration into motion in the voice of a female narrator, she adopts a position analogous to more recent attempts by male writers, such as Derrida and Barthes, to write as male.[11] The woman writer has the same two choices—to write from the perspective of the same sex or from the opposite—but by virtue of being a woman writer neither of her choices will qualify as "traditional." The male narrators of "La furia" and "El fantasma" illustrate the gender subversion of Ocampo's male narrated stories. What happens when she writes as a woman?

Ocampo's female-narrated "letters" are not precisely those of desire in Kauffman's terms. The female narrators address everyone but the beloved: a friend ("Cartas confidenciales"), a longtime enemy ("Carta perdida en un cajón"), some external authority ("El diario de Porfiria Bernal"). Instead of being love letters, addressed to a beloved about her abandonment by him, they are all explanations of someone's death. These letter writers are not the Woman Who Waits; she is the Woman Who Writes (Kauffman, 25) in preparation for becoming the Woman Who Acts, to kill herself or someone else. Ocampo's female characters frequently plot both suicide and murder; while the murders are not generally narrated via letters, the suicides are. Kauffman views suicide as a rhetorical gesture which adds to the pathos of the situation of abandonment and guarantees a reading of the letter itself. Writing postpones the moment of death; the tension between writing and death emphasizes the "metaphoric substitution of pen for sword, paper for body, ink for blood, the textual for the corporeal."[12] Ocampo's stories framed as suicide letters, such as "La continuación" and "Carta perdida en un cajón," take full advantage of the epistolary fiction's ability to recount a death infinitely postponed by writing.

"Cartas confidenciales" contains two letters, addressed, as so many in the world of the real, to women friends rather than to a beloved. It relates a tale of love and loss, but one which transcends and expands the boundaries of love as it has been traditionally conceived, and presents several twists on conventions of epistolary fiction. Like Carpentier's "Viaje a la semilla," it tells of a man living his life in reverse. But here the teller is a young woman who describes the several stages of his relationship to her family. She remembers him first as "don Toni," an old man who one day simply appeared in the household of her great-grandparents; eventually the narrator's mother and he are the same age, and finally the narrator herself knows him as a young man, a boy, and finally as the infant "Tomi." As she writes about the transformation, she says: "a veces rechazo la idea loca de que Tomi sea don Toni, que la *n* se transformó en *m,* y el hombre en niño. . . . Pasó de la adolescencia a la infancia sin que yo ni nadie de la casa lo advirtiera" (*Ldn* 32) [at times I reject the idea that Tomi is Toni, that the *n* was transformed into *m,* and the man into boy. . . . He went from adolescence to childhood without anyone in the house noticing it]. He has disappeared completely at the moment of her own child's birth. One of her final statements is "Todos somos ciegos en el amor" [We are all blinded by love]. The cliched phrase has been enriched in the context of this love story. Here it retains the association of love as crazed bias akin to madness and adds to it the blindness that fails to notice the small realities of everyday life that could allow the beloved person to change gradually without one's noticing.[13] All the female characters of the story from the grandmother, to the mother to principal narrator have loved him in most of the ways it is possible for a woman to love a man—as father, brother, friend, son. We may add lover if the highly unreliable second letter writer can be believed that far: "Me dijiste que fumaron un atado de cigarillos, encerrados en el cuarto de baño, y que te dio un beso, como de cine, cuando te desmayaste" (35) [You told me that you smoked a pack of cigarettes, locked in the bathroom, and that he gave you a kiss right out of the movies when you fainted]. Earlier the original narrator had described her mother as platonically in love with don Toni. The multiple female characters of one family all have loved the long-lived and changeable Ton(m)i in many different, possibly transgressive, ways.

The second narrator throws a bath of cold water on the elegiac quality of the first letter, providing a dose of cynical indifference to the tale. Ironically, this version, from what appears to be the world of the real, provides corroborative reinforcement for readerly belief in the fantastic for she confirms rather than denies the fantastic intrusion. Love, however, has no place in her world. Whether discussing parents, husband, children, or dogs, this narrator is as unfeeling as much of our modern culture. Love exists in the fantastic part of the story; like Ton(m)i, love crosses generations and refuses to obey the laws of propriety or of reason. This love letter breaks the rules of its genre. The absent beloved male has disappeared and the lover mourns his loss, but this is hardly the picture of male power that male authors paint of "themselves" when writing epistolary fiction. The fictional letter writer, the product of a woman author, produces an image of the absent male who has seduced and abandoned the women of the story, but disappeared as an infant. The collapse of lover and child is one Freud posited for women, however. Ocampo's story humorously depicts traditional woman's normative psychological development, according to tradition, while subverting one more convention of the master plot.

Clearly the letter as structural base for the story provides the intimate, minute, and personal context favored by Ocampo, and allows her to explore and explode gender assumptions. The letters written by female narrators poignantly illustrate what frequently happens to literary works by women: They are lost in drawers or under beds, sent to recipients who fail to understand or believe them. They deal with love in the broadest possible sense, mother love, love of friends, love for the creative process itself, and love of life in the face of imminent death. The male-voiced letters write more traditionally of seduction and abandonment; they take up the conventional female positioning in discourse and effectively demonstrate its fallacies. Ocampo's stories depicting professional writers as well as the ones representing the letters of ordinary women all offer a subversion of traditional narrative positions for the female subject. Ocampo writes stories which imagine the author as neutral, changeable, neither male nor female/both male and female; as character, the female is allowed to move out of her place as object of desire to become the absent phallic power or the all-important voice of authority. By placing her fictions in the casual letters between friends or in overheard conversations, Ocampo provides a believable feminine environment/structure, which again opens up the definition of "art" to validate the creativity often invested in ordinary activities. The experiments with both gender and genre follow a (non)tradition of a certain type which she exploits to brilliant effect. The epistolary, monologized structures provide just the site for the play with identity and subjectivity that her stories enact.

Ocampo's habit of staging her stories to foreground the first-person presence of the narrator extends to structures beyond the epistolary, and situates her within a recognizable tendency among twentieth-century writers to stretch the logic of point-of-view.[14] In some instances, as already demonstrated in "Malva" and in "La gallina de membrillo," it is difficult to say where the "voice" of the first-person narrator originates. Others, like "Las fotografías," direct themselves to a "listener" who presumes knowledge of people and events unavailable to the reader, and who is visualized within the text as present at the moment of utterance. The first-person voice of the narration is then likewise visualized as a specific character who is "talking." The stories with narratee are similar to epistolary fictions in that in both cases the reader is positioned as a secondary recipient of the message: In one case the reader "reads" a letter intended for someone else, and in the other, the reader "overhears" a conversation.[15]

The most important difference between illusions of writing and speaking rests with issues of narrative time. Ocampo's letters and other documents play endlessly with the possibilities inherent in letter writing, that the letter is already fiction by the time it is received. What is retrospective for the writer is future for reader.[16] Part of the ingenious openness of Ocampo's "El diario de Porfiria Bernal" depends on its epistolary structure: It is enclosed, framed, by Miss Fielding's "account" and, therefore, remains forever unaccountable to any reality check within its own terms. Similarly, "La carta bajo la cama" relays with building panic what looks like the impending murder of the narrator herself. On the other hand, what the speaking voice embodied as a specific character loses in such temporal ambiguity it gains in the authority of immediacy and conveys the illusion of the simultaneity of transmission and reception. What both narrative strategies have in common is the distance established between "author" and narrative voice. Genette describes the gap as a dramatization of the difference between the act of narrating and that of writing. In the letters, for instance, there is a difference between what, say, the male character of "La furia" writes and what Silvina Ocampo writes. This gap is dramatized in epistolary fiction by the presence in the text of the letter's fictional writer which allows the real author to seem to disappear. The stories that imply a specific listener or narratee also draw attention to a voice that is perceived as other than the author's. The dialogic aspects inherent in every text are complicated by the presence within the text of these fictional "others."

This illusion of the author's disappearance distances the narrative and forces attention away from the actions narrated and onto the mechanisms of transmission and reception thus foregrounded. Both spoken and written dialog strain the narrative in similar ways, for "the exigencies of the story and . . . of interpersonal discourse" are at odds with each other.[17] Many of Ocampo's narratives make no attempt to smooth over these difficulties. The artifice laid bare in both epistolary and spoken fiction reflects Ocampo's basic cynicism regarding language generally and becomes the structural equivalent of the masks and makeup which will be discussed in the mirror section. Kauffman finds that Ovid's works generally, and his *Heroides* specifically, celebrate illusion for its own sake. I would say that Ocampo also celebrates illusion based on the same skepticism regarding a unitary truth which Kauffman attributes to Ovid; Ocampo's twentieth-century skepticism extends to the expressive powers of language itself.

Ocampo's stories with narratees emphasize the difficulties of narrating. "Las fotografías" and "Voz en el teléfono" set up a disjuncture between the "voice" and the pathos of the events narrated, implying in both cases that the narrators are somehow unable to understand fully either the tragic proportions of events or their own complicity in them. "La oración" does this and more. The story stages the female voice in a most peculiar situation, in church praying; the *tú* of direct address is God. The reader "overhears" a story intended only for the secrets of prayer, making the brazen hypocrisy of the female voice all the more ironic. The ambiguous ending leads the reader to various conclusions, none favorable to the honesty of this narrator. What is clear is that she desperately wants out of her marriage, that she witnessed the murder of one little boy by another, and has hidden the young criminal in her own home. The conclusion leads the reader to believe either that she has poisoned her husband and intends for the boy to be blamed for it; or she has set the scene sufficiently (encouraging the enmity between husband and unwanted eight-year-old house guest, explaining carefully to the child which of the medicines in her cabinet are poisonous, leaving it unlocked to prove her "faith" in him) so that at the time of the prayer the child is carrying out the deed on his own. The more she attempts to persuade herself (and God) that she is hiding the young Claudio out of Christian charity, the more suspect she becomes. The hypocrisy of the narrator, her elaborate lies and lame justifications to herself, demonstrate also the malleable qualities of language itself which allow and even assist self-deception. "La oración" focuses on language's ability to lie, to tell nothing but the facts, and yet none of the truth. The problem here of transmission foreshadows the issues at stake in the final section of this chapter where in Ocampo's stories of rape the problems of reception as well as of transmission reach their crisis point. "La oración" pushes the monolog form to its limits. Though the reader is treated to an unusually clear illustration of the ways people justify their evil deeds to themselves, the positioning of reader as listener to prayer stretches the tensions between the plot and its narration for it is all too clear that the intended listener (the reader) is not the one addressed (God). Genette argues that this is, after all, the situation of all fiction. It is always addressed to someone, however obliquely. In "La oración," the reader is situated as a listener off to the side, and cannot escape an awareness of the manipulative strategies of this narrator, and by extension, all narrators.

The first sentence of "La oración," however, is not spoken by the principal narrator, but forms a one-line introduction to her speech: "Laura estaba en la iglesia, rezando" [Laura was in church praying]. Who says this? The story provides no "source" for this remark, making it yet another instance of the disruption of logical point of view already noted in Ocampo's fiction. According to Kaja Silverman's study of the female voice in classic American cinema, the disconnection between sound and body is the most radical mode of subverting codes of femininity in film. The most powerful positioning of the voice in classic Hollywood cinema is the "voice-over," which seems to originate from outside the filmic narration, and which is always male. Silverman suggests that modern cinema by women directors/producers attempts to create a female voice of authority by disconnecting the female voice from either a character or the interior of the story.[18] "La oración", published in 1959, produces that very situation within a written fiction. Making the leap from film to fiction, it is possible to argue that the unaccountable, unlocatable, ungendered voices of Ocampo's fiction are her most radical departures from the accepted mode of feminine speech.

This observation makes even more interesting the vast number of stories with no obvious narratee and, therefore, no embodied speaker. Most of Ocampo's stories have a definite speaking voice, whether the "I" is a character or not. In chapter 1 these "floating" first-person narrators were analyzed as part of Ocampo's fantastic subversion of knowledge and reality. But, is there something feminine about the retention of the "sound of a voice talking?"[19] Ocampo's stories staged with speakers and narratees (except "Voz en el teléfono") are female speakers. Certainly, staging the speaking voice in a particular situation with speaker and listener is one way to identify the genderless "I" as female. But if the voice is removed from the body, from a specific character, we are left with a strange remnant of the voice-over, or in more conventional narrative terms, the old omniscient narrator of nineteenth-century convention. These disembodied narrators of Ocampo's fiction relay their fragmented, partial knowledge with a voice which *might* be female. Ocampo has thwarted my barely suppressed desire to find a narrative voice defined as female. But Silverman argues that at least in film, when the voice acquires gender, accent or specific "grain," in other words as it gains an association with a specific body, it loses its association with phallic power.[20] Ocampo's insistence on the indeterminacy of gender and the dubiousness of narrative "authority" are effective strategies for subverting the association of the female with "lack," and for questioning the notion of phallic power itself.

Mirrors, Masks and Suicide: Identity in Crisis

Ocampo's refusal to embody the authorial voice in the specifics of gender brings to a crisis the issues arising from a gendered reading of her work.[21] The "problem" of the female body is brought into focus through the study of mirrors and mirroring.

Her last published book of short stories, *Cornelia frente al es-pejo* (1988) contains in its title the image of interest here, a woman contemplating herself in a mirror. Here at last is the present absence of her entire work, so filled with mirror substi-tutes—photos, painted portraits, statues, shadows, diaries, let-ters, and doubled characters—but few mirrors. *Cornelia frente al espejo* represents an extended meditation on the conse-quences of inhabiting a female body in contemporary culture. My focus in this section is on the gender-specific use that Ocampo makes of this device, the way in which she transforms a traditionally devalued feminine activity, self-contemplation in a mirror, to come to terms with the body as self. By way of the mirror, two other elements also become implicated in the same crisis of self-definition, masks and the threat of suicide.

Jennijoy La Belle's study of literary mirroring, *Herself Beheld: The Literature of the Looking Glass,* argues that gender differ-ence marks the ways in which male and female authors use the mirror motif.[22] She observes that for most of history a woman's physical appearance has been the most important factor govern-ing the opportunities of her life. Little wonder, then, that both women and fictional female characters have spent a great deal of time contemplating the best clue to the body's impact on others, their reflection in the mirror. La Belle quotes Ambrose Bierce's *Devil's Dictionary* to provide a condensed appraisal of gender difference regarding the mind/body split: "To men a man is but a mind. Who cares/ What face he carries or what form he wears?/ But a woman's body is the woman."[23] Instead of refuting Bierce's exaggerated comment, La Belle begins her analysis of mirrors in fiction by taking it seriously. She argues that more is at stake in a woman's reflections before the mirror than mere vanity; for female characters and many women the importance of the mirror is not limited to a single, defining moment as Lacan would suggest, but a mode of apprehending the self which sharply distinguishes male and female perceptions of body and of identity and which throughout (female) life amounts to a different, and until now, unaccounted mode of organizing real-ity: "When women look at themselves in mirrors, they partici-pate in a largely ignored panoply of body/self interactions programatically excluded from the metaphysics of masculine self-presence."[24] While Silvina Ocampo's work has never vali-dated realistic fiction's notion of a single, unitary subject, her literary use of mirrors reflects some of the gender differences cited by La Belle.

Ocampo's fictional works consciously question the normative construction of the subject that Lacan would agree is false/fictional. Her use of mirrors, therefore, becomes a vehicle for exploring what La Belle has termed rebellions against mirror identity. Several early works question the status of the subject viewed in mirrors: The perceived disassociation between mirror image and self-concept produces classic horror stories or nightmarish visions; others simultaneously develop and subvert female subjectivity by way of a split consciousness expressed in doubled characters or mirror-substitutes such as photos or autobiographical writing. Ocampo's stories provide an extended denial of normative identity formation and as a result, until 1988, depict no female character who sits at length before a mirror to wonder who she is. The evolution of Ocampo's struggles with the mirror reveal a newly imagined feminine identity.

Three stories from Ocampo's first collection, *Viaje olvidado* (1937), work through quite innovative rebellions against a mirror identity: "El mar" depicts a positive self-construction outside the mirror economy, while "La cabeza pegada al vidrio" and "El vestido verde aceituna" demonstrate that economy's dangers to women. "El mar" describes a poor family, a woman who lives with her husband, her brother and her infant son. One night the two men happen onto a scene that changes all their lives. Having planned to rob a house, they climb onto the roof and watch through a bedroom window while a woman poses in a bathing suit in front of a large mirror. When she goes to bed, the two *voyeurs*, instead of robbing something of value, steal the bathing suit. The next day they insist that their wife/sister put on the suit and bathe in the sea. The woman, after some reluctance, reacts unexpectedly. While the two men are concentrated on her exposed body, she conquers an old fear:

La mujer se olvidó de la vergüenza del traje de baño y el miedo de las olas: una irresistible alegría la llevaba hacia el mar. Se humedeció primero los pies despacito, los hombres le tendieron la mano para que no se cayera. A esa mujer tan fuerte le crecían piernas de algodón en el agua; la miraron asombrados. Esa mujer que nunca se había puesto un traje de baño se asemejaba bastante a la bañista del espejo. Sintió el mar por primera vez sobre sus pechos, saltaba sobre esa agua que de lejos la había atormentado con sus olas grandes, con sus olas chicas, con su mar de fondo, saltando las escolleras, haciendo naufragar barcos; sentía que ya nunca tendría miedo, ya que no le tenía miedo al mar. (*Vo* 160)

[The woman forgot her embarrassment about the bathing suit and her fear of the waves: an irresistible happiness carried her toward the sea. First she wet her feet slowly, the men held out their hands to her so that she would not fall. This strong woman grew legs light as cotton in the water; they looked at her astonished. That woman who had never put on a bathing suit looked rather like the bather of the mirror. She felt the sea for the first time on her breasts, she jumped through the water which from afar had tormented her with it waves big and small, with its great ocean behind, which jumped over the jettys making ships sink; she felt that now she would never be afraid, now that she was no longer afraid of the sea.]

The poor woman, in contrast to the owner of the bathing suit, remains outside any mirror identity. She seems to be completely unaware of the effect her exposed body produces. The only hint that she might be conscious at all of her physical image, the word "vergüenza" [embarrassment], is used only to say that it was forgotten in the sensual pleasure of the water. In contrast to other female characters in Ocampo's stories, this character defines herself, not as object of desire, not in a mirror nor through the eyes of her companions, but in a solitary *jouissance*. This episode produces a crisis in the family relationships. The two men begin to hate each other, and in the story's conclusion, the neighbors hear a fight and think that they see a woman escape at night with her child. It seems that conquering her fear of the sea has induced the woman to escape her situation.

The ambiguity of the ending, narrated from the perspective of neighbors, reflects the distanced quality of the entire story in which only action is described. The sole exception to this distance is the paragraph quoted, revealing the men's suprise at the sight of her body and the woman's unexpressed reaction to the sea. Otherwise, the nameless characters are viewed from outside, as in a film. The two men function as a double. All their actions are expressed in tandem, "los hombres" opposed in the narrative to "la mujer." The physical description creates a contrast between "el hombre oscuro" [the dark man] vs. "el hombre rubio" [the blonde man] but there is no way to know which is the brother and which the husband. In relation to the woman, they cannot be indistinguishable because the erotic feelings appropriate to one are taboo for the other. The sexual, incestuous tension, never openly expressed, produces an intolerable division between the doubled male characters. The crisis induced by the fetishism of the female body in the bathing suit expels the woman from her home, from the world of the fiction. The word in the story, however, is "escape," as if her departure were self-motivated and positive. The woman of "El mar" constitutes herself apart from the triangle so emblematic of Ocampo's fiction. The men, in fact, are defined by their relation to her rather than the reverse. She (re)defines herself apart from either of them in overcoming her fear and discovering a joy in the sea. This story envisions the mirror's absence as the precondition for an escape from the patriarchy.

Other stories of the same collection express the danger of the mirror image for a woman. Social approbation and even sanity are intimately linked to the mirror's reflection. La Belle observes that seeing oneself as beautiful in the mirror is a form of social acceptance, while finding something ugly or, even worse, unrecognizable, is one literary form of madness frequently elaborated by women writers: "to look in [a mirror] and see something bestial or fragmented is to fail both a social and a psychic examination" (ibid., 127). "El vestido verde aceituna" explores the social consequences of mirror reflection, while "La cabeza pegada al vidrio" describes the madness implied in a discord between the reflected image and a character's self concept. In the first story the character, Miss Hilton, sees herself but only partially, and this incomplete image brings about a crisis. A governess, she allows her student to fix her hair: "se había dejado peinar por las manos de catorce años de su discípula, y desde ese día había adoptado ese peinado de trenzas que le hacía, vista de adelante y con sus propios ojos, una cabeza griega; pero, vista de espalda y con los ojos de los demás, un barullo de pelos sueltos que llovían sobre la nuca arrugada" (*Vo*, 25) [she had allowed her fourteen-year-old student to fix her hair and from that day had adopted that braided style which when seen from the front with her own eyes looked like a Greek head; but seen from the back with the eyes of others, was a mass of loose hair which rained over her wrinkled neck]. The disorder and sensuality of her hair create an impression for others of which she is unaware. When a portrait painter copies the hairstyle for one of his nudes, the student's mother fires her from her teaching position with a note that says, "No queremos maestras que tengan tan poco pudor" [We don't want teachers who have so little modesty]. The story's ironic title names the olive green dress that Miss Hilton wears to her portrait sitting which is subsequently left off the nude, not included in the painting with her magnificent hairstyle. The governess is innocent of all but a loss of control over her public image.

"La cabeza pegada al vidrio" presents a more extreme case of disassociation between image and self concept. The main character, a director of a private school, sees the image of the title, a head of a man in flames, in a window of her bedroom. At first, the image seems to form part of the window itself, as if it were stained glass. However the head follows her all over the house, wherever she tries to sleep. In the final scene she discovers it in her mirror at the moment the narrator says, "después de apoyar su melancolía sobre la balaustrada, que fue como *una despedida a la belleza,* subió corriendo hasta el espejo de su cuarto" (*Vo* 101, emphasis mine) [after resting her melacholy on the banister as if bidding good-bye to beauty, she ran upstairs to her bedroom mirror]. Once in the bedroom, the head appears in the mirror presumably in the place where her own face should be. Ocampo's character sees something alien, deformed and tortured in her mirror, moments after bidding farewell to beauty. La Belle's analysis allows a recognition of this gesture as the equivalent to a good-bye to sanity.

La Belle states that male characters do not contemplate themselves in mirrors in search of their identity. If they look in mirrors at all, it is generally for practical ends (21). However, one of Silvina Ocampo's stories presents a male character with the same version of insanity frequently attributed to female characters. "La vida clandestina" is an experimental narrative (discussed in chapter 1) which rejects traditional plot structures as well as the notion of an integrated personality. The main character declares that neither his voice in echoes nor his mirror image correspond to his true self. But neither do the voice and the reflection form together any consistent alternative personality because the being in the mirror is male while the voice appears to be female. The disparity between his self-concept and any of its various bodily reflections creates an incoherence in the plot which parallels the character's unstable identity. "La vida clandestina" offers an extreme vision of the disassociation between body and image (representation); despite its male character, it has relayed the problem in terms specifically connoted as feminine. Imagining the quintessential female nightmare with a male character may represent one strategy for attempting to distance the problem of bodily identity from the exclusive arena of the feminine. The story subverts the accepted traditions of narration in an effort to demonstrate the precariousness of identity itself.

The short stories before 1988 offer no long, contemplative moment before a mirror in which "women look into mirrors searching for what they really are."[25] The place where that activity does occur is in a poem written by Ocampo for an anthology entitled *Retratos y autorretratos* (1973), a volume that includes a photographic portrait with the signature of each contributor and an autobiographical poem. The poem contributed by Silvina Ocampo to this volume, entitled "La cara," speaks directly of the rebellion against mirror identity already witnessed more indirectly in the short stories. The lyric *I* of the poem describes her face as an essential and yet alien part of her being. Words like "mask" and later, "tattoo," emphasize the face's aspect as costume or work of art. Verb forms in reference to the reflected image vacillate between third and first person: "en un verdadero espejito la arrinconé/ o más bien ella me arrinconó con su mirada aviesa" [In a real little mirror I cornered her/ or rather she cornered me with her perverse glance].[26] Although Labelle considers in some detail the use of the pronoun "you" in reference to the reflected image, she makes no mention of the possibility of third-person.[27] To refer to one's own image in the mirror as "she" is a more emphatic distancing device for what is otherwise taken to be a form of the "I."

The poem describes images chronologically from the first visions of the face viewed by a small child in the concave of a spoon to the more elaborate adolescent acting-out in front of a full-length mirror. The last section leaves the mirror and turns to a series of numbered photographs in which the figure in the photos grows from a small child to an adult.[28] One evolution of note in the photographs and in the poem as a whole is the degree of social stereotyping revealed at each stage. While the adolescent tries out every culturally inherited image of femininity—the queen, the slave, the beauty and the brain—one of the photos of the young adult is described by the poetic voice as deserving the title "hermafrodita" or "retrato de un espíritu bizco" [hermaphrodite, portrait of a cross-eyed spirit]. This cross-eyed spirit, this double vision of the hermaphrodite, is an image which provides, I believe, the best clue to Ocampo's (de)constructing of the feminine in fiction. Just as her images of the author in stories about writers are sexually neutral, the image she presents of herself in this poem is a complex mixture of male and female.

The poem's lyric voice stops counting photographs after the eleventh and continues describing them with the words "another" and "another" until reaching the concluding lines: "No quiero más fotografías de esa cara/que no es la misma cara que estaba adentro de una cuchara/ni en el vidrio, ni en el cuchillo, ni en el aljibe,/ni siquiera en el espejo" [I want no more photographs of that face/ which is not the same face as the one in the spoon/ nor in the glass, nor in the knife, nor in the well,/ nor even in the mirror]. The poem rejects the mirror and even the face itself (and its photographs) as an adequate mode of self-definition. The photo of Silvina Ocampo that accompanies this poem shows an elegant woman seated on the floor with her legs folded decorously around her. She appears to be barefoot. One hand, formed in a loose fist and bearing several bracelets, rests in her lap. The other is extended toward the camera with all fingers spread wide, completely hiding her face from view. This aggressive negation of the face expresses an important theme of the stories, here situated in an autobiographical frame: in a volume that refers to self-portraits, next to her signature and a photograph of "herself." For Ocampo, personal identity is a temporary, ever-changing shell, vulnerable to place, clothing, and small objects, always capable of irreparable fragmentation. The stories emphasize the multiplicity of personality and have consistently questioned an identity limited to the mirror image. The poem confirms what the stories suggest, that the mirror lies, that it has no power to form a unified, workable identity, that a person is not really identifiable even by her face.

Though Ocampo's stories depict no long, lingering moments of meditation before the mirror, they do present glimpses of briefer interaction in ways suggested by La Belle. Two stories present fleeting moments in which a woman looks into a mirror at a crucial juncture of her life. It is perhaps unsurprising that both moments of crisis involve the character's suicide. In "La continuación" the fictitious author looks rapidly at herself in a mirror while arguing with her lover "para asegurar mi presencia" (*F* 15) [to assure my presence]; the narrator of "El sótano" contemplates her face in a mirror moments before her anticipated death in the demolition of the building she refuses to leave (*F* 61). These stories combine, if tangentially, two ideas firmly associated with the feminine, mirrors and suicide. Both are greatly expanded in her final collection, where she develops as well the related issue of feminine disguise.

Cornelia frente al espejo can be viewed as a lengthy meditation on being through mirroring as if Silvina Ocampo decided to stop denying the mirror's power and to confront it directly.

Many of the stories collected here elaborate themes suggested in the poem, "La cara," including the notion of the face as mask and the uncertainty even of physical identity. The collection also makes overt a connection only suggested elsewhere between mirrors and death. Margaret Higonnet has pointed out that death traditionally has provided the most significant moment of life, the moment in which a life can be interpreted. Suicide, or the threat of suicide, has been identified as a rhetorical strategy for forcing the "reading" of a life, intimately (and inaccurately) associated with the feminine. Higonnet demonstrates the ways in which women writers of the twentieth century have sought to destabilize the certainty and closure associated with suicide to see it as something more ambiguous: "The decisive moment is no longer decisive."[29] Silvina Ocampo associates the issues of identity in both activities—thinking about suicide and gazing in mirrors—with the need to rethink issues of gender. The face, and by extention the body, becomes a necessary mask, associated with the artifice of language itself as a means of constructing a frail, always false, identity.

The title story, "Cornelia frente al espejo," combines the attempt to find identity in the mirror with the attempt to interpret a life in the moment of a threatened suicide. It reveals what these two gestures have in common: both mirror identity and suicide represent the attempt to create a wholeness that the story suggests is impossible/illusory. "Cornelia frente al espejo" performs an elaborate rupture of traditional narrative by dramatizing the impossibility of a secure identity and ultimately the failure of character. As in theater, there is no narrator: Cornelia addresses the mirror, who answers. Their dialog, set late at night in an empty millinery shop, is motivated by Cornelia's decision to kill herself. However, the dialog with the mirror is interrupted by three additional characters, a young girl who calls herself Cristina Ladivina, a hired assassin, and an architect named Daniel. The first of these is a humorous reference to other little girls who predict the future in Ocampo's fiction, her name a play on the word *adivina*.[30] The child's appearance is the first hint that the other characters may also be projections of Cornelia's imagination, part of the theater being enacted before the mirror. The child is described as a ghost; one reading will view the other characters as phantoms as well. The second intruder is a figure completely new to Ocampo's works, a hired killer. The mysterious, monosyllabic thug poses as a thief who eventually confesses that he has been hired to kill someone else; he had thought to practice on Cornelia. Though Cornelia's conversation at times appears to be that of a mad or unbalanced person, she outsmarts the assassin by having him drink the poison she had intended for herself. Just as he does so and flees to die "off-stage," Daniel enters. The sympathetic male character inspires Cornelia to tell a story within a story, the early part of her own life when she was just the age of eleven-year-old Cristina.

The story that Cornelia tells to Daniel forms a series of doubles with the framing situation and repeats plot elements and descriptive phrases by now quite familiar to attentive readers of Silvina Ocampo's other works. The story sets up an elaborate game of mirrors in which the author's previous works echo like the overture to an opera in which the music of the whole appears. For instance, the story's setting, a hat shop, is by now a familiar one while the name, Cornelia, recalls an infamous character from the story, "Los amigos." The titles of other stories or key words also appear: At one point Cornelia recites the seven deadly sins, echoing "Las invitadas"; she makes reference to a mortal sin, recalling "El pecado mortal"; one exchange has the mirror describe Cornelia as "una santa," as in "Las vestiduras peligrosas"; Cornelia recites a history of the mirror, a humorous reference to many early works, especially of poetry.[31] Various episodes also reprise earlier works—the theft of a valuable object by a friend, the friendship between a child and an older woman, the suggestion that two characters have the same dream—as well as the major themes of betrayal, doubling, rape, suicide, and murder.

Cornelia's narration in the inner story of her childhood infatuation with an older woman, Elena Schleider, is almost parodic in its familiarity. Ocampo here combines in a troubling way many recurring elements of her fiction. When the child Cornelia discovers that her two special adult friends, Elena and Pablo, are lovers, her intense feelings of betrayal inspire a revenge that translates her rage and confusion into a report of her own rape by a stranger in the woods. No one, including the reader, believes her story. The original distress, combined with outrage at not being believed leads her to ever more drastic measures. She steals Elena's gold cigarette case in order to buy Pablo an engagement ring; when he won't accept it she tells him she is pregnant. Her frantic efforts to retaliate hurt only herself, for her parents evict her from their house. She is taken in by an aunt, the one who runs the hat shop, where she has worked until the present moment and where she is about to take her life. This inner story, richly suggestive of many elements already discussed throughout this book, is almost a coded summary of Ocampo's most important literary preoccupations. The framing situation of suicidal despair is thus all the more distressingly personalized, an autobiographical gesture to which we return below.

The final segment of this long narrative finds Cornelia alone with the mirror, who no longer speaks. Having bid farewell to all the figures who have formed doubles of herself, she now shatters the mirror, the last and most important double: "Soy lo único que no conozco. . . . "Me buscaré a mí misma en todos tus pedazos: un ojo, una mano, un mechón de pelo, mis pies, mi ombligo, mis rodillas, mi espalda, mi nuca tan querida, nunca podré juntarlos" (*Cornelia* 53) [I am the only one I do not know . . . I will look for myself in all your pieces: an eye, a hand, a lock of hair, my feet, my navel, my knees, my back, the beloved nape of my neck, I will never be able to join them]. The destruction of the mirror destroys the locus for Cornelia's futile attempt to construct an image of unity and wholeness on which identity depends. That unity is what Cornelia fails to find in the mirror and now seeks in death: "La muerte de un espejo no es igual a la muerte de una persona" [The death of a mirror is not the same as the death of a person]. A mirror's "death" results in a new multiplicity, but a person's death seems to create a unity, something complete that can be understood. The enigmatic ending of this story allows the rest of the collection to refute both of Cornelia's temptations. Neither mirror identity nor suicide offer a solution to the problem of identity.

Though it has been clear in previous volumes that Ocampo orders stories carefully in order to stress certain connections, the elaborate play of titles and themes is especially obvious in this one. Two stories that intersect each other in important ways are "La máscara" and "Con pasión," which both take place the night in which a young girl dresses for carnival in a woolen Dutch-girl costume and suffers terribly from the heat. "La máscara" comes close to producing a plotless narrative for the story ends ambiguously after two pages in which the character contemplates her costumed image before a mirror:

Me miré en un espejo. No me reconocí. . . . Debajo del cartón, el sudor cayó de mi frente a mis ojos, prorrumpiendo casi en llanto, pero nadie veía lo que pasaba detrás de ese cartón, duro e interminable como la máscara de hierro. Poco a poco la careta embellecío un poco; la miré de nuevo en el espejo. . . . Nunca fui tan linda, salvo algún día de extraordinaria felicidad en que tuve una cara idéntica a otra cara que me gustaba. (94)

[I looked at myself in the mirror. I did not recognize myself. . . . Under the cardboard, the sweat fell from my forehead into my eyes, errupting almost in tears, but no one could see what was happening behind that cardboard, hard and interminable like an iron mask. Little by little the mask became more beautiful; I looked again in the mirror. . . . I was never so beautiful, except one day of extraordinary happiness in which I had a face identical to another face I liked.]

The carnival mask reflected in the mirror is almost simultaneously perceived as instrument of torture that obscures the suffering behind it and accepted as (confused with) a beautiful reflection of the self. Ocampo's character dramatizes literally what the lyric "I" of "La cara" had suggested figuratively, that the face itself is a mask. La Belle suggests that the reflected image is and is not equivalent to the self, a duality she expresses as an oxymoron because "mirroring is, quite literally, a mode of figuration or figuring-forth an image which, like metaphor, is inscribed with both identity and difference."[32] By adding the complicating factor of the mask, Ocampo questions the status of the "I" who looks as well as the "you" of the reflection.

The following story, "Con pasión," takes up where the first left off except that the carnival night is narrated here by the boyfriend. He describes his beloved as a person whose overriding passion is to inspire compassion, hence the play on words of the title ("con pasión/compasión" [with passion/compassion]). The carnival ball, one episode of a longer story, initiates the turning point in their relationship when the girl faints from the heat. This time the male narrator suggests that the girl's fainting spell was a ruse to win his declaration of love. Her actions are viewed as a manipulation, as one more mask. The two stories reflect each other in a play of mirrors; the girl's profound identity confusion in the first story is viewed as a deception in the second.

The intertwined themes of disguises, identity, and desire function also in the comic story, "Los celosos," in which a woman named Irma Peinate uses the various tricks of the womanly trade, cosmetics, as a kind of mask. The false beauty she creates to impress her husband succeeds in arousing his love and also his jealousy. One day he decides to follow her and manages to overhear a flirtatious conversation between his wife and her dentist. As she walks out of the dentist's office, he hits her over the head, knocking out her new teeth as well as her tinted blue contact lenses, false eyelashes, and wig. He then fails to recognize her: "—Discúlpeme, señora. La confundí. Creía que era mi esposa—dijo perturbado—. Ojalá fuese como usted; no sufriría tanto como estoy sufriendo. —Apresurado se alejó, sintiéndose culpable por haber dudado de la integridad de su mujer" (128) ["Excuse me, madam. I mistook you for my wife," he said, upset. "If only she were like you I would not suffer the way I am now." He hurried away feeling guilty for having doubted his wife's integrity]. The many ironies of this story illustrate the Lacanian concept of male desire governed by metonymy, the part for the whole, or even, as already seen in other of Ocampo's stories, *instead* of the whole. It also makes the point that the resulting identity confusion in women, the narcissistic viewing of themselves in parts, threatens their "integrity" in the dual sense of that word. Irma's use of feminine conventions stresses the instability of all identity, particularly one based on ideals of feminine beauty. If it is imposible for the husband to recognize his wife without her adornments, without her mask, is there anything "essential" to recognize? Ocampo suggests in "La máscara," "Con pasión" and "Los celosos" that our faces are constructed accessories, just like masks.

An understanding of the mask as a kind of metaphor for the construction of identity makes possible a highly political reading of "El banquete." In the imaginary society of this narrative, a group of young people have managed to protest a law which, if passed, would have forbidden the wearing of masks by those under fifty years of age.

Pero la ley fue rechazada gracias a las manifestaciones y los actos de violencia que se produjeron. Había gavillas de adolescentes que las usaban a escondidas. Descubrieron un arsenal de máscaras impúdicas: los menores de edad las almacenaban. El escándalo se propagó hasta en los colegios donde los alumnos las consiguieron para los exámenes, de modo que casi todos resultaban impostores. (112)

[But the law was rejected thanks to the demonstrations and acts of violence which they produced. There were gangs of adolescents who used them in secret. They discovered an arsenal of indecent masks: minors would store them. The scandal extended even to the schools where students obtained them for exams to the point that nearly all of them turned out to be imposters.]

The vocabulary used to relate official suspicion of groups of young people, which has no direct connection to the rest of the story, cannot fail to connote events of the *guerra sucia.* for readers in 1988.[33] Ocampo has presented masks in other stories as a metaphor for a constructed identity which permits the subject to form part of the symbolic. Therefore, to deny masks to a group of young people is to deny them subjectivity, the capacity to fully exist as subjects of language, as part of the political system. The political theme of "El banquete" introduces the mask's subversive potential, identified by René Girard: "Masks stand at the equivocal frontier between the human and the "divine," between a differentiated order in the process of disintegration and its final undifferentiated state—the point where all differences, all monstrosities are concentrated, and from which a new order will emerge."[34] In one small episode of "El banquete" Ocampo emphasises the mask's subversive power.

The banquet of the story's title is organized to celebrate an earthquake costing the lives of several million people, the critical number, according to the story's scientists, necessary to avoid the coming crises of air and food for the world's population. The pompous banquet speaker explains that the catastrophe is in effect a salvation for those who have survived. However, during the banquet itself, the guests become aware that a virus is sweeping the rest of the world, caused by the rotting corpses of the earthquake. The main character, upon realizing that death is imminent, makes an important discovery, "Ya ves, la eternidad no es distinta" (114) [Now you see, eternity is no different]. Here, it seems to me, lies the articulation of Ocampo's essential refusal of transcendence. This story's unusual (for Ocampo) political statement indicates that human salvation depends on the living, on individuals and on societies. But Ocampo's absurd and ironic view of politics throws solutions onto individual transformation, rather than on public activism.

Hence, the importance placed in her work on private concepts of the individual. Jennijoy La Belle argues that the specular image, never confused with the essential masculine, requires from neither male authors nor fictional characters a rebellion against its limits. Masculine consciousness perceives its essence "inside" the person, in some unreachable and invisible realm. Men define the I/not-I dichotomy as the bodily "I" versus something magic and transcendental, a soul; while women define the dilemma as wholly part of the physical world.[35] La Belle concludes that the feminine use of the mirror represents a socially constructed identity at odds with this masculine convention and, therefore, amounts to a different version of transcendence as well. La Belle quotes a dialog between an old woman and a priest from Elizabeth Taylor's novel *Hester Lilly,* in which the old woman says, "I believe in personality . . . , you believe in souls. That's the difference between us." La Belle continues:

> Personalities are constructed through human interaction, human conversations, not the creative Word of an absent God. To get out of one's self means to join with others in a communal pursuit of transformed identity, not the Vicar's heavenly notion of the same old ego levitated to some other world. The old woman's theory of identity is less isolated, less alienated from the physical world, and more open to change than the Vicar's. . . . Seneca said, "No one is free who is a slave to the body." To a very large degree, Western religion and philosophy have depended upon this basic idea of the autonomous self, one that tends to exclude women who form identities in other ways. Perhaps the paucity of female contributions to transcendentalizing traditions has some basis in a woman's unwillingness to define self through its alienation from the body.[36]

Ocampo's stories demonstrate a complex agreement with this conclusion, a refusal to deny the body, but at the same time a desire to question seriously its status in defining identity.

The final story included in *Cornelia frente al espejo,* entitled "Anotaciones," provides a meditation on death which utilizes the mirror as the marker between life and death: "El día en que me muera . . . iré corriendo por la plaza San Marco, por todas las edades, y no me reconoceré en ningún espejo" (223) [The day that I die . . . I will run through the Plaza San Marco, through all the ages, and I will not recognize myself in any mirror]. The last sentence of the story and, therefore, the last of the book itself is, "Quisiera escribir un libro sobre nada" [I would like to write a book about nothing]. Ocampo's desire to eliminate the mirror as a sign of the self turns into a wish to do without all referent in literature. This desire to push the limits of language in order to play freely with signifiers is stated in a way that simultaneously acknowledges its impossibility, for the verb tense, the imperfect subjunctive, defines its status as empty wish. In fact, the earlier image—of failing to recognize herself in the mirror—defines death in the same terms: the irrevocable separation of signified from signifier becomes Ocampo's vision of death itself. Genette, in his study of Ocampo's favorite author, Proust, concludes that the signified is inevitable: "We do not escape the pressure of the signified: the semiotic universe abhors a vacuum, and to *name* contingency is already to assign it a function, to give it a meaning."[37] The contingency which Ocampo names is the body's. Here the image of death does not imply the absence of the body, for to run and to fail to recognize oneself in a mirror does not mean to exist without the body, but rather to exist without the body's identifying limits. Death in Ocampo's image has lost its sense of closure while the body ceases to define the self.

Ocampo's stories teach us that personality is not defined nor limited by the body nor by death, but by art and by an expanded definition of love. With Kristeva, her works suggest that art is not an object but a process intimately connected to life: "A life, a work of art: are these not 'works in progress' only in as much as capable of self depreciation and of resubmitting themselves to the flames which are, without distinction, the flames of language and of love?"[38] For Ocampo it is unimportant whether the creative process produces a hat, a painted canvas, or a short story, creativity itself is the essence of being. Kristeva associates art with love, as activities always open to the other and "in progress;" melancholy, by contrast, tends toward the Real, that is, toward death. In presenting the mirror as inevitably associated with death, particularly death by suicide, Ocampo makes a complex association of these with their opposites, art and love.

Margaret Higonnet argues that suicide is falsely associated with the feminine because of nineteenth-century fictions which depoliticize the act, denying it any heroic element and turning it into an illness, due to love. The male character in "El jardín de infierno" narrates a humorous inversion of the Bluebeard myth that speculates playfully on sexual stereotypes.[39] The narrator ends by hanging himself in a secret room where he has discovered his wife's previous six husbands. The humorous tone of the story makes the point that other stories suggest, that love itself is a kind of suicide.[40] Love as loss of identity, a kind of suicide, is thematized directly in several of Ocampo's works, especially "Las ondas" and "Amada en el amado," but is a possibility, a tension, inherent in every story Ocampo has written about love. Ocampo's female characters have learned from romantic tradition that true love ends in death. Without this suicidal impulse it can't really be love. However threatening love may be to women and women artists, finally it is inseparable from identity itself. Ocampo's ultimate conception of love seeks a broader definition, freed from conventions of romantic thralldom and of narrow gender definitions.

Unlike other suicides in Ocampo's works, Cornelia's seems to offer no positive reading. Rather, her suicide suggests Kristeva's "melancholy," the turning to death. In looking in the mirror Cornelia recalls Narcissus, whom Kristeva evokes as precisely the wrong example of a healthy narcissism which aids identity. By refusing to accept a real other outside himself, Narcissus refuses loss and thus folds in on himself and dies. Cornelia's death, like that of Narcissus, reflects her failure to accept repression in language, to symbolize loss, which in turn gives birth to desire. Cornelia's search, first in the mirror then in death for truth as singular, unitary, monistic recreates the condition for Nietzsche's nihilism, "for such a view of truth opens the way to its total collapse: 'God is truth' risks becoming 'All is false.'"[41] Love and art for Kristeva, and I would say for Ocampo, are the impulses opposed to melancholy, or death, because both love and art are based on metaphor, the necessity to recognize difference. Kristeva postulates that the work of art can represent a melancholy overcome wherein the artist is drawn toward suicide, but produces art instead. And the process of creation creates the artist: it is "constitutive of the subject, rather than constituted by the subject."[42] In an interview with John Lechte, Kristeva continues:

> I would even say that signs are what produce a body, that—and the artist knows it well—if he doesn't work, if he doesn't produce his music or his page or his sculpture, he would be, quite simply, ill or not alive. Symbolic production's power to constitute *soma* and to give an identity is completely visible in modern texts. (Lechte, 25)

The process described by Kristeva reproduces the plot of Ocampo's "La continuación," in which the "writer" within the text contemplates suicide but writes the story instead. According to Kristeva, this process wherein the artist creates and is created by the work of art, is opened to the other, imitates the cure in analysis, which seeks to open the psyche to the other, to difference, "making the other an 'event' in the life of the subject. It aims to make this loving condition permanent."[43] We could speculate, like Kristeva does, that the artist, in this case Silvina Ocampo, imitates her own fiction in writing "Cornelia." "Cornelia" presents no artist within the text, as did the earlier work, "La continuación" and, therefore, leaves the reader with the spectacle of a character in the process of destruction. The very lack of fictional artist points the finger to Ocampo herself as the artist for whom this work represents, in Kristeva's words, "melancholy overcome."

John Lechte ends his article on Kristeva with her words indicating a need "to have a new loving world surface from the eternal return of historical and mental cycles" (40). In Kristeva's phrase which eerily recalls the great themes of Borges, we can glimpse the difference between his works and those of Ocampo. For Ocampo the inevitability of the body and of love contrasts with absence of these from the works of Borges.[44] Both writers view transcendence as a sacrifice of the singularity of the individual. For Borges, this implies a struggle to renounce fame, to give up authorship. Many of his best-known works—"El inmortal," "Pierre Menard," "El aleph," "Borges y yo"—conclude that a work of art is a work by everyone and no one, in which the artist, whether Homer, Cervantes, or Borges himself, disappears. Ocampo, whose vision of creative work has always been more humble and communal, renounces fame and the singularity of a name with some ease. Her many nameless characters, including the woman of "El mar," for instance, indicate the name's insignificance. Cornelia's words from the story's first page make this explicit: "¡Cornelia! Mi nombre me hace reír. . . . Podría llamarme Cornisa, sería lo mismo" [Cornelia! My name makes me laugh. . . . I could be called Cornice and it would make no difference]. She continues that she has written her name in many places—on the walls, on the garden trellis, on her own arm—but despite having written it on her own body, the name has no power to define her. The body itself is, for Ocampo, the more difficult problem.

Cornelia has surrendered, it seems, to two feminine temptations, mirror identity and suicide. Ocampo's story, "El mar," published more than fifty years earlier, presents its opposite, a character free of mirrors and of masculine domination, who escapes at story's end for parts unknown. If we still cannot envision a destination, a destiny, for the woman of "El mar" this speaks volumes about the unexpected difficulty to change a system, the patriarchy, rooted in our social customs and family life, and more important, in our very language. Kristeva argues that creating a character who succumbs to melancholy is one way to permit the author to live with love, to recognize the false illusions of the two orders in which we live, the symbolic and the imaginary. Significantly, the works in which overt contemplation in the mirror occurs, the poem "La cara" and "Cornelia frente al espejo," both draw overt connections to the author herself.

The poem is framed autobiographically by the volume's title, *Retratos y autorretratos* [Portraits and Selfportraits], while the story makes pointed reference to previous works by the author in an orgy of self-referentiality. The final story in the collection, "Anotaciones," continues this highly unusual (for Ocampo) personalization by including the initials of her husband, Adolfo Bioy Casares, in one of its statements. Italicized and in English, the statement literally stands out on the page: "Y para siempre soñaré con vos en las largas noches de mi exilio. Y aquí en el agua me muero sin esperanzas de encontrar algo mejor que el agua, soy una exiliada. *The only thing I love, A.B.C.,<< the rest is lies>>* (226) [And forever I will dream of you in the long nights of my exile. And here in the water I die without hope of finding something better than water, I am an exile. *The only thing I love, A.B.C, "the rest is lies"*]. The impulse to situate herself autobiographically in precisely these stories that foreground mirrors and death, creativity and love, makes their issues seem both more personal and more painful. For Ocampo, as for many women artists, according to La Belle, the reluctance to define self without a body is matched by the fear that the self will be limited to/defined solely by the body. Returning to "La cara," the word "hermafrodita" takes on a new significance. It indicates that she, the lyric I, considers herself simultaneously neither man nor woman/both man and woman. The body hides multitudes not revealed in its surface, in its mirror image. The word comes to define the ideal revealed in Ocampo's writing as a whole: Existing as a hermaphrodite does not imply identifying oneself beyond or without a body, but it does insist on the body's contingency, its complexity, its unexpected, invisible surprises.[45]

AMBIGUITY AND SILENCE: RAPE

Ambiguity and silence have been identified as elements of a particularly feminine writerly strategy by many critics.[46] Ocampo's creative use of these strategies can be deduced from many elements of the foregoing analysis of her work. Female characters utilize silence as resistance, rather than consent, in several works studied in detail here. More broadly the creation of ambiguity surrounding the central events of her narratives could be said to define Ocampo's works: It is the necessary ingredient for her approach to the fantastic mode and, for that matter, for the subversion of the male/female dichotomy I claim for her work. I want to concentrate, by way of conclusion, on the ambiguity implied by a subversion of narrative authority and a rejection of the monism of truth which Ocampo brings to the issue of rape. In Ocampo's stories about rape, silence goes deeper, to mark the failure of language to convey experience. The profound ambiguity of these stories makes them nearly impossible to "read." Rape is the ultimate problem of narration and interpretation: Its issues bring us to the difficulty of feminist criticism in general and of Ocampo's works in particular.

Lynn A. Higgins writes, "Viewers sympathetic both to feminism and to postmodernism must thread our way between the Scylla of univocal readings and the Charybdis of infinitely proliferating indeterminacy."[47] The implications of that statement for any representation of rape become clear, as Higgins later elaborates, in that rape is the only crime which leaves no verifiable evidence that a crime was committed: "A rape defense case can rest on the claim that what occurred was not a rape and so the question is not *who committed* the crime, but *whether a crime occurred at all*."[48] Though Higgins suggests that such narrative indeterminacy provides the perfect subject for experimental film, I contend that the same can be said for fiction. Silvina Ocampo utilizes the dynamics described by Higgins to explore female stories of rape, and thereby produces her most ambiguous, and in my mind, most misread stories. The confluence of Ocampo's recognition of female desire with the use of ambiguity and silence as feminine strategies and her postmodernist insistence on a plurality of meaning, lead to major gaps in the narrative, gaps into which readers are irresistibly drawn.[49]

Women writers face a complex set of cultural assumptions in any attempt to fictionalize rape. Pornography, and here I include women-authored soft porn, such as the Harlequin series' bodice rippers, as well as the "hard," deal with the specifics of the act of sexual violation in order to titillate readers.[50] Writers with other interests must struggle to speak of violation apart from the sexual. Most feminist literary critics who have dealt with this issue have studied male-authored texts, primarily mythical representations of rape. In offering new ways to read the stories of violated and silenced women of our most ancient heritage, these critics suggest ways in which rape is still perpetuated in our time.[51] Our mythic inheritance burdens any reading of rape with a weight of purity, silence, or monstrosity: the stories of Philomela and Arachne, Lucrece, Leda, Helen, Medusa, et al., turn out to be stories of the men and what it means, on the one hand, to have one's property stolen or damaged, and on the other, to imagine fears of female revenge. Mythic rapes stake out who (the virtuous, the virginal) can be raped and its consequences (death). What it means to the female can be heard only by a feminist reading attentive to the power relations surrounding the speakers of rape.[52]

The ancient mythic discourse of the patriarchy finds its most radical equivalent in modern women writers of Latin America. Jean Franco has noted that the testimonial literature written by women goes to great lengths to avoid the titillation of the reader in describing rape during torture. The accounts of historical events narrate the scenes of rape in language that emphasizes the brutality and violence of the act.[53] Isabel Allende's *La casa de los espíritus* is the best-known fictional example of a silencing of the actual scene of rape. The vivid descriptions of lesser forms of violation that precede the novel's torture scenes, the minute account of other forms of physical attack that accompany the rapes make the silencing of the rape itself all the more chilling. Although the details are omitted, there is no doubt about what happened; the effect of silence in this case emphasizes the real purpose of attack, to inflict humiliation and pain. What do mythic story and modern torture have in common? They both depict what our culture has agreed to call "real rape." These are the most unambiguous cases, one from the voice of the ancient patriarchy, the other from the voice of modern women. In the first, the avowedly virginal or virtuous daughters of the aristocracy come to grief wholly against their will. The case of rape as part of torture is its modern counterpart, the extreme of modern life in which the woman's pleasure (or even the man's) is not at issue, her unpleasure being, in fact, the point. In between the two historical periods our culture has contemplated more complicated cases which oppose rape to seduction thereby acknowledging the potential of female desire. In these, a disparity of interpretation surrounding the same event has frequently found a woman who speaks rape and a man who speaks seduction. The problem of speaking rape leads to the heart of language itself: The weight of mythological, religious, erotic, and narrative forces combine to repress and rewrite the act of rape.[54]

The ambiguity of Silvina Ocampo's rape stories creates doubt, not just in terms of how the act happened, but in the very terms at issue for modern courts: Is what happened "really" rape? The irony and black humor that Ocampo occasionally brings to the

subject (as already mentioned regarding Artemia of "Las vestiduras peligrosas") and her willingness to subject the female narrator of rape stories to the same unreliability of all narrators are
both aspects of her stories guaranteed to make North American
feminists uneasy.[55] Ocampo's ambivalent approach is more common in Spanish-American women writers who are far more willing to blur the distinctions between seductress and victim, truth
and fiction, self-deception and lies, desire and equivocation than
their North American counterparts.[56]

Many of Silvina Ocampo's stories, as we have seen, validate
female desire, often seen in her stories in transgressive or even
perverse directions. Ocampo subjects the dichotomy rape/seduc-
tion to an exploration which runs the gamut between the desiring female who after an act of consensual sex responds with
anger and revenge ("Albino Orma" and "La furia," for instance),
to Artemia of "Las vestiduras peligrosas," whose perverse desires
take her deliberately into danger and death. Other stories discussed earlier also present problematic views on the depiction
of rape. "Cornelia frente al espejo," for example, presents a
would-be child victim who has lied about her experience. The
adult Cornelia who narrates this episode from her childhood
depicts herself as liar, but also as furious about the disbelief
evoked by her story. "Cornelia frente al espejo" suggests that the
child is relaying a deflected version of what she perceives to be
true: Her adolescent crush on Pablo and friendship with Elena
explode with the discovery of their love affair; her feelings of
violation and betrayal make her grope for a literal, bodily version
of her complex emotional reaction. The potential for the narrator of any story to cast the truth in highly selective terms is the
point of many Ocampo narratives, which here and elsewhere
she brings to the issue of rape. Within the world of Ocampo's
fiction, the rape of a child, whether presented to the reader as
true or false, is never accepted as true by the characters within
the fiction. In other words, the child is never believed whether
or not she is lying. Two stories do depict "real rape," but with
such extreme ambiguity that it is difficult to say what happens
with any assurance. The gaps, or holes, in the narrative occur
just as Robbe-Grillet suggested, at the moment in which the
absence swallows everything. The ambiguity in both cases results in part from the fact that the victim is a child and the
crime is told from the point of view of one who fails to understand completely the events as they unfold.

"La calle Sarandí" is told as a reminiscence of an adult "I" of one autumn afternoon "when I was a little girl." From the child's point of view, she describes having to walk along a sidewalk near her house where a man was always standing. But unlike the other, ever-present objects to which she compares him, a stair step or a fence railing, she is afraid of him, in part, because of his "sticky words" ("palabras pegajosas") and, in part, because of a willow branch he uses to swat her legs as she passes. Her reaction to this fear is an extreme passivity, "que me obligaba a pasar por la misma vereda de su casa con lentitud de pesadilla" (*Vo* 119) [which forced me to pass along the same side of the street as his house with the slowness of a nightmare]. One afternoon, he pulls her into the house. Though the reader knows that she was there for several hours and that she escaped by running as though for her life, the events of those hours, between being hauled into a room with a bed and tipping over a chair as she runs out, remain untold. This is the gap in narration that the reader must struggle to fill.

The story continues: Her entire family has died except for the son of her oldest sister. She has raised this boy, always referred to as "el hijo que fué casi mío" [the son who was almost mine], until the present moment, some sixteen or more years later. Now she is horrified at his changed voice, the voice that reminds her of the man with the willow stick. Just as she hid "en el cuartito de mis manos" [in the little room of my hands] during the unnamed horror of many years before, in the story's conclusion she declares her intention to stay hidden behind those same hands until her own death. The boy has grown into a man, the enemy. Whether he is her nephew or really her own child known by that polite fiction, he is a baby she has loved who has grown into a man for whom she feels nothing but fear and loathing. By deduction, the reader may guess that the painful memories of the past frame a rape, which remains the silence of this text.

The story's past and present are divided midway by the word "Ahora" [Now]. Identification between the scene of rape in the first half and the scene of death in the conclusion is made through several identifying features: the iron bed, the image of shoes at its edge, and the man's voice. The associations involving the boy's voice are another highly ambiguous aspect of the story; she confuses its sudden drop at puberty with the voice of a radio announcer and with the memory from her past. The concluding lines of the story put all these elements and objects together to create this narrator's personal horror:

> No quiero ver más nada. Este hijo que fue casi mío, tiene la voz desconocida que brota de una radio. Estoy encerrada en el cuartito obscuro de mis manos y por la ventana de mis dedos veo los zapatos de un hombre en el borde de la cama. Ese hijo fue casi mío, esa voz recitando un discurso político debe de ser, en la radio vecina, el hombre con la rama de sauce de espantar mosquitos. Y esa cuna vacía, tejida de fierro . . . (*Vo* 123)

> [I don't want to see anything more. This son who was almost mine has the unknown voice which flows from a radio. I am locked in the little dark room of my hands and through the windows of my fingers I see a man's shoes at the edge of the bed. That son who was almost mine, that voice reciting a political speech might be, on the neighbor's radio, the man with the willow branch for shooing mosquitos. And that empty cradle of wrought iron . . .]

The narrator associates the boy with the rapist through the careful association of the elements essential to the two moments in time. The ellipsis at paragraph's end allows for a characteristic openness of interpretation: It is entirely consistent with the text to read the boy as the product of the rape, that his birth is another of the text's silences. The insistently repeated phrase, "ese hijo que fue casi mío," seems to suggest such a reading. A more literal understanding, however, makes a more radical statement: The victim, as an adult, views all men as sons of the rapist, the political speech on the radio as emblem of the patriarchal system that perpetuates rape, and the empty cradle as a miniature version of the rapist's bed.

Several elements of this early story reappear in Ocampo's later masterpiece, "El pecado mortal": the narration of the episode by an adult woman from the perspective of her childhood memory, the silencing of the actual scene of rape, the extreme passivity of the female character, as child and as adult. I read "El pecado mortal" as a most painful and terrifying story of child abuse. The mute helplessness, terror, fascination, and almost unbearable guilt portrayed never fail to fill me with heart-palpitating anxiety. I confess my own reader reaction at the outset, in part, because the story elicits it from me, in part, because my reaction is at odds with those of its other (published) readers. This story is mentioned by most if not all commentators on Ocampo's works; it provides the title for an anthology of Ocampo's stories edited in 1966 by José Bianco and serves as a primary focus for two articles about Ocampo's works published more recently.[57] Considering the relative slimness of the bibliography on Ocampo's writing in general, such attention represents a considerable percentage of available commentary on her more than two hundred short stories. Clearly, I am not the only reader to react strongly; my purpose here, then, is to contrast my reading to those of others and then try to understand how this work permits and even invites such a variety of responses. In placing this story in the book's concluding section, I intend that my reader bring together the argmuents of the whole, for this work combines issues of desire, doubling, mirroring, and details, as well as what is more overtly discussed, ambiguity and silence.

The central source of ambiguity of this work, and a point at which different readings diverge sharply, is the identity of the narrator who addresses the hapless child character as "tú." The first and last paragraphs contain first-person verbs, moments that offer insight about the narrator's relationship to events. In the opening the narrator says: "Dios me lo perdone, pues fui en cierto modo tu cómplice y tu esclava" (*I* 138) [God forgive me, since I was to a certain extent your accomplice and your slave], a statement, which however mystifying at this juncture, does identify the *yo* as female ("esclava") and intimately connected to the action. In the story's concluding lines, she says: "Te buscaría por el mundo entero a pie como los misioneros para salvarte si tuvieras la suerte, que no tienes, de ser mi contemporánea" (142) [I would look for you around the whole world on foot like the missionaries in order to save you if you had the luck, which you don't have, of being my contemporary]. The events narrated between these two statements could be known only by the child herself; most of the story takes precisely the child's point of view with a child's limited understanding. The narrative positioning together with these two oblique self-references indicate, to me, that the child character and the narrator are one and the same: An older voice narrates events as only her younger self could have experienced them. The adult narrator feels herself to have been complicit with her childish self, and yet slave to her; unable to help her because they are not "contemporaries," her adult comprehension cannot help the child she once was.[58] The narrative strategy of dividing the "I" from the "you" provides a doubled vision, a version of events that replicates the position of the child in terms of curiosity, enthrallment, confusion, helplessness, and terror, while allowing the reader to "hear" the ambivalent feelings expressed by her adult voice. In addition, the repeated *tú* of the narration, as Anderson-Imbert has pointed out, creates an intensified impression of being addressed directly by the narrative voice, a sensation which at once incorporates the reader into the subject position of the main character and creates a subtle sense of accusation and guilt. Anderson-Imbert compares the reader's position in second-person narration to an interrogation by police or a psychologist. His remarks uncannily reflect my claims regarding Ocampo's strategy: "Dirigirse a un 'tú' significa adjudicar la aventura a un cualquiera; equivale a decir: 'lo que ocurre en este cuento podría ocurrirte a ti'" [To address oneself to a "you" means to attribute the adventure to anyone; it is as if to say, "what occurs in the story could happen to you"].[59]

As in "La calle Sarandí," the gaps in the narrative extend the ambiguity of the story to the plot for it is difficult to say just what happens here. Briefly, the story relates the rape of a very young girl by one of the male servants employed in her parents' house. But such a straightforward, simplified version is open to question both in the context of the story itself and of other accounts of it. The voice of the narrator explains in the first lines that she does not mention the "technical name" for what happens just as the child to whom it happens could not name it. The ambiguity of the story depends, then, on a silence, the absence of a technical term. Language creates reality, so if it has no name, it does not exist. Even the voice of authority, the catechism, has no word for this child's reality. Ignorant of the word *rape,* she relates events, of necessity, couched in terms that she does know. And these are the words of traditional romance, which irrevocably distort the implications of what is narrated: "conociste en aquel tiempo el placer—diré—del amor, por no mencionarlo con su nombre técnico" [you knew at that time the pleasure—I will say—of love so as not to mention it with its technical name]. A few lines later she uses the expression "goce inexplicable" [unexplainable pleasure] to describe the same mysterious experience. The child instinctively understands that what happened is wrong, but since she cannot name the "sin" as rape, a crime placing blame on another, she internalizes the sin as her own, and relates the tale as a secret and disgusting confession of her complicity with evil. Years later, the adult narrator who tells the tale to herself repeats the error.

Framing the narration is the religious iconography of the first communion, the institutional positioning of child as emblematic of untarnished innocence, which makes her confession all the more impossible: "No hallaste fórmula pudorosa ni clara ni concisa de confesarte. Tuviste que comulgar en estado de pecado mortal" (141) [You found no modest nor clear nor concise formula for confession. You had to take communion in a state of mortal sin]. As always in Ocampo's narrative, the list of elements, in this case the various white objects used as symbols of purity, are listed with obsessive precision and repeated in contrast to the sordid evil of the narration: "el vestido blanco, lleno de entredoses" [the white dress with panels], "los guantes de hilo y el rosario de perlitas" [the linen golves and the peal rosary] and especially "el libro de misa de tapas blancas (un cáliz estampado en el centro del la primera página y listas de pecados en otra)" [the missal bound in white (a chalice stamped on the center of the first page and lists of sins on the other)] are repeated throughout. The ironic association of the list of sins inside the missal is anticipated in the story's first sentence which recognizes that symbols of purity are at times more titillating than overt pornography. Among the religious objects Ocampo adds another repeated element, the "flor roja, llamada plumerito" [the red flower called "plumerito"], a symbol of innocence taken from the natural world and one used traditionally to symbolize (loss of) virginity. The insistent framing of this story in terms of *the child*'s culpability and sin is one important source, I believe, of its misreading.

Another source of misreading, or multiple readings, are the silences in the narration, of which rape is only one. The child, nicknamed "La muñeca" [The Doll], watches the servant, Chango, as he comes and goes from the servants' bathroom, which is located between her nursery and a workroom, curious because he seems to linger longer than others within this forbidden space ("recinto vedado"). Furthermore, she catches him more than once, "solo, enajenado, deslumbrado, en distintos lugares de la casa, de pie, arrimándose incesantemente a la punta de cualquier mesa" (139) [alone, absent, dazed, in different places in the house, standing, pressing incessantly against the corner of any table]. "La muñeca" sees Chango masturbating, but the narration makes clear that she does not understand completely, has no name for what she sees, even though we, the readers, do. All these images of the child's watching and observing what she only partially understands, which obviously place her in the position of desiring subject, come together when Chango invites her to look at him through the keyhole of the aforementioned bathroom door. Though we assume that she sees the genitals he no doubt shows her, what gets narrated is the smell: "un aliento de animal se filtró por la puerta" [an animal breath filtered through the door]. Since Gallop has pointed out that female desire is triggered by smell, it is clear that Ocampo presents her child in the position of desiring subject, a subject that gazes in fascination at the object of desire and also is aroused by its smell. To these details, Ocampo includes a reference to the romantic legend of Pyramus and Thisbe, adding to the discourse of religious morality that of poetry and myth, making "reality" all the more untellable.

The moments following this episode just before the rape narrate the child as object of another's desire: Chango approaches her with a "mirada turbia" [turbulent gaze]. An earlier phrase remembers a symbolic anticipation of the event about to be narrated: "Tú lo espiabas, pero él también terminó por espiarte: lo descubriste el día en que desapareció de tu pupitre la flor de plumerito, que adornó más tarde el ojal de su chaqueta de lustrina" (139) [You spied on him, but he ended up spying on you: you discovered it the day that the plumerito flower disappeared from your desk, and later adorned the lapel of his wool jacket]. Combined with images of entrapment—a room isolated from the rest of the house, the absence of all other household members except servant and child—Ocampo adds those of a small animal hunted by its prey: "no tenías la menor intención de huir. Un ratón o una rana no huyen de la serpiente que los quiere; no huyen animales más grandes" (140) [you had no intention of fleeing. A mouse or a frog does not flee from the serpent who wants them; larger animals don't flee]. The child, admittedly a desirous one, finds herself like the mouse or the frog in a perilous situation from which she cannot escape.

The rape itself is narrated by an accumulation of objects and images at close range:

Baños consecutivos de rubor cubrieron tu rostro, como esos baños de oro que cubren las joyas falsas. Recordaste a Chango hurgando en la ropa blanca de los roperos de tu madre, cuando reemplazaba en sus tareas a las mujeres de la casa. Las venas de sus manos se hincharon, como de tinta azul. En la punta de los dedos viste que tenía moretones. Involuntariamente recorriste con la mirada los detalles de su chaqueta de lustrina, tan áspera sobre tus rodillas. Desde entonces verías para siempre las tragedias de tu vida adornadas con detalles minuciosos. No te defendiste. Añorabas la pulcra flor del plumerito, tu morbosidad incomprendida, pero sentías que aquella arcana representación, impuesta por circunstancias imprevisibles, tenía que alcanzar su meta: la imposible violación de tu soledad. (*I* 141)

[Repeated washes of red covered your face like those washes of gold that cover fake jewely. You remembered Chango digging in the underwear of your mother's dresser when he replaced the women of the house in their work. The veins of his hands bulged as if with blue ink. On the tips of his fingers you saw that he had bruises. Involuntarily your glance went over the details of his wool jacket, so rough on your knees. From that moment you would always see the tragedies of your life adorned with minute details. You did not defend yourself. You longed for the delicate plumerito flower, your misunderstood morbidness, but you felt that that arcane performance, imposed by unforeseen circumstances, had to achieve its goal: the impossible violation of your solitude.]

The technical name, "violación," is now used, but is displaced in the paragraph and its meaning obscured. More significant for the child's understanding is the flower, which earlier she had associated with "el placer—diré—del amor" (138) [the pleasure—I will say—of love]. The rape, the de-flowering, of this child is enacted without technical names but with a series of visual images that reproduce what Lacan describes about mental process of early childhood: the imaginary is organized in just such images, such objects. Like the montage of a film, the rape is deduced from the man's face with an expression of obscene delight in forbidden pleasures (going through her mother's underwear), the veins on his hands, the bruises on his finger-tips, the pattern on his jacket as it brushes her knees, the removal of the flower from her writing desk. Ocampo's details here reproduce the possible thought processes of a child in this situation, and more important, the impossibility for the victim, even as adult, to modify the original version for herself.

The horror and sadness of this story, then, is compounded by its recounting of a terrible event *and* the process by which the child victim fails to understand fully, and in fact, blames herself, names herself even years later as evil, as una "joya falsa" [a fake jewel]. The story has an uncanny relationship to what we know about victims of sexual abuse in real life, about their over-whelming feelings of complicity and guilt. They name their desire as the equivalent of their guilt, and thus the victim joins culture generally in erasing a story of rape and rewriting it as a story of seduction.

This story shows better than any other I know how the victim blames herself. However, its readers have understood it not as a plea for the protection of female desire, but precisely as a story of an evil child or an evil narrator. Barbara Aponte reads Ocampo in the context of two other stories both by men—Arguedas and Roa Bastos—about male children's fall from grace. She finds Ocampo's voice, a story by a woman about a little girl, at odds with theirs and concludes that, of the three, Arguedas's is the most universalizing tale of the broadly human problem of alienation, while "the somewhat frivolous tone" of Ocampo's narrator lacks what Todorov calls "moral appreciation."[60] Helena Araújo reads "El pecado mortal" as participating in an ideological process similar to Bataille's in which he attempts to liberate the human spirit from restrictive social norms of purity and decency by way of erotic excess.[61] Araújo comes close to Matamoro who also suggests that La Muñeca expresses desire for what is repressed in her life, that is, a desire for her own forbidden body. My reading does not conflict with either of theirs until Araújo concludes: "A través del tiempo, sin embargo, esta transgresión, será a la vez un estigma y un trofeo, por haber constituido una experiencia iniciática" [In time, however, this transgression will be at once a stigma and a trophy for having constituted an experience of initiation.][62] Though I agree that Ocampo's impulse here and elsewhere attacks the limitations of church-defined female purity, I cannot agree that her work recommends the rape of six-year-olds as a corrective.

These critics compare Ocampo's story to those of men. Even Araújo, whose title seems to read it with Alba Lucía Angel's novel, *Misiá Señora,* really compares both of these to Bataille. Aponte describes both Arguedas's and Roa Bastos's young male characters as torn between forces of good and evil, between their moral sense and temptation awakened by desire. Her analysis considers the women characters of each story to be evil and the young male adolescents, though weak, to be good. But when the narrator of "El pecado mortal" voices her character's ambivalence to the scene of corruption, Aponte feels that in spite of the "sordid eroticism" of the story, this narrator's "involvement can be reduced to delectation in the obscenity of the theme."[63] The notion that a young male may be both desiring and innocent is acceptable; male desire in itself is not considered to be evil. Females in representation, however, are still polarized between desirous women of pleasure (representatives of evil in Aponte's other two examples) and the virtuous (because) undesiring. Because this particular story juxtaposes desire and innocence in a female incarnation, we can only read it in the accustomed way: We are conditioned to read the female as "asking for it."

Ocampo presents the reader with a complex juxtaposition of desire and innocence, exploitation and knowledge which deconstructs female nullity (lack of desire). Her narrator's problems with telling the tale is the story's plot, the problem rooted in our use of language. Binary oppositions oppose female goodness, innocence, weakness, and passivity (lack of desire) to evil, knowledge, power, and activity (desire). The child La Muñeca is desirous and knowledgeable but surely still innocent, deserving of protection. Because of her knowledge of evil, she implicates herself in that evil. It is an irrevocable loss, which the narrator's sadness and cynicism make evident. This story is about a rape victim who relates with pain, sadness, and resignation a story she knows will not be understood. It was not understood in her first attempts to tell it with or without words: "Cuando alguna amiga llegaba para jugar contigo, le relatabas primero, le demostrabas después, la secreta relación que existía entre la flor del plumerito, el libro de misa y tu goce inexplicable. Ninguna amiga lo comprendía, ni intentaba participar en él, pero todas fingían lo contrario, para contentarte, y sembraban en tu corazón esa pánica soledad (mayor que tú) de saberte engañada por el prójimo" (*I* 139) [When a friend would come to play with you, you would tell her first, then show her, the secret relationship which existed between the plumerito flower, the missal and your unexplainable pleasure. No friend understood it, nor attempted to participate in it, but all pretended to, in order to please you, and sowed in your heart that panicked solitude (older than you) of knowing yourself to be deceived]. The misunderstandings surrounding the event are as traumatic as the event itself.

Aponte and Araújo exhibit two extremes: One blames the victim (the narrator) the other applauds the perpetrator for at least having broken through the limits of the traditional female role. Neither mourns the abuse of this small spark of female desire, or the damage which the story demonstrates as permanent. That La Muñeca and her adult voice garner so little sympathy from her erudite readers convinces me that we still are a long way from nurturing and protecting—or reading—female desire. This story is received like the narratives of children who tell similar tales in the world of the real; like La Muñeca they continue to be abused, misjudged, and disbelieved. Silvina Ocampo has overcome the mental trap of viewing the desirous female as evil. Now we, her readers, must do the same.

Notes

INTRODUCTION

1. Matilde Sánchez, ed. *Las reglas del secreto* (Mexico: Fondo de Cultura Económica, 1991), 8.

2. "Mi vida no tiene nada que ver con lo que escribo," quoted in Noemí Ulla, *Encuentros con Silvina Ocampo* (Buenos Aires: Belgrano, 1982), 137.

3. See, for example, *Páginas de Silvina Ocampo,* ed. Enrique Pezzoni (Buenos Aires: Celtia, 1984), 248, and *Las reglas del secreto,* 615. Silvina Ocampo clarified her date of birth for me in an interview of March 1980; Enrique Pezzoni explained his own ambiguous reference to Marta, saying that she was Bioy's daughter with another woman. Apparently Silvina Ocampo adopted the baby in Sept. of 1954 in France. Marta's two children were introduced to me in 1980. Aged four and six at the time, they addressed the nearly eighty-year-old author as "Silvi," and played quietly in a nearby room while she and I talked.

4. The works by Pezzoni, Sánchez and Ulla contain biographical information; Sánchez's anthology contains a series of photographs of Ocampo and her circle. I also found useful the following: Doris Meyer, *Victoria Ocampo: Against the Wind and the Tide* (New York: George Braziller, 1979); Ofelia Kovacci, *Adolfo Bioy Casares* (Buenos Aires: Ediciones Culturales Argentinas, 1963); and Oscar Hermes Villordo, *Genio y figura de Adolfo Bioy Casares* (Buenos Aires: EUDEBA, 1983). A general sense of the intellectual *milieu* can be found in John King, *"Sur": A Study of the Argentine Literary Journal and its Role in the Development of a Culture, 1931–1970* (Cambridge: Cambridge University Press, 1986).

5. Julio E. Payró, "La escuela de París," *Sur* 71 (1940): 80–85. His brief comments regarding Ocampo mention that her subjects consist primarily of women and children, sketched in a manner he describes as "sculptural."

6. See, for instance, Janet Greenburg, "A Question of Blood: The Conflict of Sex and Class in the *Autobiografía* of Victoria Ocampo," in Seminar on Feminism and Culture, *Women, Culture, and Politics in Latin America* (Berkeley: University of California Press, 1990), 130–50.

7. Villordo, *Genio y figura,* 47.

8. Danubio Torres Fierro, "Correspondencia con Silvina Ocampo," *Plural* 50 (1975): 60.

9. She is shown photographed with Marta in Sánchez and in Bioy Casares's recent memoir, *Memorias* (Barcelona: Tusquets, 1994).

10. Torres Fierro, 58.

11. Victoria Ocampo, review of *Viaje olvidado, Sur* 35 (1937): 118–21; Ezequiel Martínez Estrada, review of *Espacios métricos, Sur* 137 (1946): 82–

86; Rosa Chacel, review of *Los que aman odian, Sur* 143 (1946): 75–81; and Eduardo González Lanuza, review of *Autobiografía de Irene, Sur* 175 (1949): 56–58.

12. Ulla, *Encuentros,* 34.

13. *Antología de la literatura fantástica,* eds. Jorge Luis Borges, Adolfo Bioy Casares and Silvina Ocampo (Buenos Aires: Sudamericana, 1940); *Antología poética argentina,* eds. Jorge Luis Borges, Adolfo Bioy Casares and Silvina Ocampo (Buenos Aires: Sudamericana, 1941).

14. *Los que aman odian* (Buenos Aires: Emecé, 1946).

15. *Enumeración de la patria* (Buenos Aires: Sur, 1942); *Espacios métricos* (Buenos Aires: Sur, 1946); *Los sonetos del jardín* (Buenos Aires: Sur, 1946).

16. Ulla, *Encuentros,* 83.

17. King, *"Sur": A Study of the Literary Journal,* 90. Helena Araújo, in a different context, has also argued that influence is most likely to have been mutual rather than going just one direction: "De la misma manera que a nadie se le ocurre comparar *Los recuerdos del porvenir* de Elena Garro con *Al filo del agua* de Agustín Yáñez, a nadie se le ocurre pensar que ciertos temas de Borges o Bioy Casares los pudo inspirar Silvina Ocampo." (32) [Just as it never occurs to anyone to compare Elena Garro's *Recuerdos del porvenir* to Agustín Yáñez's *Al filo del agua,* it never occurs to anyone to think that certain themes of Borges or Bioy Casares could have been inspired by Silvina Ocampo], "Narrativa femenina latinoamericana," *Hispamérica* 32 (1982): 23–34.

18. *Poemas de amor desesperado* (Buenos Aires: Sudamericana, 1949); *Los nombres* (Buenos Aires: Emecé, 1953); *Los traidores* (Buenos Aires: Losange, 1956); *Lo amargo por dulce* (Buenos Aires: Emecé, 1962). Ulla's book, cited above, discusses the poetry as does Helena Percas in "La original expresión poética de Silvina Ocampo," *Revista Iberoamericana* 38 (1954): 283–98.

19. Eugenio Guasta and Mario A. Lancelloti, "Dos juicios sobre *La furia,*" *Sur* 263 (1960): 62–66.

20. Review of *Las invitadas, Sur* 278 (1962): 74–76.

21. *El pecado mortal,* ed. José Bianco (Buenos Aires: Eudeba, 1966); *Informe del cielo y del infierno,* ed. Edgardo Cozarinsky (Caracas: Monte Avila, 1970).

22. Silvia Molloy, "La simplicidad inquietante en los relatos de Silvina Ocampo," *Lexis* 2, no. 2 (1978): 241–51.

23. *El cofre volante* [The Flying Trunk] (Buenos Aires: Estrada, 1974); *El tobogán* [The Slide] (Buenos Aires: Estrada, 1975); *El caballo alado* [The Winged Horse] (Buenos Aires: De la Flor, 1976); *La naranja maravillosa: Cuentos para chicos grandes y grandes chicos* [The magic orange: Stories for children of all ages] (Buenos Aires: Sudamericana, 1977). This is the only body of narrative works, other than the detective novel, not considered in the present study. See Enrique Pezzoni, "La nostalgia del orden: Silvina Ocampo y sus historias para niños," review of *La naranja maravillosa, La nación* 21 de agosto 1977, sec. 4, p. 2.

24. Alejandra Pizarnik, "Dominios ilícitos," review of *El pecado mortal* by Silvina Ocampo, *Sur* 311 (1968): 91–95; Silvia Molloy, "Silvina Ocampo: La exageración como lenguage," *Sur* 320 (1969): 15–24; Rosario Castellanos, "Silvina Ocampo y el más acá," *Mujer que sabe latín* (Mexico: SepSetentas, 1973), 149–64; Blas Matamoro, "La nena terrible," *Oligarquía y literatura* (Buenos Aires: Ediciones del Sol, 1975), 193–221.

25. *Faits Divers de la terre et du ciel,* trans. Francois-Marie Rosset, preface by Jorge Luis Borges, introduction by Italo Calvino (Paris: Gallimard, 1974).

26. Giulia Poggi, "'Las vestiduras peligrosas' di Silvina Ocampo: Analisi di un'antiflaba," *Studi Ispanici* 3 (1978): 145–62.

27. Silvina Ocampo, *Leopoldina's Dream,* trans. Daniel Balderston (Ontario, Canada: Penguin Books, 1988).

28. "Sábanas de tierra," *Sur* 42 (1938): 36–40; "La inauguración del monumento," *Sur* 49 (1938): 22–33. Both appear unchanged in *Y así sucesivamente.*

29. Thomas C. Meehan, "Los niños perversos en los cuentos de Silvina Ocampo," *Hispanic Literatures,* Proceedings of 4th Annual Conference, 20–21 Oct. 1978, ed. J. Cruz Mendizábal (Indiana University of Pennsylvania, 1979) 1: 57–68; Daniel Balderston, "Los cuentos crueles de Silvina Ocampo y Juan Rudolfo Wilcock," *Revista Iberoamericana* 49 (1983): 743–52.

30. Barbara A. Aponte, "The Initiation Archtype in Arguedas, Roa Bastos, and Ocampo," *Latin American Literary Review* 11, no. 21 (1982): 45–56; Helena Araújo, "Ejemplos de la niña impura en Silvina Ocampo y Alba Lucía Angel," *Hispamérica* 13, no. 38 (1984): 27–35.

31. Susan Bassnett, "Coming Out of the Labyrinth: Women Writers in Contemporary Latin America" in *On Modern Latin American Fiction,* ed. John King (New York: Noonday Press, 1987), 251.

32. Patricia N. Klingenberg, "The Grotesque in the Short Stories of Silvina Ocampo," *Letras Femeninas* 10 (1984): 49–52; "The Twisted Mirror: The Fantastic Stories of Silvina Ocampo," *Letras Femeninas* 13 (1987): 67–78; "Portrait of the Writer as Artist: Silvina Ocampo," *Perspectives in Contemporary Literature: Literature and the Other Arts* 13 (1987): 58–64; "The Mad Double in the Short Stories of Silvina Ocampo," *Latin American Literary Review* 16, no. 2 (1988): 29–40; "The Feminine 'I': Silvina Ocampo's Fantasies of the Subject," *Romance Languages Annual* 1(1989): 488–94.

33. Cristina Ferreira-Pinto, "El narrador intimista de Silvina Ocampo: 'La continuación'," *Revista de Estudios Hispánicos* 17–18 (1990–91): 309–15.

34. Marjorie Agosín, "Mujer, espacio e imaginación en Latinoamérica: dos cuentos de María Luisa Bombal y Silvina Ocampo," *Revista Internacional de Bibliografía/Inter-American Review of Bibliography* 41, no. 4 (1991): 627–33.

35. Cynthia Duncan, "Double or Nothing? The Fantastic Element in Silvina Ocampo's 'La casa de azúcar,'" *Chasqui* 20, no. 2 (1991): 64–72.

36. Alejandra Rosarossa, "Espacio y acontecimiento en la focalización de 'La red' de Silvina Ocampo," *Estudios de narratología,* ed. Mignon Domínguez (Buenos Aires: Biblos, 1991), 123–35.

37. Noemí Ulla, *Invenciones a dos voces: Ficción y poesía en Silvina Ocampo* (Buenos Aires: Torres Agüero, 1992), 23.

38. Graciela Tomassini, *El espejo de Cornelia: La obra cuentística de Silvina Ocampo* (Buenos Aires: Plus Ultra, 1995). I am grateful to an anonymous reader of my manuscript for informing me of this publication.

39. Ibid., 24.

40. Cynthia Duncan, "A Eye for an 'I': Women Writers and the Fantastic as a Challenge to Patriarchal Authority," 233–46; María B. Clark, "Feminization as an Experience of Limits: Shifting Gender Roles in the Fantastic Narrative of Silvina Ocampo and Cristina Peri Rossi," 249–68; Patricia N. Klingenberg, "Silvina Ocampo frente al espejo," 273–86, all in *Inti: Revista de Literatura Hispánica* 40–41 (1994–95).

41. Alberto Manguel, ed. *Other Fires. Short Fiction by Latin American Women* (New York: Clarkson N. Potter, Crown, 1986), 3.

42. John King, "Victoria Ocampo (1890–1979): Precursor," in *Knives and Angels: Women Writers in Latin America,* ed. Susan Bassnett (London: Zed, 1990), 18.

43. Eduardo González Lanuza, review of *Autobiografía de Irene, Sur* 175 (1948), 58.

44. Debra Castillo, *Talking Back: Toward a Latin American Feminist Criticism* (Ithaca: Cornell University Press, 1992); Amy Kaminsky, *Reading the Body Politic: Feminist Criticism and Latin American Women Writers* (Minneapolis: University of Minnesota Press, 1993). See also Eliana Rivero, "Precisiones de lo femenino y lo feminista en la práctica literaria hispanoamericana," *Inti: Revista de Literatura Hispánica* 40–41 (1994–95): 21–46.

45. All but the last of these are taken up as separate chapters; the maternal appears in the chapter called "Surfacing"; see especially 157–58, 169–75.

46. Ibid., 51–52.

47. Naomi Schor, *Reading in Detail: Aesthetics and the Feminine* (New York & London: Methuen, 1987), 22.

48. Jane Gallop, *Thinking Through the Body* (New York: Columbia University Press, 1988), 135.

49. Sylvia Molloy, "Sentido de ausencias," *Revista Iberoamericana* 51 (1985): 485.

50. Josefina Delgado, "Presencia de la mujer en la literatura," in *Mujeres y escritura,* ed. Mempo Giardinelli (Buenos Aires: Puro Cuento, 1989), 137.

51. Enrique Pezzoni, "Silvina Ocampo," *Enciclopedia de la literatura argentina.* Ed. Pedro Orgamide y Roberto Yanui (Buenos Aires: Sudamericana, 1970), 474. The reader will notice my inconsistent translation of the word *infiel:* its most literal, *unfaithful,* is a term not generally used in a literary sense in English; hence, my modification to "unreliable." In an earlier article I wanted a more striking word, and chose *twisted,* as in a carnival mirror.

52. The conference proceedings have been published as *Mujeres y escritura,* ed. Mempo Giardinelli, (Buenos Aires: Puro Cuento, 1989).

53. Martha Mercader, "¿Existe la literatura femenina?," in Giardinelli, 12.

54. Naomi Schor, "Dreaming Dissymmetry: Barthes, Foucault, and Sexual Difference," in *Coming to Terms: Feminism, Theory, Politics,* ed. Elizabeth Weed (New York and London: Routledge, 1989), 47–58.

55. Teresa de Lauretis, *Alice Doesn't: Feminism, Semiotics, Cinema.* (Bloomington: Indiana University Press, 1984), 164.

CHAPTER 1. THE FANTASTIC AND THE GROTESQUE

1. Bioy Casares's oft-quoted statement to this effect appears in his prologue to the original 1940 edition of the *Antología de la literatura fantástica:* "Viejas como el miedo, las ficciones fantásticas son anteriores a las letras," [Old as fear, supernatural fiction precedes literature] (Buenos Aires: Sudamericana, 1940), 7.

2. Rosemary Jackson summarizes Freud's argument regarding the parallel development of individuals and societies in *Fantasy: The Literature of Subversion* (London: Methuen, 1981), 71–72.

NOTES TO CHAPTER 1

3. Frederic Jameson, "Magical Narratives: Romance as Genre," *New Literary History* 7, no. 1 (1975): 138.

4. Ibid., 145.

5. Frederic Jameson, "Imaginary and Symbolic in Lacan: Marxism, Psychoanalytic Criticism, and the Problem of the Subject," in *Literature and Psychoanalysis: The Question of Reading: Otherwise,* ed. Shoshonna Felman (Baltimore: Johns Hopkins University Press, 1982), 357.

6. "The fantastic is that hesitation experienced by a person who knows only the laws of nature, confronting an apparently supernatural event," Tzvetan Todorov, *The Fantastic: A Structural Approach to a Literary Genre,* trans. Richard Howard (Ithaca: Cornell University Press, 1970), 25.

7. Tzvetan Todorov, *Poetics of Prose,* trans. Richard Howard (Ithaca: Cornell University Press, 1977), 157–59. Shoshona Felman provides a thorough history of critical appraisal of *Turn,* particularly the history of heated debate regarding the interpretation of the ghosts. See the section of her article subtitled, "The Conflict of Interpretations: The Turns of the Debate" (113–19) in "Turning the Screw of Interpretation," *Literature and Psychoqnalysis,* ed. Shoshonna Felman, 94–207.

8. Indeed, as Flannery O'Conner has said, it is almost easier to say what is not grotesque as what is, Flannery O'Conner, "Some Aspects of the Grotesque in Fiction" (Wesleyan College, Macon, GA, 29 October 1960, typescript located in the library of the University of Illinois at Urbana-Champaign), 2. In the vast literature on the grotesque, C. Hugh Holman's *Handbook to Literature* offers a good working definition: "The interest in the grotesque is usually considered an outgrowth of contemporary interest in the irrational, distrust of any cosmic order, and frustration at man's lot in the universe. In this sense, the grotesque is the merging of the comic and tragic, resulting from our loss of faith in the moral universe essential to tragedy and in a rational social order essential to comedy" (New York: Odyssey Press, 1972), 245–46.

9. Lee Byron Jennings, *The Ludicrous Demon* (Berkeley: University of California Press, 1963), 17.

10. I am indebted to Jackson's articulation of the connections between fantastic, uncanny, and grotesque, especially 68–69.

11. "It has already been implied that what Bakhtin terms carnivalistic and official selves can be made equivalent to Lacan's distinction between different stages of development, the imaginary and the symbolic" (Jackson, 135).

12. Jackson, 89.

13. Jackson, 9. Sylvia Molly's early article on Ocampo makes the same claim: "No hay para estos relatos una salida—una asimilación a la "realidad"—decorosa. Una vez sometidos a las acrobacias éticas y lingüísticas que les impone la autora pierden la posibilidad de volver, como las tragedias, al orden tranquilizador del que se han alejado [In these tales there is no decorous exit—no assimilation to "reality." Once submitted to the ethical and linguistic acrobatics that the author imposes on them, they lose the possibility of return, as in tragedy, to the reassuring order from which they were distanced.], "Silvina Ocampo: La exageración como lenguaje," *Sur* 320 (1969): 22.

14. Originally published in *Sur* 42 (1938): 36–40; it was later included in *Y así sucesivamente.*

15. The works of Rank, Rogers, and Irwin, listed in the bibliography are representative of the vast critical literature on the theme of the double. Keppler's categories are especially intriguing, see C. F. Keppler, *The Literature of*

the Second Self (Tucson: University of Arizona Press, 1972). An earlier version of this and related arguments is in my "The Mad Double."

16. Eduardo González Lanuza, Review of *Autobiografía de Irene, Sur* 175 (1949): 56. Enrique Pezzoni dubs its narrative technique as an "empresa anti-proustiana" [anti-Proustian enterprise]: "No se trata de recuperar el tiempo perdido, sino de invertir la proyección hacia el futuro en una retrospección que trasciende la historia del Yo, reinventándola a partir del desenlace" [It is not a matter of recuperating time past, but of inverting the projection toward the future to a retrospection which transcends the story of the I, reinventing it from the ending], *Páginas de Silvina Ocampo, seleccionadas por la autora,* ed. Enrique Pezzoni (Buenos Aires: Celtia, 1984), 29.

17. Other comparisons to Borges seem inevitable here: While Borges's Funes (of "Funes el Memorioso") is a figure trapped by the past, Ocampo's Irene is similarly trapped by images of the future.

18. It hardly "fits" anywhere by virtue of its genre: its eighty-page length makes it a short novel rather than a short story; the only other narrative that approaches it in length is "Cornelia frente al espejo" at forty-two pages.

19. In contrast to Borges's story, "La intrusa," in which two brothers try to deceive each other in the attempt to share the same woman, Ocampo's identical twins attempt to deceive the woman.

20. *The Fantastic,* 124–39.

21. Chapter 2 discusses the female doubles in greater detail. In their influential study of women's writing of the nineteenth century, *The Madwoman in the Attic* (New Haven: Yale University Press, 1979), Sandra Gilbert and Susan Gubar take up the issue of doubling in literature by women whereby they suggest that women authors have a different relation to the culturally constituted ideal self than do male writers. In literary representations of the split between the ideal and the real, the male writer sees himself embodied in the socially defined ideal self and sees his double as representative of evil. Female writers, on the other hand, insist on multiple division of character and resist more insistently any closure of meaning, even identifying themselves with their own fictional monsters. The fantastic stories under discussion here exhibit similar dynamics and might well be included in the subsequent argument.

22. Keppler's discussion of the "Second Self as Beloved" (130–60) takes for his example in this category Emily Brontë's *Wuthering Heights,* the only female-authored work mentioned in his book.

23. The famous line from San Juan's mystical poem refers to the union of the soul with God. See chapter 2 for further commentary regarding Ocampo's ironic association of human men with the divinity. Ulla points out (*Invenciones* 79) that the plot hinges on the word omitted from Ocampo's title, "transformada" [transformed].

24. These problems have been persistent preoccupations in Ocampo's works as well as in those of Borges, Bioy Casares, and Cortázar. Their approach to the illusions of individual identity, truth, and illusion, however, has been to examine them through another illusion, time. Ocampo has preferred to dwell, not on human unity/repetition in time, but on fragmentation in space. See Chapter 4's mirror section for related arguments.

25. Molloy, "Simplicidad," 241.

26. "El vestido verde aceituna," "El vestido de terciopelo," and "Las vestiduras peligrosas" contain velvet dresses important to the plot. The "Detail" section of chapter 3 discusses this recurring motif.

27. This story first appeared in *Sur* 49 (1938): 22–33. It was later included in *Y así sucesivamente.*

28. Originally published as "Yo" in *Sur* 272 (1961): 41–57.

29. Jackson, 87.

30. All quoted phrases here are from Jameson's description of the imaginary realm in "Imaginary and Symbolic," 356. Jameson's article is extremely useful in articulating the ideological aspects of Lacan's theory.

31. See in particular his brief account of the polemic between Lacan's analysis of Poe's "Purloined Letter" and Derrida's response (374–75).

32. Jonathan Culler uses this phrase to describe Genette's attempts to account for Proust's ruptures of the system of point of view, in Gerard Genette, *Narrative Discourse: An Essay in Method,* trans. Jane E. Lewin, intro. Jonathan Culler (Ithaca: Cornell University Press, 1980), 12. Genette compares Proust's distancing techniques, the insistent framing of narrative in "a narration doubly, sometimes triply, retrospective" (168) to the musical or artistic polymodalities of Stravinsky and Picasso (210). The "presence of the narrator himself, the disturbing intervention of the narrative source—of the narrating in the narrative"(210)—is also characteristic of Ocampo's fictions which will be discussed further in chapter 4's section on Voices.

33. Wolfgang Kayser, *The Grotesque in Art and Literature,* trans. Ulruch Wesstein (Bloomington: Indiana University Press, 1963). See "The Word and its Meaning," especially 20–22 and his conclusion, "An Attempt to Define the Nature of the Grotesque" (180–88). Kayser utilizes Spanish paintings, particularly those of Goya and Velázquez, to illustrate his points; he also mentions one of Silvina Ocampo's art teachers, Chirico, as a modern proponent of the grotesque.

34. Jennings, 160.

35. Mikhail Bakhtin, *Rabelais and His World* (Bloomington: Indiana University Press, 1984), 18.

36. Kayser, Todorov, and Felman all cite this essay, as does Lacan in his "Desire and the Interpretation of Desire in *Hamlet,*" where he clarifies that the uncanny "crosses the limits originally assigned to it," in *Literature and Psychoanalysis,* ed. Shoshonna Felman, 22.

37. Jackson, 65.

38. Quoted in Jackson, 68–69.

39. Ocampo's interest in madness is more extensive than I am able to develop here. For instance, three stories of madness from *Viaje olvidado,* "El corredor ancho de sol," "Florindo Flodiola," and "Nocturno," fall outside the analysis of this book since they are not properly grotesque nor do they invite a feminist reading. In other cases my focus on feminine subversion mutes an awareness of the subversive potential of madness *per se.*

40. Bakhtin, 39–40.

41. An earlier story, "La sibila," describes a seamstress also named Clotilde Ifrán who has died by the time the narration begins. This story is discussed in chapter 3.

42. Ocampo's stories make a sustained play on the nature of both God and the devil. The young protagonist of "La sibila," identifies a bearded thief as God. Two other stories, "La paciente y el médico" and "El asco," suggest humorously that a photo of a bearded man is related to the divinity.

43. Bakhtin, 49.

44. Various kinds of animals appear together with circus performers, and seem to incorporate some small essence of Bakhtin's carnivalesque. Though the circus is a performance, not a street festival in which all social boundaries are broken down, it does seem to retain the freedom of imagination and an escape from the laws of human necessity that Bakhtin considers essential to the carnival spirit. Ocampo uses circus performers, such as trapeze artists ("Los funámbulos") and animal trainers ("Paisaje de trapecios," "Keif," "Miren cómo se aman") and dancers ("Los pies desnudos") as images of the ideal form of creativity. For that reason, these images will be discussed more fully below in chapter 3's section entitled "Artists."

45. See especially Bakhtin, 20–21. His concept of grotesque realism encompasses the idea of "degradation," which in addition to its gesture against official culture, takes the human body as its principle metaphor. The head and face obviously represent the spiritual or heavenly, while the earthly is represented by those body parts most concerned with life and death: "To degrade is to bury, to sow, and to kill simultaneously, in order to bring forth something more and better. To degrade also means to concern oneself with the lower stratum of the body, the life of the belly and the reproductive organs; it therefore relates to acts of defecation and copulation, conception, pregnancy and birth" (21).

46. Blas Matamoro, "La nena terrible," *Oligarquía y literatura* (Buenos Aires: Ediciones del Sol, 1975), 195. The word *terrible* in Spanish retains more of its connotation with evil than its English equivalent, hence, "wicked children" and "evil parents" are possible translations of these phrases.

47. Matamoro's chapter on Bioy Casares, for instance, is titled "El niño mimado" [the little rich boy], and refers to the author as well as to certain aspects of his fiction. It is worth noting that Silvina Ocampo is the only author of whom Matamoro speaks positively in his study of ideology.

48. The flower named is "el nardo." The seamstress's description of this flower as sad probably refers to its use at funerals. The woman compares the flower to the velvet fabric, claiming to love things that are cleary harmful to her: "El nardo es mi flor preferida, y sin embargo me hace daño. Cuando aspiro su olor, me descompongo. El terciopelo hace rechinar mis dientes, me eriza como me erizaban los guantes de hilo en la infancia y, sin embargo, para mí no hay en el mundo otro género comparable" (108) [The lilly is my favorite flower, and yet it makes me ill. When I breathe its odor, I become nauseated. Velvet sets my teeth on edge, it makes me bristle just like linen gloves did when I was a child, and yet, for me there is no other fabric in the world comparable].

49. Molloy, "Simplicidad," 248.

50. Kaja Silverman, *The Acoustic Mirror: The Female Voice in Psychoanalysis and Cinema* (Bloomington: Indiana University Press, 1988), 49.

51. An early version of this argument was published as "The Feminine 'I': Silvina Ocampo's Fantasies of the Subject," *Romance Languages Annual* 1(1989): 488–94.

52. James's frame provides a trap for the reader by giving authority to its inner narrator, the governess. Douglas's statements about her invite the reader into her version with confidence even as the framing context, telling ghost stories around a fire, sets the stage for a tale of the supernatural. The structure masks an equally convincing tale of madness.

53. I had searched for a more specific reference for this name with no success until I happened to read Isabel Allende's memoir, *Paula* (Barcelona: Plaza & Janés, 1994). Allende refers to "porfiria" as a hereditary blood disorder,

the condition which lead to her daughter's untimely death at the age of twenty-seven. Needless to say, the more specific medical term is an important connotation to Ocampo's character's name, a layer of meaning which adds ominously to those suggested here.

54. My reading of Miss Fielding as representative of the symbolic also in some ways glosses Gallop's chapter, "Keys to Dora." Gallop's discussion of three women involved with Freud's famous case, Dora, her mother and the nurse, at one point describes a drama similar to the one at issue in Ocampo's story. In discussing the nurse, Gallop argues: "As threatening representative of the symbolic, the economic, the extra-familial, the maid must be both seduced (assimilated) and abandoned (expelled). . . . The nurse is desirable. . . . But the desire for her is murderous," *The Daughter's Seduction* (Ithaca: Cornell University Press, 1982), 147.

55. Ibid., 14.

56. This reading is indirectly confirmed by Silverman's reformulation of Kristevan/Lacanian theories of symbolic castration in chapter 4 of the *Acoustic Mirror* that "the third term need not be male" (243n38), and her analysis of "Riddles of the Sphinx," 126–40.

57. The words in quotation are taken from critical articles describing Ocampo's child characters. I refer to Blas Matamoro's chapter title and Meehan's and Araujo's articles specifically.

58. Anika Lemaire, *Jacques Lacan,* trans. David Macey (London: Routledge, 1977), 124.

59. Matamoro, 211.

60. "No hay solidaridad en el mal," Matamoro, 221.

61. Mary Russo, "Female Grotesques: Carnival and Theory," *Feminist Studies/Critical Studies,* ed. Teresa de Lauretis (Bloomington: Indiana University Press, 1987), 215.

62. Ibid., 227.

CHAPTER 2. THE FEMININE: SUBVERTING THE MASTER PLOT

1. In addition to those works specifically cited, I have found particularly useful the following general studies, listed in their entirety in the Bibliography: Benstock, Jardine, Nancy K. Miller's *The Poetics of Gender,* Showalter, Suleiman, and Weed.

2. Feminist analysis of film has provided intriguing approaches to fictional narrative which also serve as background to my understanding of issues of gender. Studies by Doane, de Lauretis and Silverman are listed in the Bibliography.

3. Virginia Woolf, *A Room of One's Own,* 1929 (New York: Harcourt, Brace & Co., 1957), 85.

4. Peter Brooks, *Reading for the Plot* (New York: Vintage, 1984), 323.

5. Brooks, 314.

6. Rachel Blau DuPlessis, *Writing Beyond the Ending* (Bloomington: Indiana University Press, 1985), 16.

7. I refer to the female doubles identified with the angel/monster dynamic which centers their argument in *The Madwoman in the Attic* (New Haven: Yale University Press, 1979).

8. Mitchell and Rose provide two lengthy introductions to Lacanian thought as it pertains especially to the feminine: Jaques Lacan, *Feminine Sexuality,* eds. Juliet Mitchell and Jacqueline Rose (New York: W. W. Norton, 1982). Most useful to me has been Kaja Silverman's critique of Lacan in *The Subject of Semiotics* (New York: Oxford University Press, 1983).

9. Mary Daly's *Beyond God the Father* (Boston: Beacon Press, 1973) argues this point. Among Ocampo's stories, "La sibila" also makes ironic use of this association between beards and the divinity by having the child narrator say to a thief breaking into her house, "Ud. es el Señor porque tiene barba crecida" (*F* 58). The child's "mistake" resides in Spanish usage which employs the word *señor* for any man and for God.

10. See especially *The Daughter's Seduction,* 26–30, where Gallop discusses what she calls Freud's "smelly footnotes" and Michelle Montrelay's related argument that the "odor di femina" produces a threat to the "achievements of repression and sublimation" attained by way of the visual modes of representation (27). Gallop concludes that feminine sexuality operates in a different register from the male: "Unlike 'desire,' unlike Freudian masculine libido, feminine sexuality is *not* subject to metonymy, mediation and sublimation. Desire may always be masculine, but not sexuality. If the sexuality of desire (mediated, sublimated) is *phallocentric,* if desire is *eccentric,* feminine sexuality (immediate, olfactory), is . . . *concentric*" (28). And later, "Feminine sexuality, unlike the mediation of the visible that sustains phallic desire, is of the register of touching, nearness, presence, immediacy, contact" (30).

11. The photograph reveals something offputting or even menacing that is not obvious to the narrator in viewing the man himself. Only after looking carefully at a visual representation ("al rato de mirar el retrato") does the duality divine/devilish occur to her. Ocampo's insistence on representation rather than on the "real" man is important here and below in the discussion of "La paciente y el médico."

12. Kaja Silverman summarizes the operations of metaphor and metonymy in the functioning of desire (*Subject,* 109–22). She concludes that "desire is in effect nothing more than a series of metaphors and metonymies, displacements away from an unconscious point of origin in which one term replaces another which it either resembles or adjoins before being subjected to a similar fate" (115).

13. Several places where Silverman discusses the irrational, unconscious origin of desire, she utilizes a reading of Proust. See "Desire and Signification," especially 83–85, and "Metaphor and Metonymy" (115–22). The possibility that Ocampo is parodying Proust is a notion beyond the scope of this work, but deserves serious consideration, especially in light of Ocampo's comments to me and others that directly name him as an influence.

14. Mary Ann Doane, "Film and Masquerade," *Screen* 23, nos. 3–4 (1982): 82.

15. Lacan's insistence on the Law as distinct from the biological father is discussed in his "Meaning of the Phallus" (available in Mitchell and Rose), where he famously states "the phallus can only play its role as veiled" (82). Gallop's *The Daughter's Seduction* elaborates on his position (20–22) and throughout her chapter entitled, "The Ladies' Man," especially 36–39. The issue specifically of woman's infidelity and the Name of the Father is discussed in her chapter "Encore, *encore*" (47–49).

16. Molloy, "Simplicidad," 244.

17. Doane, "Film and Masquerade," 82. See related arguments in *Desire to Desire* (Bloomington: Indiana University Press, 1987), 23.

18. An earlier version of this argument appeared as "The Mad Double" in *Latin American Literary Review* 16, no. 2 (1988): 29–40.

19. See, for example, the list of feminist studies of the double in Naomi Schor's conclusion to "Dreaming Dissymmetry," in *Coming to Terms*, ed. Elizabeth Weed (New York and London: Routledge, 1989), 58 and n24.

20. Juliet Mitchell says of Lacan's subject: "Lacan's human subject is not a 'divided self' . . . , but a self which is only actually and necessarily created within a split—a being that can only conceptualise itself when it is mirrored back to itself from the position of another's desire" (5). Ocampo's stories are a perfect illustration of Lacan's insistence on desire as "impossible" because it originates in the unconscious, is filtered through signification to emerge into the symbolic in quite altered forms. Desire is always the desire of the Other, a desire created from elsewhere and defined by the larger symbolic field (Silverman, *Subject*, 176–78).

21. C. F. Keppler, *The Literature of the Second Self* (Tucson: University of Arizona Press, 1972), 15.

22. This particular narrative reads like a fairy tale, and in fact appears later in slightly altered form in Ocampo's story collection for children, *La naranja maravillosa* (1979).

23. These qualities have been noted as general characteristics of literary doubles. Keppler discusses the "unmotivated animosity" of the doubles in his chapter entitled "The Second Self as Pursuer."

24. Sandra M. Gilbert and Susan Gubar, *The Madwoman in the Attic*, 17.

25. For discussion of the implications of the angel myth particularly in Hispanic tradition, see Bridget Aldaraca, "El ángel del hogar: The Cult of Domesticity in Nineteenth-Century Spain," in *Theory and Practice of Feminist Literary Criticism*, eds. Gabriela Mora and Karen S. Van Hooft (Ypsilanti, Mich.: Bilingual Press/Editorial Bilingüe, 1982), 62–87.

26. *Madwoman*, 78.

27. Keppler, 186.

28. *Madwoman*, 38–39.

29. Mitchell's introduction says of the castration complex: "Henceforth, the girl will desire to have the phallus and the boy will struggle to represent it . . . for both sexes, this is the insoluble desire of their lives" (7). Gallop, Silverman, and others point out that cultural production is ever at pains to cover over this "insoluble desire" on the part of the male.

30. Some corroboration for this reading appears in remarks by Josefina Delgado who also reads a woman's message behind the male characters: "Cuando termino de leer las últimas líneas de "El impostor" de Silvina Ocampo, . . . advierto que a veces la alianza consiste en no hablar de lo que se quiere. Mostrarlo en esquince, disfrazarlo de otra cosa. . . . Porque Silvina Ocampo está metiéndose en un modo de relación, que, más allá del sexo de sus protagonistas, es el que agota y marchita las relaciones convencionales aceptadas. Una parte es la que piensa, otra es la que siente. No, así no, nos dice Silvina, a veces pueden darse las cosas mezcladas. Y los roles sexuales se vuelven más ricos, menos asfixiantes" [When I finish reading the last lines of Silvina Ocampo's "El impostor," I realize that at times the alliance consists of not talking about what one wants to. Showing it indirectly, disguising it as something else. . . . Because Silvina Ocampo is dealing with a type of relationship,

which beyond the sex of her characters, is what shrivels conventional relationships. One part is the one that thinks, the other is the one that feels. No, not like that, Silvina tells us, at times things are mixed. And sexual roles become richer, less asphixiating], in *Mujeres y escritura,* ed. Mempo Giardinelli (Buenos Aires: Puro Cuento, 1989), 137.

31. The notion of "crime" expressed here has been analyzed by Carol Gilligan, who studies the heavy penalty which women levy on themselves for avoiding precisely these kinds of obligations. Gilligan discusses the conflict between "passion and duty" and "the verdict of selfishness [which] impales" both fictional characters created by women writers and women assessing their own lives (131).

32. The title story of *La furia* also lends itself to analysis here (see my "The Mad Double") especially when we remember that the wicked Winifred murdered her friend Lavinia during a Christmas pageant in which both were dressed as angels. I study "La furia"'s structural issues of doubling in chapter 4's section on epistolary fiction. At this juncture, it can be observed that several of the stories discussed here are framed as letters.

33. *Madwoman,* 26.

34. Jessica Benjamin, *The Bonds of Love* (New York: Pantheon Press, 1988), 23.

35. Ibid., 107

36. *Daughter's Seduction,* 79.

37. Benjamin, 89.

38. In males the mother's perceived lack results in a debasement of the female which prevents a desire of the true other and perpetuates the homoerotic circulation of women as objects; in women it results primarily in idealization of the male and accompanying masochism (80–82).

39. Two stories with significant fathers are discussed below, "El goce y la penitencia" and "El incesto."

40. Nancy K. Miller's "Emphasis Added" makes the connection between mimesis and ideology, in *New Feminist Criticisms,* ed. Elaine Showalter (New York: Pantheon, 1985), 339–60.

41. Quoted in Doane, *Desire to Desire,* 119.

42. Benjamin, 109–10.

43. Gallop, *Daughter's Seduction,* 120. Gallop argues that any body contradicts images of power, which is what Lacan means when he says the phallus can only exert its power when veiled. The phallus represents an "impassive neuter mask of power" which cannot display desire. Both mother and father command images of phallic power for children, which are "impostures" eventually revealed by their sexed bodies "which fall short of that representation" (120).

44. Benjamin, 165.

45. Sara Ruddick, "Maternal Thinking," *Feminist Studies* 6 (1980): 354–55.

46. Bruno Bettelheim discusses this splitting of the mother figure between good and evil in standard fairy tales in his section, "The Fantasy of the Wicked Stepmother," *The Uses of Enchantment* (New York: Vintage Books, 1975), 66–73.

47. My point here is that the mother may be viewed as the agent of Miss Fielding's destruction rather than Porfiria. But the question of the chocolate as magical potion is an interesting one as well. Many indigenous cultures of

the Americas considered chocolate to be a sacred drink, while recent popular lore has proposed it as an aphrodisiac for women.

48. See especially chapter 4, "The Fantasy of the Maternal Voice: Female Subjectivity and the Negative Oedipus Complex," for a thorough description and critique of Kristeva's concept of the *chora*. For the female, the concept of the *chora* is closely associated with the negative Oedipus, identification with the parent of the same sex. The *chora*'s paradoxical nature is "the 'place' where the subject is both generated and annihilated" (103). Silverman concludes: "Feminism can't really manage without the negativity, which is an indispensable weapon not only against the name, meaning and law of the father, but against the female subject's unconscious investment in those things. . . . We may also need the positivity of the *chora* . . . a powerful image both of women's unity and of their at times necessary separatism" (125).

49. My contradictory images of the maternal bond in this story mimic (Silverman's assessment of) Kristeva's account of the *chora*: For an Oedipal child, it is the *chora* (the bond with the mother) which is the order under attack from the symbolic (Miss Fielding); for the adult that Porfiria is becoming by story's end, the situaton is reversed. It is the *chora* which "assails language and meaning, the negativity that threatens to collapse both the *je* and the *moi*" (104). In this way, I have been able to have my cake and eat it too: I have read the figure of Miss Fielding as an image of the triangulation imposed by the Symbolic on the mother-child duo and also as a splitting of the mother herself.

50. Yet another theoretical assessment of the mother seems compatible with this story. Gallop's analysis of the nurse in Dora concludes by suggesting that the nurse allows the child to hold on the image of the all-powerful phallic mother, to "believe that there is some mother who is not a governess" (147). Though Lacan would view this belief, along with the Imaginary itself, as "regressive" (Gallop's word), Gallop concludes with a careful call to reevaluate the hierarchy of symbolic over imaginary, "which tends to support the valuation of men over women" (149), my argument of chapter 1 of this study. Gallop's suggestion that the servant is simultaneously a threat to the family (she associates Freud's position as analyst to that of governess), makes this a figure of interest on several levels.

51. Silverman, *Subject,* 190.

52. *Mi mejor cuento* (Buenos Aires: Orión, 1973), 187.

53. Gallop, after Irigaray, uses this term to describe his theory's weakness regarding the gender formation of the little girl, assuming that she, like the little boy, suffers from a view of herself as "lacking" what is not there, i.e., a penis, which both mistake for the phallus (56–58).

54. Silverman, *Subject,* 142–43.

55. The centaur, combination of man/horse, is a well-known mythological figure. The several stories in which Zeus disguises himself as a bull seem always to have produced male offspring. Though I am unaware of a specific Hija del Toro to which Ocampo may refer, mythic imagination has already associated the human female with a sexualized father (god) as bull.

56. This is from *Emma,* a frequently quoted defense of woman in Austen's works spoken movingly by the title character about Jane Fairfax, a character who has acted improperly out of personal desperation (over the potential fate of having to "sink" to the level of governess!). In defense of Jane's transgressive behavior, Emma speaks for all such powerless women: "Of such, one may almost say, that 'the world is not theirs, nor the world's law'" (chapter 46).

57. The narrator addresses the main character directly, as *tú*, a narrative position duplicated in "El pecado mortal," which also deals with a "love affair" crossing class lines. See final section of chapter 4.

58. The highly suggestive quality of many character names—which is touched on briefly by Silvia Molloy's article—is worthy of further study. In this case, the word "horma" is defined as "molde en que se fabrica o hace alguna cosa. La usan más comunmente los zapateros y sombrereros" [a mold on which something is made. Commonly used by shoemakers and milliners], *Diccionario enciclopédico e ilustrado Ercilla,* 2d ed., s.v. "horma." The name is unmistakably and quite imaginatively phallic. In other passages Ocampo makes use of the sexualized motion of the park swing to create a believably childish version of eroticism (see especially *Ldn* 95).

59. Ocampo's stories never deal directly with homoeroticism, but its suggestion here just below the surface is the most explicit example of its veiled or partially obscured possibility in this and other of Ocampo's texts.

60. Chapter 4 discusses several stories of rape in the context of Ocampo's deliberately ambiguous language, all narrated from the perspective of the child herself. The stories in the following section present the child's abuse from a more distanced vantage.

61. Gallop, *Daughter's Seduction,* 79.

62. Louise J. Kaplan, *Female Perversions* (New York: Doubleday, 1991), 10.

63. Chapter 3 discusses at some length the various seamstresses of Ocampo's fiction. But the shop itself has already been seen in "La gallina de membrillo" as a familial setting.

64. The name, Livia, was utilized in "Las invitadas" for the little girl representing "lujuria," the mortal sin of lust.

65. My close readings of individual stories give some indication of the importance of mythological references in Ocampo's works, an element even more pronounced in her poetry.

66. Ocampo confirmed for me (March 1980) that she paid careful attention to story order within each collection. See also chapter 4's discussion of story order in *Cornelia.*

67. This is her argument in *The Daughter's Seduction,* chapter 2: "Of Phallic Proportions: Lacanian Conceit," especially 15–20; she later concludes: "Rather than deny the 'fact' of phallic privilege, Lacan flaunts it. And that just may be the path to accede to some sort of place for feminine sexuality to manifest itself" (32).

68. Silverman, *Acoustic Mirror,* 17.

CHAPTER 3. AESTHETIC FANTASIES

1. In *A Room of One's Own* Woolf creates Mary Carmichael, an imaginary author representative of women writers of Woolf's own day, whose equally imaginary novel veers sharply from male literary tradition: "Mary is tampering with the expected sequence. First she broke the sentence; now she has broken the sequence," Virginia Woolf, *A Room of One's Own* (1929) (New York: Harcourt Brace & Co., 1957), 85.

2. Ibid., 79.

3. For remarks suggesting the difficulty of reading women's writing, see especially Woolf's chapter 5 where she confesses that the woman writer's

changes in the expected "twitched me away" and that instead of allowing a readerly recognition of the cliched "common stuff of humanity," she felt herself accused of being "lazy minded and conventional" (95). Chapter 6 declares, in relief, "Indeed, it was delightful to read a man's writing again. It was so direct, so straightforward after the writing of women" (103).

4. Sandra M. Gilbert and Susan Gubar, *No Man's Land: The War of the Words* (New Haven: Yale University Press, 1988), 239.

5. Kaja Silverman makes a complex reassessment of the notion of androgyny in the final chapter of *The Acoustic Mirror*; see especially her analysis of Liliana Cavani's film, *Milarepa* (224–33).

6. Woolf, 96 and 108.

7. "Hay textos femeninos porque hay una situación femenina." Quoted by Eliana Rivero, "Precisiones de lo femenino y lo feminista en la práctica literaria hispanoamericana," *Inti: Revista de Literatura Hispánica* 40–41 (1994–95), 24.

8. Silverman's commentary on Irigaray demonstrates the temptation to confuse these two concepts, and indeed, the tenuous nature of that difference. See *Acoustic*, 146–47.

9. Ibid., 210.

10. *Alice Doesn't*, 186.

11. See especially Silverman's discussion of Irigaray, *Acoustic*, 141–48.

12. Ibid., 149.

13. "Robar el fuego," in *Mujeres y escritura*, ed. Mempo Giardinelli, 132.

14. Josephine Donovan, "Toward a Women's Poetics," *Tulsa Studies in Women's Literature* 3, nos. 1–2 (1984): 101. An early version of my argument here was published as "Portrait of the Writer as Artist: Silvina Ocampo," *Perspectives in Contemporary Literature* 13 (1987): 58–64.

15. See Kathryn Allen Rabuzzi, *The Sacred and the Feminine: Toward a Theology of Housework* (New York: Seabury, 1982) and John Lechte, "Art, Love, and Melancholy in the Work of Julia Kristeva," in *Abjection, Melancholia, and Love: The Work of Julia Kristeva*, eds. John Fletcher and Andrew Benjamin (London and New York: Routledge, 1990), 24–41.

16. Rabuzzi, 105.

17. Naomi Schor's book-length study, *Reading in Detail: Aesthetics and the Feminine* (New York & London: Methuen, 1987), provides numerous examples of such statements. See especially two, both in reference to Hegel's *Aesthetics*: "Hegel condemns any art . . . that remains mired in the material and the contingent" (25); "the contempt Hegel flaunts for 'the little stories of everyday domestic existence' he lumps under the dismissive heading 'the prose of the world" (32).

18. I refer, in chronological order, to: "Los funámbulos," "Paisaje de trapecios," "Los pies desnudos" (*Vo*) "Keif" (*Ldn*),"La pista de hielo y de fuego" (*Y así*), and "Miren cómo se aman" (*Cornelia*). This idea particularly enriches my reading of "Keif" (see chapter 2) as the ideal solution to the problems of female subjectivity.

19. Sylvia Molloy, "La simplicidad inquietante en los relatos de Silvina Ocampo," *Lexis* 2, no. 2 (1978): 245–46.

20. Noemí Ulla's interview with Silvina Ocampo (*Encuentros*) confirms my readings of the complex associations in her work between sewing and other household tasks, a redefinition of motherhood, and artistic expression. See especially the section entitled "Primeros recuerdos" (61–65) in which Ocampo

recalls her childhood and remarks, "Yo la descubrí a mi mamá después que quise a varias niñeras" (65) [I discovered my mother after loving various baby-sitters]. In subsequent sections Ocampo describes in detail her relationship with specific servants (see 117 for discussion of Eulalia) and their activities: "Me gustaban mucho los movimientos, la máquina de coser. . . . Realmente tenía una gran atracción por distintos trabajos. Me gustaban los ornatos . . . estaban asociados al dibujo. De chica yo hacía un dibujito y después me parecía que de ese dibujo podía salir un saco, el corte de un saco" (76) [I liked the movement, the sewing machine. . . . I felt a great attraction for different work. I liked ornaments . . . they were related to drawing. As a little girl, I would make a sketch and then it would occur to me that it could be a jacket, the cut of a jacket]. In reference to the use of rhyming couplets in Spanish verse, Ocampo makes a connection to sewing: "Es un sistema más bien de perezoso, la hebra de la costurera que se dice. La hebra de la perezosa, larga, para no volver a enhebrar la aguja" (83) [It is a system for the lazy person, the basting stitch as one might say. The basting stitch of the lazy person, long, so as not to have to rethread the needle].

21. In Spanish Aurora's sentence is far more ambiguous; the spoken phrase could be understood as, "You are the man," which allows the thug to misunderstand her.

22. The *Diccionario Manual de la Real Academia,* 2d ed., gives this definition: "dominante o señor de un estado pequeño" [dominating or lord of a small state]; one of its secondary meanings is "quim. parte más pura de los minerales después de separadas las impuras" [chemical. purest part of minerals after they have been separated from their impurities], s.v. "régulo." These levels of meaning suggest the contradictions of her character.

23. The *Oxford Classical Dictionary,* 2d ed., s.v. "Artemis," explains that the goddess Artemis is "a daughter of Zeus, 'lady of wild things,' and a 'lion unto women,' because their sudden deaths are ascribed to her." The *Larousse Encyclopedia of Mythology* explains that her long and complex story includes demanding the sacrifice of Iphigenia, transforming the hunter Actaeon into a stag, killing her twin brother Apollo's lover Chion, and murdering all twelve of Niobe's children, both of these latter done to punish each woman's boast about the beauty of her children. She jealously guarded the chastity of her nymphs as well as her own, one aspect of her "dark and vindictive character."

24. The *Larousse Encyclopedia of Mythology* at first states that the second Artemis is "a striking image of a fertility goddess who has nothing to do with the Greek Artemis" (130); however the editor later concedes that "by their warlike habits and their horror of men the Amazons offer some resemblance to the Greek Artemis, which is doubtless the reason why their great goddess was given the same name" (133).

25. Carol Gilligan's *In a Different Voice* (Cambridge: Harvard University Press, 1982) discusses gender differences regarding both the concept and consequences of personal success. Many women interview subjects expressed what interviewers called "fear of success." While standard explanations argue that a "perceived conflict between femininity and success" may be responsible for such a response (14), Gilligan contemplates the possiblity that female subjects are more aware of the "emotional costs" of worldy sucess (15).

26. *Leopoldina's Dream,* trans. Daniel Balderston (Ontario, Canada: Peguin Books, 1988), xi.

27. Poggi argues that Piluca/Régula is, in fact, the main character. See Giulia Poggi, "'Las vestiduras peligrosas' di Silvina Ocampo: Analisi di un'antiflaba," *Studi Ispanici* 3 (1978): 145–62.

28. Jane Gallop, "Annie Leclerc Writing a Letter with Vermeer," in *Poetics of Gender,* ed. Nancy K. Miller (New York: Columbia University Press, 1986), 152.

29. Ibid., 150.

30. "Emphasis Added," in *New Feminist Criticisms,* ed. Elaine Showalter (New York: Pantheon, 1985), 340.

31. Nancy J. Vicker's essay, "The Mistress in the Masterpiece" in *Poetics of Gender,* ed. Nancy K. Miller, 19–41, gives a history of the myth's utilization by artists.

32. *The Bonds of Love* (New York: Pantheon Press, 1988). See especially the chapter entitled "Master and Slave," from which I am paraphrasing page 73.

33. Gerard Genette, *Narrative Discourse* (Ithaca: Cornell University Press, 1980), 228.

34. This passage is quoted by Cristina Ferreira-Pinto, "El narrador intimista de Silvina Ocampo: 'La continuación,'" *Revista de Estudios Hispánicos* 17–18 (1990–91): 311, to illustrate the same point I want to make, that the narrator is identified as female even without traditional gender markers in the text. She concludes: "O sea, la identificación con el personaje es como un enamoramiento: el Yo del enunciado es una mujer que ha escrito una narrativa cuyo protagonista es un hombre" [In other words, the identification with the character is a kind of love affair: the ennunciating I is a woman who has written a narrative whose protagonist is a man].

35. Harold Bloom's argument of *The Anxiety of Influence* (New York: Oxford University Press, 1973) that (male) writers create original works in oppostion to the previous generation provided the initial impetus for seveal feminist responses which suggest that women writers have a different relationship to predecesors.

36. Louise J. Kaplan, *Female Perversions* (New York: Doubleday, 1991). Kaplan argues in her chapter entitled "Stolen Goods" that kleptomania operates like other perversions: "the item filched by a kleptomaniac has a symbolic structure very much like the structure of any other fetish. In fetishism, the blue velvet bathrobe, the green earrings, the fur wrap are memorials to absences and losses from every level and dimension of experience. In kleptomania, the stolen goods are also versatile memorials to a variety of absences and losses" (285). If stealing objects is a perverse strategy for acquiring power, its related opposite is the fear that any power actually possessed is "stolen": "some adult women will reawaken the infantile fantasy that the intelligence they hide under the skirts, or pants, is a stolen trophy that can be stolen back from the stealer" (296). Kaplan is careful to argue that kleptomania, like other perversions, has no gendered essence, that they are all "indoctrinations" from the larger world of social and gender roles (514).

37. "La fuente del Asilo" is a phrase rich in potential meanings: The capitalization of the word "Asilo" indicates that it is a place, and hence may be translated "the fountain of Asilo." However, the Spanish word *fuente* means *source* while *asilo,* asylum, means "lugar de refugio para los delincuentes; fig. amparo, protección; establecimiento de beneficencia para recoger pobres, enfermos, huérfanos" (*Diccionario enciclopédico ilustrado Ercilla,* 2d ed.) [place of refuge for delinquents; fig. rescue, protection; charitable establishment to house the poor, sick, orphans]. The second set of meanings, of sanctuary or refuge,

I have adopted above; the first and last correspond well with my argument in the "Detail" section and elsewhere in this study that Ocampo validates marginalized beings both in her thematics and aesthetics.

38. Shari Benstock, "From Letters to Literature," *Genre* 18 (1985): 265.

39. See the section of chapter 4 on "Epistolary fiction" for the "feminization" of writers of both suicide and love letters.

40. This, of course, is close to Hegel's theory of the origins of artistic expression; the following section on "Details" discusses the Hegelian features of Ocampo's aesthetics.

41. The Gallimard anthology of selected Ocampo stories contains a preface by Borges and an introduction by Calvino. While the first page indicates that the collection is translated into French from a work whose original title is "El destino en las ventanas," I have been unable to locate this collection in Spanish. The French translation, dated 1974, contains works selected from *Autobiografía de Irene, La furia,* and *Las invitadas.*

42. Schor's study of most interest to me here is *Reading in Detail,* but in an earlier work she describes the clitoris as the detail par excellence: see "Female Paranoia," *Yale French Studies* 62 (1981): 204–19.

43. Schor, *Reading in Detail,* 21.

44. Ibid., 20.

45. If a late eighteenth-century figure like Reynolds (Schor dates his remarks between 1769 and 1790) seems a strange detour regarding Silvina Ocampo, it should be noted that the cover of her 1988 volume, *Cornelia frente al espejo,* reproduces, quoting the inside jacket cover, "detalle de *Retrato de Mrs. Lloyd* (c. 1775) de Sir Joshua Reynolds" [detail of *Portrait of Mrs. Lloyd* by . . .]. The painting depicts an elegantly dressed woman in the act of carving words on a tree trunk. It is likely, of course, that Ocampo had little to do with the choice of design for the jacket cover, but even on the level of accident, I take it as partial justification for my arguments in this section.

46. Molloy, "Simplicidad," 247.

47. The *Enciclopedia* says that the reason for the manufacturer's having sent two statues is unknown. The other statue proceeded to its original destination, Sumampa, near San Jerónimo de Córdoba, where she has been known as Nuestra Señora de la Consolación. The hidden story of a double may also account for Ocampo's interest in the figure.

48. The editors describe the image's growing popularity, which on 4 December 1910 inspired the innauguration of a basilica to which numerous pilgrimages are made by people from throughout the region, including Paraguay, Uruguay y Argentina (1981 ed.).

49. The word *escarapela* is defined as a "divisa de cintas para un sombrero" [flat, round adornment made of ribbons for a hat], (*Diccionario Manual,* 2d ed.).

50. Stephen Bungay, *Truth and Beauty: A Study of Hegel's "Aesthetics"* (New York: Oxford University Press, 1984), 95.

51. Readers of Latin American fiction will think perhaps of Remedios la Bella (García Márquez's character of *Cien años de soledad).* This story, published in 1959, predates García Márquez's masterpiece by eight years.

52. *The Annual Obituary 1987* (ed., Patricia Burgess, Chicago and London: St. James Press, 1990, 439–40) states that she "collapsed, black-swathed," at Valentino's funeral. The entry traces Pola Negri's career from her native Poland, to German silent films of director Ernst Lubitsch, to Hollywood, where

"her talent was mishandled so that it sank beneath the weight of coiffure, gowns and jewellery" (439). She was reputed to be romantically involved with Charlie Chaplin as well as with Valentino. The editors conclude: "Turbans, high boots and painted toenails were among her innovations, and in the pre-talkie days, that and the rest of her colourful, mysterious style cut a serious deal of ice. The Hollywood films have frozen her into a succession of heavy, silly attitudes, but she was an actress with talent. How much did she conspire to obscure it?" (440).

53. *Oxford Classical Dictionary*, s.v. "Nestor."

54. Readers unfamiliar with Argentina should note that the poncho, knife, riding equipment, and *mate* and *bombilla* together evoke the figure of the gaucho. The two latter items, untranslatable, are sold as a set: The *mate*, traditionally made of a gourd, is frequently decorated with silver trim, and serves as a kind of cup; the *bombilla*, usually made entirely of silver and copper, serves as a straw. Together they were traditionally used to drink a hot tea made of an herb also called *mate* or *yerba mate* (which is also mentioned in the first sentence of this story, quoted above) from horseback.

55. Molloy, in "La exageración," 18–20, discusses the disparity between the endings of certain stories and the events leading up to them as well as the apparent irrelevance of episodes. The ending of "El almacén negro" and the implications regarding the narrator's motivation are very similar to what Molloy describes in "La propiedad."

56. Rosario Castellanos, "Silvina Ocampo y el más acá," *Mujer que sabe latín* (Mexico: SepSetentas, 1973), 154.

57. Jameson, "Magical Narratives," *New Literary History* 7, no. 1 (1975): 146.

CHAPTER 4. FEMININE STRATEGIES

1. In addition to the ones identified by their titles—"Carta perdida en un cajón," "Carta bajo la cama," "Carta de despedida," "Cartas confidenciales"— "La furia," "La continuación," "El fantasma," and "La pluma mágica" are similarly framed as epistolary fictions, as explained below.

2. Several critics and writers have commented at length on the implications of gender in amatory epistolary tradition. I have found Nancy K. Miller's "'I's in Drag: The Sex of Recollection," *The Eighteenth Century* 22 (1981): 47–57, and her *Heroine's Text* (New York: Columbia University Press, 1988), Linda Kauffman's *Discourses of Desire* (Ithaca: Cornell University Press, 1986), as well as Shari Benstock's "From Letters to Literature: *La Carte postale* in the Epistolary Genre," *Genre* 18 (1985): 257–95, particularly helpful, although they refer primarily to French and English epistolary traditions, including more recent contributions by Barthes and Derrida.

3. "The epistolary *genre* sentenced woman to a literary fate in which she was created by the male author, made to write under his dictation, made to serve his fictional purposes (as object of man's desire), existing as a male fiction, written into the text in translation, her creativity simultaneously appropriated and denied by the literary form," ("Letters to Literature," 265).

4. Both Miller and Benstock refer to this phrase from Kristeva's *Le Texte du roman* (The Hague: Mouton, 1970).

5. Benstock, "Letters," 263.

6. Kauffman also offers evidence to support Ovid's debt to Sappho for the genre he claims to have invented. See chapter 1: "Ovid's *Heroides*: 'Genesis and Genre'," *Discourses of Desire,* especially 50–61.

7. Ibid., 33.

8. See Benstock, 259, on the play on these two English words in contrast to the French *genre.* In this case French and Spanish work from the same Latin root and have the same double meaning—the Spanish word, *género,* is used for both biological/grammatical difference and categories of literary form. Both Kaminsky (9–13) and Castillo (306–9) discuss less playful implications of this multiplicity of meaning.

9. It is also tempting to read it with Octavio Paz's "Arcos," which he dedicated to Silvina Ocampo, discussed in *La Nación,* 17 April 1994, as part of an interview regarding the dedications to his poems. For her part, Ocampo discusses the two poems that she and Paz dedicated to each other (Ulla, *Encuentros,* 147) without mentioning the dedication to "La furia." It is speculation on my part to suggest that Ocampo's story is a sly response to Paz's well-known machismo.

10. "I's in Drag," 55. Miller concludes with the speculation that a male-voiced lover's discourse (following Barthes) may be "too painful, too threatening to be assumed in a masculine identity. Perhaps the miraculous feminization which attends the man who speaks the suffering of absence resembles inversion too closely in a century preoccupied with the grammar of sexual identity to be spoken with comfort even in fiction" (57).

11. Jacques Derrida's *La Carte Postale: de Socrate à Freud et au-delà* (Paris: Flammarion, 1980) and Roland Barthes's *Fragments d'un discours amoureux* (Paris: Éditions du Seuil, 1977) subvert the conventions of traditional epistolary fiction by having a male author write as a man to a beloved, what Barthes describes as a feminizing role. Benstock's analysis suggests that Derrida subverts the traditional gender structure by writing love letters signed by a man and allowing the silent female to be obviously so instead of positioned as fetish in a homoerotic situation in which man writes to himself in the disguise of a woman (269). Later she notes the possibility that "toi, mon amour," the addressee of Derrida's postcards, might be Derrida himself or a male lover (274). We should note that Ocampo's experiments with the epistolary mode precede both of these works.

12. Kauffman, 59.

13. The reader will also conclude that Tomi has been reincarnated as her own child, but this possibility is never mentioned by the story's characters.

14. Genette's comments about the fluidity of twentieth-century fiction with regard to narrative voice culminates with a reference to Borges which is equally applicable to Ocampo: "The Borgesian fantastic, in this respect emblematic of a whole modern literature, does *not accept person*," *Narrative Discourse* (Ithaca: Cornell University Press, 1980), 247.

15. Genette makes this association between epistolary fiction and fictionalized "speech" in his section, "The Narratee," which concludes significantly by associating Proust with Borges's "Pierre Menard, autor del Quijote": "the real author of the narrative is not only he who tells it, but also, and at times even more, he who hears it. And who is not necessarily the one it is addressed to: there are always people *off to the side*" (262). The voice of the first-person speaker is presented in a dramatized situation with a fairly obvious narratee

in these stories by Ocampo: "La red," "Las fotografías," "Voz en el teléfono" and "La oración."

16. See Benstock, "Letters," 262.

17. Kauffman, 26.

18. Silverman's *Acoustic Mirror* (Bloomington: Indiana University Press, 1988) demonstrates the gender system of Hollywood's vocal register in her chapter entitled "Body Talk," where she argues that "to embody a voice is to feminize it" (50) and further, that "in his most exemplary guise, classic cinema's male subject sees without being seen, and speaks from an inaccessible vantage point. These qualities can be most efficiently designated through the disembodied voice-over, but they are also recoverable from the much more terrestrial uses to which Hollywood generally puts the male voice" (51). Experiments with the female voice by women film makers are discussed in her chapter, "Disembodying the Female Voice: Irigaray, Experimental Feminist Cinema, and Femininity" (141–86).

19. I am paraphrasing Frank O'Conner who identifies a marginalized "sound of a *man* talking" (my emphasis) as the very definition of the short story in *The Lonely Voice* (Cleveland and New York: World Publishing, 1962).

20. Silverman, *Acoustic Mirror,* 49.

21. An early version of this argument appeared in Spanish as "Silvina Ocampo frente al espejo," *Inti: Revista de Literatura Hispánica* 40–41 (1994–95): 273–86.

22. Jenijoy La Belle, *Herself Beheld: The Literature of the Looking Glass* (Ithaca: Cornell University Press, 1988).

23. Quoted by La Belle, 14.

24. Ibid., 172.

25. La Belle, 2.

26. *Retratos y autorretratos,* eds. Sara Facio and Alicia D'Amico (Buenos Aires: Crisis, 1973), 116.

27. La Belle, 36 and 41–42.

28. The photograph is used here and throughout the book as a substitute for the mirror, earlier as another "false" double, and here as a means by which the subject constructs and is constructed by bodily representation. The complex differences (and similarities) between photographic and specular representation can be glimpsed from Silverman's remarks regarding Lacan's description of the inevitable structuring status of the gaze of the cultural Other as a kind of photograph. Silverman concludes: "There are thus two crucial ways of understanding the subject's relation to visual representation, both of which stress his or her captation—the mirror stage and the 'photo session.' In the former he or she incorporates an image, and in the latter, he or she is appropriated as image. (Interestingly, the 'photo session' is implicit even within the mirror stage, since the child meets up with its own reflection only through the confirming look of the Other.)" (*Acoustic,* 161).

29. Margaret Higonnet, "Speaking Silences: Women's Suicide," in *The Female Body in Western Culture,* ed. Susan Rubin Suleiman (Cambridge: Harvard University Press, 1986), 81.

30. The child's name, Cristina Ladivina, forms a double or triple play on words with divination and the divine; *la adivina,* and *la divina* are pronounced alike in Spanish. The story makes the connection overt in one of Cornelia's comments: "Las santas son todas adivinas" (27) [Saints are all seers].

As in the English word, *divine,* colloquial speech looses its association with the sacred.

31. Frequent reference to Classical history is typical of her early poetry, especially of *Enumeración de la patria,* the stories included in *Autobiografía de Irene* and the verse drama *Los traidores.*

32. La Belle, 42.

33. Another oblique reference to contemporary Argentine politics of the "dirty war" is intended perhaps in "Cornelia frente al espejo" when Daniel encourages Cornelia to continue her story:

—¿Por qué no sigue?
—No sé. Me parece que hablo en vano.
—¡Por favor! Me hace olvidar el mundo horrible en que vivimos, las torturas.
—¿Las torturas?
—Sí, las torturas. Siga. (41)

[Why don't you go on? I don't know, it seems useless. Please, it makes me forget the horrible world we live in, the torture. The torture? Yes, the torture. Go on]

34. René Girard, *Violence and the Sacred* (Baltimore: Johns Hopkins University Press, 1977), 168.

35. La Belle, 170. A similar argument appears, with different emphasis, in Silverman's *Acoustic Mirror:* "female interiority is basically an extension of the female body" (67). Earlier she states: "Modern male sexuality would thus seem to be defined less by the body than by the negation of the body" (25).

36. La Belle, 172.

37. Genette, 268.

38. Quoted by John Lechte, "Art, Love, and Melancholy in the Works of Julia Kristeva," *Abjection, Melancholia, and Love,* eds. John Fletcher and Andrew Benjamin (New York and London: Routledge, 1990), 25.

39. Silvina Ocampo mentions in her interview with Ulla her fascination with this story and with the possibility of writing an inverted version. She also adds, "La curiosidad es pecado. . . . Hay dos pecados en pugna en 'Barba Azul,' la curiosidad y la crueldad" (*Encuentros,* 108) [Curiosity is a sin. . . . There are two sins in conflict in Blue Beard, curiosity and cruelty].

40. Higonnet suggests that for women in history, erotic desire must have been strongly associated with death in pregnancy. She argues that "love can be considered a kind of suicide for women" and that "identity itself [is] the cost of female desire" (73). Kauffman's chapter on *Clarissa,* "Passion as Suffering: The Composition of Clarissa Harlowe," makes similar points (119–58). Silvina Ocampo herself says, "Eso es el amor, el eco. Es el poder de encerrar en algo, algo precioso. Es el poder de poder vivir dentro de un deseo que nunca parece realizarse, inagotable. . . . Es un suicidio" (Ulla, *Encuentros,* 145) [That is love, an echo. It is the power to enclose in something, something precious. It is the power to be able to live within a desire that never comes true, inexhaustable. . . . It is a suicide].

41. Lechte, 38.

42. Ibid., 24.

43. Lechte, 33. Some echo of Kristeva's words is found in one of Ocampo's statements quoted by Ulla: "Es un acto de amor escribir. Y cuando nos falta el amor, y escribimos, eso nos salva. Nos salva de muchas cosas escribir" (*En-*

cuentros, 118) [Writing is an act of love. And when we lack love and we write, that saves us. Writing saves us from many things].

44. Mary Ann Reis summarizes a variety of explanations by his many commentators for "the dearth of female character or love interest" in Borges's works: "Dearth and Duality: Borges' Female Fictional Characters," *Revista Hispánica Moderna* 17–18 (1990–91): 281.

45. Jane Gallop ends *The Daughter's Seduction* with a consideration of the bisexuality proposed by Hélène Cixous and Catherine Clémont as a new mode of directing desire. Gallop concludes that our ideal should be "neither the fantasmatic resolution of difference in the imaginary, nor the fleshless, joyless assumption of the fact of one's lack of unity in the symbolic, but an other bisexuality, one that pursues, loves and accepts both the imaginary and the symbolic, both theory and flesh" (150). I see Ocampo's image of the hermaphrodite as an attempt to resolve on the level of identity the same problem expressed by Gallop on the level of desire.

46. For recent discussion in the context of Latin American women writers see Debra Castillo, *Talking Back* (Ithaca: Cornell University Press, 1992), chapter 1 (37–43) and all of chapter 2 ("On Silence: Helena María Viramontes").

47. Lynn A. Higgins, "Screen/Memory: Rape and Its Alibis in *Last Year in Marienbad,*" in *Rape and Representation,* ed. Lynn A. Higgins and Brenda R. Silver (New York: Columbia University Press, 1991), 305.

48. Higgins, 307.

49. Higgins quotes Robbe-Grillet's comments regarding narrative gaps: "Everything up to the 'hole' is told—then told again after the hole—and we try to reconcile the two edges in order to make this annoying emptiness disappear. But what happens is the exact opposite: it's the emptiness that overruns, that fills everything" (320).

50. Louise J. Kaplan's chapter entitled "For Female Eyes Only" (*Female Perversions* (New York: Doubleday, 1991) discusses at length the relationship between popular romance fiction intended for female readers and more standard (male) pornographic publications. The Spanish-language equivalent of the Harlequin series, the mass-produced works by "Corín Tellado" are analyzed with different emphasis but in similar terms by Virginia Erhart, "Corín Tellado: La Cenicienta en la sociedad de consumo," *Crisis* 3 (1974): 71–80.

51. See Alicia Ostriker, "The Thieves of Language: Women Poets and Revisionist Mythmaking," in *The New Feminist Criticism,* ed. Elaine Showalter (314–38); Nancy J. Vickers, "'This Heraldry in Lucrece' Face'," in *The Female Body in Western Culture,* ed. Susan Rubin Suleiman (209–21); Nancy K. Miller, "Arachnologies: The Woman, the Text, and the Critic," in *The Poetics of Gender,* ed. Nancy K. Miller (270–93); Patricia Klindienst Joplin, "The Voice of the Shuttle Is Ours," and Coppélia Kahn, "The Sexual Politics of Subjectivity" in *Rape and Representation* (35–66 and 141–59, respectively).

52. See especially Higgins and Silver's introduction to *Rape and Representation* (2–11), which begins, "What does it matter who is speaking?"

53. Jean Franco appeared with Alicia Partnoy on a panel about testimonial literature during the 1987 MLA convention in which she made this point (session no. 143, "Literature of the Disappeared: Politics and Writing"); Kaminsky discusses pornography versus testimonial in Alicia Partnoy's *The Little School* in similar terms, *Reading the Body Politic* (Minneapolis: University of Minnesota Press, 1993), 57.

54. I am paraphrasing Higgins, 317.

55. Ellen Rooney's provocative article on Hardy's *Tess of the d'Urbervilles* lucidly articulates the debate among North American feminists: Catherine McKinnon's influential work attempts to undo the distinction rape/seduction, and tends, as Rooney shows, toward a denial of female desire/subjectivity (in *Rape and Representation,* see especially 91–92).

56. I am unaware of any single study which addresses the issues of this admittedly sweeping statement. The essay by Marta Peixoto on Clarice Lispector, "Rape and Textual Violence in Clarice Lispector" from *Rape and Representation* (182–203), suggests similarities to the ambivalence and violence that I find in Ocampo. See also María Clark's "Desirous Fiction," *Romance Languages Annual* 4 (1992): 404–10 and Castillo's analysis of Valenzuela (*Talking Back,* 96–136). All of these critics find perspectives on rape from various Latin American women writers that differ markedly from anything I have found in English-language tradition.

57. I refer to the following articles, which are discussed below: Helena Araújo, "Ejemplos de la niña impura en Silvina Ocampo y Alba Lucía Angel," *Hispamérica* 13, no. 38 (1984): 27–35; and Barbara A. Aponte, "The Initiation Archtype in Arguedas, Roa Bastos, and Ocampo," *Latin American Literary Review* 11, no. 21 (1982): 45–56.

58. Neither Araújo, Aponte nor Molly seem to read it this way. Silvia Molloy refers to the narrative positioning of "El pecado mortal" as "una suerte de *voyeurisme* gramatical" ("Simplicidad," 250) [a kind of grammatical voyeurism]. But the context of other of Ocampo's stories, such as "Voz en el teléfono," "Cornelia" and "Lección de dibujo," reinforces my reading as does this story's most direct predecessor, "La calle Sarandí." Each of these stories is narrated at least in part by an adult who views events from a child-like perspective of his or her own past.

59. Enrique Anderson Imbert, *Teoría y técnica del cuento* (Buenos Aires: Marymar, 1979), 95.

60. Aponte, 54.

61. Though I cannot agree with the conclusions Araújo makes regarding this particular story, I believe the reading of other of Ocampo's works with Bataille's would be very interesting. The two authors have in common a transgressive view of textual and sexual practice. Readers interested in a feminist appraisal of Bataille can find Susan Rubin Suleiman's "Pornography, Transgression, and the Avant-Garde: Bataille's *Story of the Eye*" in *The Poetics of Gender* (117–36).

62. Araújo, 35.

63. Aponte, 54.

Works by Silvina Ocampo
in Chronological Order

Viaje olvidado. Buenos Aires: Sur, 1937.

Antología de la literatura fantástica. With Jorge Luis Borges and Adolfo Bioy Casares. Buenos Aires: Sudamericana, 1940.

Antología poética argentina. With Jorge Luis Borges and Adolfo Bioy Casares. Buenos Aires: Sudamericana, 1941.

Enumeración de la patria. Buenos Aires: Sur, 1942.

Espacios métricos. Buenos Aires: Sur, 1945.

Los sonetos del jardín. Buenos Aires: Sur, 1946.

Los que aman odian. With Adolfo Bioy Casares. Buenos Aires: Emecé, 1946.

Autobiografía de Irene. Buenos Aires: Sur, 1948.

Poemas de amor desesperado. Buenos Aires: Sudamericana, 1949.

Los nombres. Buenos Aires: Emecé, 1953.

Los traidores. With Juan Rudolfo Wilcock. Buenos Aires: Losange, 1956.

La furia y otros cuentos. Buenos Aires: Sur, 1959.

Las invitadas. Buenos Aires: Losada, 1961.

Lo amargo por dulce. Buenos Aires: Emecé, 1962.

Los días de la noche. Buenos Aires: Sudamericana, 1970.

Amarillo celeste. Buenos Aires: Losada, 1972.

"La cara." *Retratos y autorretratos,* eds. Sara Facio and Alicia D'Amico, 114–18. Buenos Aires: Crisis, 1973.

"Silvina Ocampo." *Mi mejor cuento.* Buenos Aires: Orión, 1973.

El cofre volante. Buenos Aires: Estrada, 1974.

El tobogán. Buenos Aires: Estrada, 1975.

El caballo alado. Buenos Aires: De la Flor, 1976.

La naranja maravillosa: Cuentos para chicos grandes y grandes chicos. Buenos Aires: Sudamericana, 1977.

Canto escolar. Buenos Aires: Fraterna, 1979.

Arboles de Buenos Aires. Buenos Aires: Crea, 1979.

Breve Santoral. Con dibujos de Norah Borges. Prólogo de Jorge Luis Borges. Buenos Aires: Ediciones de Arte Guaglianone, 1984.

Y así sucesivamente. Barcelona: Tusquets, 1987.

Cornelia frente al espejo. Barcelona: Tusquets, 1988.

Anthologies of Silvina Ocampo's Short Stories

Pequeña antología. Buenos Aires: Ene, 1954.

El pecado mortal. Ed. José Bianco. Buenos Aires: Eudeba, 1966.

Informe del cielo y del infierno. Ed. Edgardo Cozarinsky. Caracas: Monte Avila, 1970.

Faits Divers de la terre et du ciel. Trans. Francois-Marie Rosset. Préface de Jorge Luis Borges. Introduction d'Italo Calvino. Paris: Gallimard, 1974.

La continuación y otras páginas. Ed. Noemí Ulla. Buenos Aires: Centro Editor de América Latina, 1981.

Páginas de Silvina Ocampo, seleccionadas por la autora. Ed. Enrique Pezzoni. Buenos Aires: Celtia, 1984.

Leopoldina's Dream. Trans. Daniel Balderston. New York: Penguin Books, 1988.

Las reglas del secreto. Ed. Matilde Sánchez. México: Fondo de Cultura Económica, 1991.

Bibliography on Silvina Ocampo

Agosín, Marjorie. "Mujer, espacio e imaginación en Latinoamérica: dos cuentos de María Luisa Bombal y Silvina Ocampo." *Revista Internacional de Bibliografía/Inter-American Review of Bibliography* 41, no. 4 (1991): 627–33.

Aponte, Barbara A. "The Initiation Archtype in Arguedas, Roa Bastos, and Ocampo." *Latin American Literary Review* 11, no. 21 (1982): 45–56.

Araújo, Helena. "Ejemplos de la niña impura en Silvina Ocampo y Alba Lucía Angel." *Hispamérica* 13, no. 38 (1984): 27–35.

———. "Erotismo y perversión en un cuento de Silvina Ocampo." *Río de la Plata* 1 (1985): 141–45.

Balderston, Daniel. "Los cuentos crueles de Silvina Ocampo y Juan Rudolfo Wilcock." *Revista Iberoamericana* 49 (1983): 743–52.

Castellanos, Rosario. "Silvina Ocampo y el más acá." *Mujer que sabe latín.* Mexico: SepSetentas, 1973. 149–64.

Chacel, Rosa. Review of *Los que aman odian* by Silvina Ocampo. *Sur* 143 (1946): 75–81.

Clark, María B. "Feminization as an Experience of Limits: Shifting Gender Roles in the Fantastic Narrative of Silvina Ocampo and Cristina Peri Rossi." *Inti: Revista de Literatura Hispánica* 40–41 (1994–95): 249–68.

Duncan, Cynthia. "Double or Nothing? The Fantastic Element in Silvina Ocampo's 'La casa de azúcar'." *Chasqui* 20, no. 2 (1991): 64–72.

———. "A Eye for an 'I': Women Writers and the Fantastic as a Challenge to Patriarchal Authority." *Inti: Revista de Literatura Hispánica* 40–41 (1994–95): 233–46.

Ferreira-Pinto, Cristina. "El narrador intimista de Silvina Ocampo: 'La continuación.'" *Revista de Estudios Hispánicos* 17–18 (1990–91): 309–15.

Fox-Lockert, Lucía. "Silvina Ocampo's Fantastic Short Stories." *Monographic Review/Revista Monográfica* 4 (1988): 221–29.

Gonález Lanuza, Eduardo. Review of *Antología poética argentina,* eds. Jorge Luis Borges, Adolfo Bioy Casares, and Silvina Ocampo. *Sur* 89 (1942): 68–69.

———. Review of *Autobiografía de Irene,* by Silvina Ocampo. *Sur* 175 (1949): 56–58.

Guasta, Eugenio and Mario A. Lancelloti. "Dos juicios sobre *La furia.*" Review of *La furia y otros cuentos,* by Silvina Ocampo. *Sur* 263 (1960): 62–66.

Klingenberg, Patricia. "'El infiel espejo': The Short Stories of Silvina Ocampo." Ph.D diss., University of Illinois, 1981.

———. "The Grotesque in the Short Stories of Silvina Ocampo." *Letras Femeninas* 8 (1984): 49–52.

———. "The Twisted Mirror: The Fantastic Stories of Silvina Ocampo." *Letras Femeninas* 13 (1987): 67–78.

―――――. "Portrait of the Writer as Artist: Silvina Ocampo." *Perspectives in Contemporary Literature: Literature and the Other Arts* 13 (1987): 58–64.

―――――. "The Mad Double in the Short Stories of Silvina Ocampo." *Latin American Literary Review* 16, no. 2 (1988): 29–40.

―――――. "The Feminine 'I': Silvina Ocampo's Fantasies of the Subject." *Romance Languages Annual* 1(1989): 488–94.

―――――. "Silvina Ocampo frente al espejo." *Inti: Revista de Literatura Hispánica* 40–41 (1994–95): 273–86.

Lancelloti, Mario A. Review of *Las invitadas,* by Silvina Ocampo. *Sur* 278 (1962): 74–76.

Martínez Estrada, Ezequiel. Review of *Espacios métricos,* by Silvina Ocampo. *Sur* 137 (1946): 82–86.

Matamoro, Blas. *Oligarquía y literatura.* Buenos Aires: Ediciones del Sol, 1975.

Meehan, Thomas C. "Los niños perversos en los cuentos de Silvina Ocampo." *Hispanic Literatures.* 4th Annual Conference. 20–21 October 1978. 2 vols. Edited by J. Cruz Mendizábal. Indiana, PA: Spanish Section, Foreign Languages Department, Indiana University of Pennsylvania, 1979. 1: 57–68. Reprint, *Essays on Argentine Narrators.* Valencia and Chapel Hill: Albatros Hispanófila, 1982. 31–44.

Molloy, Sylvia. "Silvina Ocampo: La exageración como lenguaje." *Sur* 320 (1969): 15–24.

―――――. "La simplicidad inquietante en los relatos de Silvina Ocampo." *Lexis* 2, no. 2 (1978): 241–51.

―――――. "Sentido de ausencias." *Revista Iberoamericana* 51 (1985): 484–87.

Ocampo, Victoria. Review of *Viaje olvidado,* by Silvina Ocampo. *Sur* 35 (1937): 118–21.

Payró, Julio E. "La escuela de París. Gustavo Cochet. Norah Borges, Xul Solar y Silvina Ocampo, Ramón Gómez Conet." Review of art exhibit, "La escuela de París." Museo Müller, Buenos Aires. *Sur* 71 (1940): 80–85.

Perassi, Emilia. "Retratto e fotografia: Note per due racconti di Silvina Ocampo." *Quaderni Ibero-Americani* 53–56 (1982–83): 387–90.

―――――. "Mito e foclore in Silvina Ocampo." *Quaderni Ibero-Americani* 59–60 (1985–86): 105–11.

Percas, Helena. "La original expresión poética de Silvina Ocampo." *Revista Iberoamericana* 38 (1954): 283–98.

―――――. *La poesía femenina argentina (1810–1950).* Madrid: Cultura Hispánica, 1958.

Pezzoni, Enrique."Silvina Ocampo." *Enciclopedia de la literatura argentina.* Ed. Pedro Orgamide y Roberto Yanui. Buenos Aires: Sudamericana, 1970. 473–77.

―――――. "La nostalgia del orden: Silvina Ocampo y sus historias para niños," Review of *La naranja maravillosa,* by Silvina Ocampo. *La Nación* [Buenos Aires] 21 de agosto 1977, sec. 4: 2.

―――――. "Estudio preliminar." *Páginas de Silvina Ocampo, seleccionadas por la autora.* 1984. Reprint, "Silvina Ocampo: orden fantástico, orden social." *El texto y sus voces.* Buenos Aires: Sudamericana, 1986. 187–216.

Pizarnik, Alejandra. "Dominios ilícitos." Review of *El pecado mortal,* by Silvina Ocampo. *Sur* 311 (1968): 91–95.

Poggi, Giulia. "'Las vestiduras peligrosas' di Silvina Ocampo: Analisi di un'anti-flaba." *Studi Ispanici* 3 (1978): 145–62.

Revol, E. L. "Silvina Ocampo, narradora mágica." *La Gaceta* [Tucumán] 19 de setiembre de 1976, sec. 2: 1–2.

Rosarossa, Alejandra. "Espacio y acontecimiento en la focalización de 'La red' de Silvina Ocampo." In *Estudios de narratología,* ed. Mignon Domínguez, 123–35. Buenos Aires: Biblos, 1991.

Schoó, Ernesto. Review of *Los traidores,* by Silvina Ocampo. *Sur* 243 (1956): 97–101.

Tomassini, Graciela. *El espejo de Cornelia: La obra cuentística de Silvina Ocampo.* Buenos Aires: Plus Ultra, 1995.

Torres Fierro, Danubio. "Correspondencia con Silvina Ocampo: Una entrevista que no osa decir su nombre." *Plural* 50 (1975): 57–60.

Trevia Paz, Susana Norma. "Contribución a la bibliografía del cuento fantástico argentino en el siglo XX." *Bibliografía Argentina de Artes y Letras (Compilaciones Especiales)* 29–30 (1966): 30–31.

Ulla, Noemí. *Encuentros con Silvina Ocampo.* Buenos Aires: Belgrano, 1982.

———. *Invenciones a dos voces: Ficción y poesía en Silvina Ocampo.* Buenos Aires: Torres Agüero, 1992.

V. P. "Silvina Ocampo y su perro mágico." Review of *No sólo el perro es mágico. Sur* 253 (1958): 108–9.

Zapata, Mónica. "En torno a la ley: perversión, juego, y horror." *Récits* 10 (1988–89): np.

———. "L'Esthétique de l'horreur dans le récit court du Río de la Plata: Silvina Ocampo et la beauté femenine." *La Beauté—Convergences* 5 (1989): 195–206.

———. "Versions de l'horreur: les motifs du cadavre et du meurtre dans quelques nouvelles d'Armonía Somers et de Silvina Ocampo." *Tigre* (Travaux Iberiques de l'Université des Langues et Lettres de Grenoble) 5 (1990): 105–34.

———. "L'Esthétique de l'horreur dans le récit court de Silvina Ocampo." Ph.D diss., Université de Toulouse-Le Mirail, 1992.

General Bibliography

Anderson Imbert, Enrique. *Teoría y técnica del cuento.* Buenos Aires: Marymar, 1979.

Araújo, Helena. "Narrativa femenina latinoamericana." *Hispamérica* 11, no. 32 (1982): 23–34.

Bakhtin, Mikhail. *Rabelais and His World.* Bloomington: Indiana University Press, 1984.

Bassnett, Susan. "Coming Out of the Labyrinth: Women Writers in Contemporary Latin America." In *On Modern Latin American Fiction.* Edited by John King, 247–67. New York: The Noonday Press, 1987.

Benjamin, Jessica. *The Bonds of Love: Psychoanalysis, Feminism, and the Problem of Domination.* New York: Pantheon Press, 1988.

Benstock, Shari. "From Letters to Literature: *La Carte postale* in the Epistolary Genre." *Genre* 18 (1985): 257–95.

———, ed. *Tulsa Studies in Women's Literature* 3, nos. 1–2 (1984). Reprint, *Feminist Issues in Literary Scholarship,* Bloomington: Indiana University Press, 1987.

Bettelheim, Bruno. *The Uses of Enchantment: The Meaning and Importance of Fairy Tales.* New York: Vintage Books, 1975.

Bioy Casares, Adolfo. *Memorias: Infancia, adolescencia, y cómo se hace un escritor.* Barcelona: Tusquets, 1994.

Booth, Wayne C. "Freedom of Interpretation: Bakhtin and the Challenge of Feminist Criticism." *Critical Inquiry* 9 (1982): 45–76.

Brooks, Peter. *Reading for the Plot: Design and Intention in Narrative.* New York: Vintage, 1984.

Bungay, Stephen. *Truth and Beauty: A Study of Hegel's "Aesthetics."* New York: Oxford University Press, 1984.

Castillo, Debra. *Talking Back: Toward a Latin American Feminist Criticism.* Ithaca: Cornell University Press, 1992.

Cixous, Hélène. "La fiction et ses fantôme: une lecture de l'*Unhemliche* de Freud." *Poetique* 10 (1973): 199–216.

Clark, María. "Desirous Fiction or 'El hombre del túnel' by Armonía Somers." *Romance Languages Annual* 4 (1992): 404–10.

de Lauretis, Teresa. *Alice Doesn't: Feminism, Semiotics, Cinema.* Bloomington: Indiana University Press, 1984.

———. *Technologies of Gender: Essays on Theory, Film, and Fiction.* Bloomington: Indiana University Press, 1987.

———, ed. *Feminist Studies/Critical Studies.* Bloomington: Indiana University Press, 1986.

279

Doane, Mary Ann. "Film and Masquerade: Theorising the Female Spectator." *Screen* 23, nos. 3–4 (1982): 74–87.

———. *The Desire to Desire: The Woman's Film of the 1940s.* Bloomington: Indiana University Press, 1987.

Donovan, Josephine. "Toward a Women's Poetics." In *Feminist Issues in Literary Scholarship,* ed. Shari Benstock, 99–110. Bloomington: Indiana University Press, 1987.

Duncan, Cynthia, ed. *The Configuration of Feminist Criticism and Theoretical Practices in Hispanic Literary Studies.* Special Issue of *Inti: Revista de Literatura Hispánica* 40–41 (1994–95).

DuPlessis, Rachel Blau. *Writing Beyond the Ending: Narrative Strategies of Twentieth-Century Women Writers.* Bloomington: Indiana University Press, 1985.

Erhart, Virginia. "Corín Tellado: La Cenicienta en la sociedad de consumo." *Crisis* 3 (1974): 71–80.

Felman, Shoshonna. "Turning the Screw of Interpretation." In *Literature and Psychoanalysis: The Question of Reading: Otherwise* Edited by Shoshonna Felman. 94–207. Baltimore: Johns Hopkins University Press, 1982

Freud, Sigmund. "The Uncanny." *The Standard Edition of the Complete Psychological Works,* Translated and edited by James Strachey, 24 vols. 17:317–52. London: Hogarth Press, 1953.

Gallop, Jane. *The Daughter's Seduction: Feminism and Psychoanalysis.* Ithaca: Cornell University Press, 1982.

———. "Annie Leclerc Writing a Letter with Vermeer." In *The Poetics of Gender.* Edited by Nancy K. Miller. 137–56. New York: Columbia University Press, 1986.

———. *Thinking Through the Body.* New York: Columbia University Press, 1988.

García Pinto, Magdalena. *Women Writers of Latin America. Intimate Histories.* Austin: University of Texas Press, 1988.

Genette, Gerard. *Narrative Discourse: An Essay in Method.* Translated by Jane E. Lewin with an introduction by Jonathan Culler. Ithaca: Cornell University Press, 1980.

Giardinelli, Mempo, ed. *Mujeres y escritura.* Buenos Aires: Puro Cuento, 1989.

Gilbert, Sandra M., and Susan Gubar. *The Madwoman in the Attic: The Woman Writer and the Nineteenth-Century Literary Imagination.* New Haven: Yale University Press, 1979.

———. "Sexual Linguistics." *New Literary History* 16 (1984–85): 515–43.

———. *No Man's Land: The War of the Words.* New Haven: Yale University Press, 1988.

Gilligan, Carol. *In a Different Voice: Psychological Theory of Women's Development.* Cambridge: Harvard University Press, 1982.

Girard, René. *Violence and the Sacred.* Translated by Patrick Gregory. Baltimore and London: Johns Hopkins University Press, 1977.

Higgins, Lynn A. "Screen/Memory: Rape and Its Alibis in *Last Year in Marienbad.*" In *Rape and Representation.* Edited by Lynn A. Higgins and Brenda R. Silver, 303–21. New York: Columbia University Press, 1991.

Higonnet, Margaret. "Speaking Silences: Women's Suicide." In *The Female Body in Western Culture*. Edited by Susan Rubin Suleiman, 68–83. Cambridge: Harvard University Press, 1986.

Hirsch, Marianne. *The Mother/Daughter Plot: Narrative, Psychoanalysis, Feminism*. Bloomington: Indiana University Press, 1989.

Irwin, John T. *Doubling and Incest/Repetition and Revenge: A Speculative Reading of Faulkner*. Baltimore: Johns Hopkins University Press, 1975.

Jackson, Rosemary. *Fantasy: The Literature of Subversion*. London: Methuen, 1981.

Jameson, Frederick. "Imaginary and Symbolic in Lacan: Marxism, Psychoanalytic Criticism, and the Problem of the Subject." In *Literature and Psychoanalysis*. Edited by Shoshonna Felman, 338–95. Baltimore: Johns Hopkins University Press, 1982.

———. "Magical Narratives: Romance as Genre." *New Literary History* 7, no. 1 (1975): 133–63.

Jardine, Alice. *Gynesis: Configurations of Woman and Modernity*. Ithaca: Cornell University Press, 1985.

Jennings, Lee Byron. *The Ludicrous Demon: Aspects of the Grotesque in German Post-Romantic Prose*. Berkeley: University of California Press, 1963.

Kaminsky, Amy. *Reading the Body Politic: Feminist Criticism and Latin American Women Writers*. Minneapolis: University of Minnesota Press, 1993.

Kaplan, Louise J. *Female Perversions: The Temptations of Emma Bovary*. New York: Doubleday, 1991.

Kauffman, Linda. *Discourses of Desire: Gender, Genre, and Epistolary Fiction*. Ithaca: Cornell University Press, 1986.

Kayser, Wolfgang. *The Grotesque in Art and Literature*. Translated by Ulruch Wesstein. Bloomington: Indiana University Press, 1963.

Keppler, C. F. *The Literature of the Second Self*. Tucson: University of Arizona Press, 1972.

King, John. *"Sur": A Study of the Argentine Literary Journal and Its Role in the Development of a Culture, 1931–1970*. Cambridge: Cambridge University Press, 1986.

———. "Victoria Ocampo (1890–1979): Precursor." In *Knives and Angels. Women Writers in Latin America*. Edited by Susan Bassnett, 9–25. London: Zed, 1990.

Kovacci, Ofelia. *Adolfo Bioy Casares*. Buenos Aires: Ediciones Culturales Argentinas, 1963.

Kristeva, Julia. *Desire in Language: A Semiotic Approach to Literature and Art*. Translated by Thomas Gora, Alice Jardine, and Leon S. Roudiez. New York: Columbia University Press, 1980.

La Belle, Jenijoy. *Herself Beheld: The Literature of the Looking Glass*. Ithaca: Cornell University Press, 1988.

Lacan, Jacques. *Ecrits: A Selection*. Translated by Alan Sheridan. New York: W. W. Norton, 1977.

———. *Feminine Sexuality: Jacques Lacan and the "école freudienne."* Edited by Juliet Mitchell and Jacqueline Rose. New York: W. W. Norton, 1982.

Lechte, John. "Art, Love, and Melancholy in the Work of Julia Kristeva." In *Abjection, Melancholia, and Love: The Work of Julia Kristeva.* Edited by John Fletcher and Andrew Benjamin, 24–41. London and New York: Routledge, 1990.

Lemaire, Anika. *Jacques Lacan.* Translated by David Macey. London: Routledge, 1977.

Manguel, Alberto, ed. *Other Fires. Short Fiction by Latin American Women.* New York: Clarkson N. Potter, Crown, 1986.

Meyer, Doris. *Victoria Ocampo: Against the Wind and the Tide.* New York: George Braziller, 1979.

Miller, Nancy K. *The Heroine's Text.* New York: Columbia University Press, 1980.

————. "'I's in Drag: The Sex of Recollection." *The Eighteenth Century* 22 (1981): 47–57.

————. "Emphasis Added: Plots and Plausibilities in Women's Fiction." In *The New Feminist Criticisms: Essays on Women, Literature and Theory.* Edited by Elaine Showalter, 339–60. New York: Pantheon, 1985.

————. "Arachnologies: The Woman, the Text, and the Critic." In *Poetics of Gender.* Edited by Nancy K. Miller. 270–95. New York: Columbia University Press, 1986.

————, ed. *Subject to Change: Reading Feminist Writing.* New York: Columbia University Press, 1988.

Mora, Gabriela, and Karen S. Van Hooft, eds. *Theory and Practice of Feminist Literary Criticism.* Ypsilanti, Mich.: Bilingual Press/Editorial Bilingüe, 1982.

Noakes, Susan. "On the Superficiality of Women." In *The Comparative Perspective on Literature.* Edited by Clayton Koelb and Susan Noakes. Ithaca: Cornell University Press, 1988.

O'Conner, Flannery. "Some Aspects of the Grotesque in Fiction." Presentation at Wesleyan College, Macon, Ga., 29 October 1960. Typescript located in the library of the University of Illinois at Urbana-Champaign.

O'Conner, Frank. *The Lonely Voice: A Study of the Short Story.* Cleveland and New York: World Publishing, 1962.

Praz, Mario. "Introduction: Genre Painting and the Novel." *The Hero in Eclipse in Victorian Fiction.* Translated by Angus Davidson, 1–33. Oxford: Oxford University Press, 1969.

Rabuzzi, Kathryn Allen. *The Sacred and the Feminine: Toward a Theology of Housework.* New York: Seabury, 1982.

Rank, Otto. *The Double: A Psychoanalytic Study.* Translated by Harry Tucker, Jr. Chapel Hill: University of North Carolina Press, 1971.

Reiss, Mary-Ann. "Dearth and Duality: Borges' Female Fictional Characters." *Revista Hispánica Moderna* 17–18 (1990–91): 281–90.

Rivero, Eliana. "Precisiones de lo femenino y lo feminista en la práctica literaria hispanoamericana." *Inti: Revista de Literatura Hispánica* 40–41 (1994–1995): 21–46.

Rogers, Robert. *A Psychoanalytic Study of the Double in Literature.* Detroit: Wayne State University Press, 1970.

Ruddick, Sara. "Maternal Thinking." *Feminist Studies* 6 (1980): 342–67.

Russo, Mary. "Female Grotesques: Carnival and Theory." In *Feminist Studies/ Critical Studies,* edited by Teresa de Lauretis, 213–29. Bloomington: Indiana University Press, 1986.

Schor, Naomi. "Female Paranoia: The Case for Psychoanalytic Feminist Criticism." *Yale French Studies* 62 (1981): 204–19.

———. "Reading Double: Sand's Difference." In *Poetics of Gender,* edited by Nancy K. Miller, 248–69. New York: Columbia University Press, 1986.

———. *Reading in Detail: Aesthetics and the Feminine.* New York & London: Methuen, 1987.

———. "Dreaming Dissymmetry: Barthes, Foucault, and Sexual Difference." In *Coming to Terms.* Edited by Elizabeth Weed, 47–58. New York and London: Routledge, 1989.

Seminar on Feminism and Culture in Latin America. *Women, Culture, and Politics in Latin America.* Berkeley: University of California Press, 1990.

Showalter, Elaine, ed. *The New Feminist Criticisms: Essays on Women, Literature, and Theory.* New York: Pantheon, 1985.

Silverman, Kaja. *The Acoustic Mirror: The Female Voice in Psychoanalysis and Cinema.* Bloomington: Indiana University Press, 1988.

———. *The Subject of Semiotics.* New York: Oxford University Press, 1983.

Suleiman, Susan Rubin, ed. *The Female Body in Western Culture.* Cambridge: Harvard University Press, 1986.

Todorov, Tzvetan. *The Fantastic: A Structural Approach to a Literary Genre.* Translated by Richard Howard. Ithaca: Cornell University Press, 1970.

———. *Poetics of Prose.* Translated by Richard Howard. Ithaca: Cornell University Press, 1977.

Villordo, Oscar Hermes. *Genio y figura de Adolfo Bioy Casares.* Buenos Aires: EUDEBA, 1983.

Weed, Elizabeth, ed. *Coming to Terms: Feminism, Theory, Politics.* New York and London: Routledge, 1989.

Woolf, Virginia. *A Room of One's Own.* 1929. New York: Harcourt Brace & Co., 1957.

Zapata, Celia de. "One Hundred Years of Women Writers in Latin America." *Latin American Literary Review* 3, no. 6 (1975): 7–16.

Index